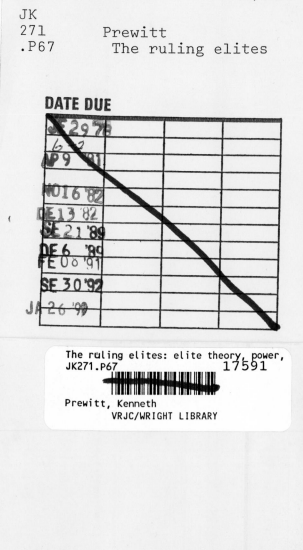

THE RULING ELITES

Elite Theory, Power, and American Democracy

KENNETH PREWITT
University of Chicago

ALAN STONE
Rutgers University

Harper & Row, Publishers
New York, Evanston, San Francisco, London

CONTENTS

FOREWORD

C. Wright Mills published *The Power Elite* (1956) about a dozen years too soon—or twenty years too late. He was between two phases of a special intellectual cycle.

In the 1930s many books by serious social scientists were unabashedly elitist in theoretical orientation and assumptions. Three such authors who are still widely respected among political scientists are Robert Brady, Charles Beard, and Harold Lasswell. Three other political scientists who became the most influential spokesmen of the later decade of pluralist orientations were nevertheless brought up on a strong elitist view of things. It is generally forgotten that David Truman, V. O. Key, and Robert Dahl all did dissertations in the field of policy and administration. They were elitist in a transitional sense but nevertheless express strongly in their training and early orientations the kind of social science that was strong in the 1930s.

Thanks in part to the influence of Truman, Key, and Dahl on the field of political science, and thanks even more to a general spirit of pluralism, in the 1950s works of an elitist orientation were treated either with indifference or hostility. Floyd Hunter's *Community Power Structure* (1953), methodologically unsound and theoretically weak, brought on one of the largest outpourings of good research modern social science has seen—all to refute an easily refutable book. (Even Mills, who shared many of Hunter's general views, failed to make any use of Hunter's book three years later.)

Political scientists were troubled less by Hunter's methods and data than by his point of view. It was a view that could neither be proven nor disproven; but that is exactly the case also with the pluralist view. As in all theory, the question is not what theory is true but which is more fruitful. It simply turns out that until the early 1960s, pluralism was considered so fruitful as to be virtually true.

In the 1960s, social scientists slowly began to look upon elitist writings with greater receptivity. Changes in my own attitudes are probably a good case in point, because they were shaped largely at Yale, which in the 1950s was the center of pluralist political analysis and the source of the very best studies within the pluralist framework. This shared framework, by the way, was not something imposed upon the students by the faculty. It was quite literally in the air. A good case can be made that it was the students who pushed many members of the faculty toward systematic community research as a reaction to the "Hunter thesis." Yale was the most exciting graduate center in the country precisely because the faculty had not made up its mind on what the best methods and theories were. In any event, while many graduate students remained in New Haven to pursue community and related politics research, I followed Herbert Kaufman to New York to try to grapple in some small way with a larger city. Partly because New York was larger, and partly because New York government was "over the hill" while New Haven government was entering into some kind of golden age, my experience in New York was distinguishable from the New Haven experience in two extremely significant ways. First, I discovered a much more highly structured, indeed hierarchical, distribution of power in New York than my colleagues discovered in New Haven. Second, I encountered the frequent failure of governments, whereas my colleagues in New Haven encountered a whole series of successes. The only way these two overwhelming facts could be accommodated to any kind of pluralist values was to suggest that while indeed there were plural centers of power, these centers of power were not only hierarchical in character but were also separated from one another, each independently governing its own special domain without too much interaction with the hierarchies that were governing in the other domains. Sayre and Kaufman dealt with the same phenomenon as a series of administrative structures surrounded by pluralist "satellite groups." Since I insisted that the political situation did not necessarily center completely on the bureaucratic structures of the city government, I formulated a variation of Sayre and Kaufman that involved only four centers of power rather than a center of power for each major administrative department. These I called "arenas of power," and their formulation arose out of a patently strong effort to accommodate purposive power structures to the organized chaos of pluralist political patterns. But whether or not this accommodation was successfully brought about, the fact remains that a pluralist must change his posture a great deal even to get this far.

The contrast between my colleagues' experiences in New Haven and my experience in New York goes far toward suggesting, it seems to me, the reasons why political scientists in general are now more receptive to elitist and structural approaches than they had been. It helps to explain why there is probably a special intellectual cycle into which such works as *The Power Elite* fell at a wrong phase. It seems to me that it has to do with the occasional failure of governments to perform their expected functions and the revival of the critical spirit in response to those failures. During the period of governmental failures in the 1960s, it was probably inevitable that political science would be deeply affected. Since the problems of the 1960s were in fact political and governmental, unlike the disorders of the 1930s, well-established theories of politics were likely to suffer, just as well-established theories of economics suffered during the Depression. This must have softened up many hundreds of graduate students and professors to alternative approaches. Something else happens during a period of governmental reverses. In the community it is called the "reform cycle," and there is probably a variant among social scientists that we might call a cycle of criticism. It is basically an effort to attribute responsibility, and that requires some research to find out who indeed is responsible. But note what a large change this requires in social science outlook. In a self-contained, balanced, self-correcting universe—the pluralist political system—the whole notion of responsibility is expendable. The notion might be evoked, but it is not intrinsic; it is quite possible to elaborate upon the scheme without using it at all. And this indeed may have been the most troublesome thing about C. Wright Mills, as well as the young political science dissenters of the early 1960s, who insisted on analyzing and criticizing governments for the public policies that they were fashioning. It wasn't that science and behavioralism had to go. It was the larger perspective that had to be changed, and in order to keep from changing it the elite viewpoints had to be resisted with particular strength. The elite point of view is enjoying a revival now because it is part of the spirit of criticism. It is adopted as a point of view precisely because it allows for a more systematic form of treating political phenomena in a combined empirical and normative way. Those who adopt this posture adopt it largely because they want to be empirical and critical simultaneously.

The reemergence of elitist theory in political science should be a welcome development even for those who, like myself, are not yet fully convinced that it is the most fruitful approach. It is necessary for the full enjoyment and the full cultivation of the upcoming phase in the cycle of political science. And this volume by Prewitt and Stone should be particularly welcomed because it is such a candid and dispassionate assessment of the elitist context as well as the insights that the elitist context is supposed to produce. The collaboration itself was almost ideally designed for a balanced reintroduction of elite theory to political science. Prewitt was trained as a behavioral scientist with a strong survey research orientation and a mastery of the study of political phenomena in those very segments of the political system that Mills called the "middle levels of power." But as one who started out as a student preparing for the ministry, Prewitt never fully escaped an old moralistic strain, and it eventually had to surface.

Stone was trained in the law and turned to political science only after ten years of what was to have been a career as a public lawyer with the Federal Trade Commission. He brought into political science a very concrete sense of the failure of public institutions and a most urgent sense of both the influence and the frailties of the top leadership. By methods and by values, both men have proved that you don't have to like elites to study them.

Their review and assessment of the elitist literature is especially timely in that it is both systematic and has a point of view. They have brought together the mighty structural concepts of Marx, Mosca, and Lasswell and the best aspects of organization leadership from Schumpeter and the pluralists. They owe a great debt to Mills, to Marx, and to the British counterpart of Mills, Miliband. Yet, they are none of these.

If I had to voice a single criticism of their work, it would be that they do not express enough outrage against contemporary American elites. There should no longer be any question in anybody's mind that elites of the public and the private sphere, of government, business, religious, and university spheres—not even to mention the most obvious sphere, the military—have failed us. They have learned about communications media only to use them for mass exercises in duplicity and manipulation. They have learned about computers and used them mainly as leverage for market power or self-aggrandizement, or both. They have learned to profit by the excitation of false expectations, and they have learned how to use bureaucracies in order to evade responsibility as well as to gain higher efficiency. Any book that analyzes elites must take the data of failure more fully into account. This is in fact the beauty of focusing on elites rather than masses, on elites rather than on large parties and the interactions among organizations. Elites are in fact people who rationally govern themselves as well as the rest of us. Elites are, as we would call them, variables in the political system. But they are purposive, so that they can be assessed as variables and judged as human beings at the same time. Elites reintroduce the human dimension —I would go so far as to say that the study of elites helps rehumanize political science without desciencing it. But the whole advantage of the thing is that one's own exercise of moral responsibility can once again come into play.

Another aspect of the same criticism is that the authors may rely too heavily in their analysis on the composition and background of elites, and they may rely too heavily in their criticism and hope for change on the processes of selection and circulation of elites. In a sense, I would say that they are being a bit too behavioristic in their approach to these highly calculating individuals. More reliance, in my opinion, should be placed upon the structure within which elites operate, no matter who they are. I think their ideologies play a stronger role in all this, especially in international matters; and I think it can be shown that more explicit imposition of limits and directions by laws that can be passed by the "middle levels of power" can in fact affect the behavior of elites. This is true because the Constitution does mean something, it is true because elites in the past one or two centuries want to be legitimate, and it is also true because whenever one segment of the elite fails to agree with another segment of the elite, they prefer to rely upon formal means of resolution wherever possible. Ever since there was a bourgeoisie, elites throughout the Western world have discovered all too often that their woes began whenever they abandoned formal contracts in favor of "old boy" relationships. And even if my impressions are not borne out by additional research, it is nevertheless true that intellectuals, as members of the influential segment of the mass, ought to impose higher and higher expectations on elites. This simply reexpresses the special value of focusing on the elite segment in political research. Since elites are political forces that can learn by experience and by education, we must take into account the possibility of the researcher having some influence upon his data. In this sense every act of political science is a political act.

Prewitt and Stone do, up to a point, play the game as I would like to see it played. They simply lack the killer instinct. They are gentlemen to the end and that inevitably leaves the bloodthirsty retributionists frustrated. In the long run, their way may be the proper way. That is for each reader to determine for himself, however, and that is precisely why I introduce this criticism here rather than later in a book review.

Dahl and Lindblom introduce their seminal work, *Politics, Economics, and Welfare,* with the modest prayer that they would measure the contribution of their book in terms of the speed with which later research rendered it obsolete. I would make the same prayer on behalf of Prewitt and Stone with the very strong expectation that their time will not be long. They have pulled together important legal and behavioral techniques in new and very promising ways. They cannot be taken lightly either as to method or to substance, and they will make a mighty contribution toward unbalancing the old and stalemated battle between the elitists and the pluralists. Criticism and research generated by this book are not likely to be far behind. With this kind of work, things are going to be better and better in the postbehavioral era.

Theodore J. Lowi
Cornell University

PART ONE

INTRODUCTION TO ELITE THEORY

The word elite *grates on the ears of most Americans. Like* racism *or* socialism, elite *is too harsh and un-American a term to gain wide acceptance. It is to be expected that the term infrequently appears in political reporting and political speeches. To use a phrase such as "political elite" is to come too close to denying that all men are created equal, and this is to deny the founding charter itself. Persons who cultivate public favor do not willingly step on cherished traditions.*

The scholar, however, cannot be so choosy. He uses words for their descriptive rather than emotional content. And the term elite *is descriptive. In the first place, it describes a theoretical perspective that holds that every society can be divided into those who rule and those who are ruled. To understand the culture of the society is to first understand the character of the ruling elite; to describe social change is to first describe changes in the structure and composition of the ruling elite; to explain social policies is to first explain the commitments of the ruling elite. In this perspective, the elites are the important actors on the historical stage; all others are passive observers or, at best, sporadic participants, but never the directing agents. Part I specifies the elite perspective in greater detail. The term* elite *is descriptive in a second manner as well. It describes common political practices and happenings, as will be made clear in our discussion. Whether it describes most important practices and happenings in the United States is, however, not a foregone conclusion. The descriptive accuracy of the elite perspective in the U.S. must be tested against evidence. This we intend to do throughout the book.*

CHAPTER 1
THEORETICAL PERSPECTIVES

In all societies—from societies that are very meagerly developed and have barely attained the dawnings of civilization, down to the most advanced and powerful societies—two classes of people appear—a class that rules and a class that is ruled. The first class, always the less numerous, performs all political functions, monopolizes power and enjoys the advantages that power brings, whereas the second, the more numerous class, is directed and controlled by the first.[1]

In this passage, the Italian political sociologist Gaetano Mosca dispelled the previously unchallenged Aristotelian classification of political systems. Aristotle had held that rule was one of three types: rule by the one (monarchy), by the few (aristocracy), or by the many (democracy), each of which had a degenerate form—tyranny, oligarchy, mobocracy. For centuries, political theorists had largely accepted this classification and considered it to be accurate and useful.

The Aristotelian concept, however, was not accepted by the elite theorists of the late nineteenth and early twentieth centuries, who denied that there could be rule by the one or by the many. One person could never rule without the active support and involvement of a governing class, whether made up of party bureaucrats, militarists, administrators, or priests. And certainly the people were too disorganized and too incompetent ever to manage themselves and the collective affairs of society. In denying the Aristotelian classification, the elite theorists liberated political sociology from one of its most ancient assumptions.

In urging the universality of rulers and ruled, or of elite and mass to use Pareto's terms, the elite theorists went much further than simply proposing the replacement of one classification, that of Aristotle, by another, their own. They advanced an entire theory of politics. Because our essay is concerned with this theory and its adequacy in explaining democratic politics in the United States, we do not need to restate the entire theory at this early stage, but an overview will be helpful.

THE ELITE PERSPECTIVE

The history of politics is the history of elites. The character of a society —whether it is just or unjust, dynamic or stagnant, pacifistic or mili-taristic—is determined by the character of its elite. The goals of society are established by the elite and accomplished under their direction.

The elite perspective does not deny social change; even radical trans-formations of society are possible. The elitists only point out that most change comes about as the composition and structure of the elite is transformed. History is the interminable struggle among elites to con-trol the society. This struggle results in the circulation of elites, with established elites giving way to new ideas and new interests. Thus is social change wrought.

Elite theory is in conflict with the marxian idea of class struggle. Where the *Communist Manifesto* claims that "The history of all hitherto existing society is the history of class struggles," the elitist manifesto claims that "The history of all hitherto existing society is the history of elite struggles." Moreover, the elitist would add, so matters will remain. The non-elite are passive observers of this struggle, or, at best, are pawns to be mobilized for the temporary advantage of a counter-elite battling against the entrenched elite. In the following statement, Pareto sum-marizes the argument, and dismisses the masses from serious considera-tion:

Let A be the elite in power, B the social element seeking to drive it from power and to replace it, and C the rest of the population, com-prising the incompetent, those lacking energy, character and intelli-gence: in short, that section of society which remains when the elites are subtracted. A and B are the leaders, counting on C to provide them with partisans, with instruments. The C on their own would be impotent: an army without commanders. They become important only if guided by the A or B. Very often—in fact almost always—it is the B who put themselves at the head of C, the A reposing in a false security or despising the C.[2]

The elitist thesis is likewise well-stated in a passage from Alexandre Dumas (fils), a French author influential in the latter part of the nineteenth century. Having observed that every human advance was, at its outset, opposed by 99 percent of humanity, he continues: "But this is of no importance, seeing that that hundredth to which we belong has, since the beginning of the world, made all the reforms for the ninety-nine others who are well pleased with them but who nevertheless go on protesting against those which still remain to be carried out." Elsewhere he writes that "Majorities are only the evidence of that which is," whereas "minorities are often the seed of that which will be." [3]

Although we shall wish to qualify, modify, and criticize features of the elite theory as we proceed, for the present we can summarize the theory in terms of two principles:

First, no matter what the dominant political ideology or the manner of organizing the State, every society can be divided into the small number who rule and the larger number who are ruled.

Second, the character of society and the direction it is taking can be understood in terms of the composition, structure, and conflicts of the ruling group.

A DIFFERENCE OF OPINION WITHIN THE ELITE PERSPECTIVE

If today many observers of society accept the two principles of the elitist perspective, not all observers draw the same conclusions. Some see the power and privileges of the ruling class and conclude that the rulers exploit and manipulate the ruled for personal benefit. The rulers monopolize power and enjoy advantages by demanding deference and tribute. They live—and live well—from the efforts of others.

There is a contrary view that rulers perform necessary and socially beneficial tasks. If rulers monopolize power, they do so to serve better all the members of society. The general welfare can be provided and protected only if the rulers can give uniform direction to society and have the force necessary to withstand attacks from enemies within or enemies without. And if the rulers enjoy many special advantages, these are only the just rewards for the special skills they bring to the task of governing and for the effort they expend on behalf of the entire society.

We can provide a simple diagram of these two viewpoints:

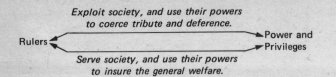

Both viewpoints accept the fruitfulness of distinguishing between the rulers and ruled, and both recognize that power and privilege are heavily concentrated in the ruling group. They differ sharply, however, in describing the type of relationship that exists between the rulers and the ruled. In these differing views is one of the enduring paradoxes of politics: that these two views can be so divergent and at the same time correct.

Let us go back, way back, into the history of man. We will see that this paradox is as old as the State itself.

SOCIAL SURPLUS AND THE ORIGIN OF THE STATE

We can ignore about 99 percent of the history of man. During the whole of what the geologists call the *Pleistocene Period* and the archeologists term the *Palaeolithic Age* (Old Stone Age), there was nothing remotely resembling what today we accept as the institutionalization of political authority. The most extensive forms of "society" were nomadic bands of hunters and food gatherers who lived as parasites by catching and collecting what happened to be provided by nature. Seldom numbering more than two dozen adults, these bands roamed the forests, lake edges, and plains in a constant effort to find food to stay alive. Our knowledge of such peoples is more extensive than might be thought because there are still hunters and gatherers in remote places of the earth who continue to live much as their ancestors did a million years ago. Anthropologists who have reported on these societies of Western Australia or Central Africa or the Arctic regions tell us that social cooperation does take place, but that it does not involve a social division into what could be called rulers and ruled.

To understand the ancient origins of the State, we need go back only eight or ten thousand years to the time that primitive man discovered how to breed animals and cultivate crops. These discoveries had enormous implications and were supplemented by the development of horticultural societies which permitted the production of surplus foodstuffs. Once men were able to control their own food supply, they were free to create a wide variety of social and cultural institutions that were totally unknown to their food-collecting predecessors. As a result, man developed several new skills.

As social surpluses were created, men were no longer obligated to spend all their time in sustenance activities; they could apply their abilities to such other occupations as pottery or masonry or weaving. More important, if there were sufficient surplus and some means of regulating its distribution, not everyone would have to cultivate. Some could live off the surplus produced by others and thus it was possible to have a division of labor. Some would cultivate and some would weave and some would fire pottery; baskets could be exchanged for grain and grain for pottery.

The production of social surplus is also related to more settled ways of living. If gardens could be cultivated, then villages could be built and the nomadic existence of those who followed the food supply could be replaced by the settled existence of those who planted and bred their food supply. Moreover, if not everyone had to cultivate, then some could live away from the land. Craftsmen, then, could congregate and barter their products for foodstuffs. This in turn would lead to the accumulation of possessions, because a settled people can afford to possess. As these developments came to pass, utilitarian goods such as tools and weapons, ceremonial artifacts such as masks and musical instruments, and even status symbols such as trophies and decorative clothing became desirable.

These three factors—the division of labor, a settled existence, and the accumulation of possessions—became the foundation for one of the most enduring of all human institutions, systems of social stratification based on wealth and property.[4]

The social surplus created by horticultural societies had a second far-reaching consequence. If the surplus were properly managed, it was possible for the community to support specialists who made no productive contribution at all. Best known of such early specialists were members of the priestly class, those persons who organized and officiated at the elaborate ceremonies that were so important to the cultural life of agricultural societies. Even before the advent of the advanced agricultural societies that sustained the enormous empires spreading over Mesopotamia, Egypt, India, and Middle America, occupants of priestly offices often devoted all their time to their specialty and were relieved of the task of growing their own food. Put differently, they were supported by the surplus of the community.

The specialists who most interest us are the chiefs and their administrators and soldiers, because, along with the priests, they constituted the first ruling classes. It has been said that the "first person who was able to stay put while commanding others to work had invented government."[5] Archeologists are generally agreed that this "invention" was not possible until surplus above subsistence needs could be produced. As well-stated by the influential British archeologist, Gordon Childe, "Chiefs cannot rule over a community unless that community can produce a social surplus above the needs of domestic consumption, sufficient to support the chieftain in idleness—i.e., as full-time ruler."[6]

Such a portrait of the surplus available to a chieftain is vividly painted by an observer of the Ngwato people of Southern Africa:

> As head of the tribe, [the chief] formerly received tribute from his subjects in corn, cattle, wild animal skins, ivory and ostrich feathers, retained most of the cattle looted in war, and kept all unclaimed stray cattle and part of the fines imposed in his court, especially for cases of assault. He could also confiscate the entire property of tribesmen conspiring against him or banished for any other serious offence. In addition, he could through the regimental system command the services of his people for personal as well as tribal purposes. He further had a large number of servants directly attached to him and doing most of his domestic work.[7]

This arrangement would, of course, be impossible were the tribesmen not able to produce foodstuffs at above a subsistence level, and therefore able to sustain a division of labor which permitted cattle raids, the collection of prestige items such as ivory, the institutionalization of a court system, and the availability of domestic servants.

The origin of the State and thereby the origin of the division of society into rulers and ruled correspond to the production of social surplus. This far the archeological evidence can take us. It cannot answer the more troublesome question that initiated our glance back into history: In what respect do rulers exploit and in what respect do they serve?

The origin of the State is sometimes explained as a social contract. This account, particularly influential among theorists of the seventeenth and eighteenth centuries, suggests that men voluntarily enter a social agreement that provides for collective defense and a division of political labor. Man initially lived under conditions of "statelessness" or what was termed the state of nature, but such living had its discomforts, obstacles, and difficulties. These were often traced to the darker side of man's nature. Self-love, writes John Locke, "will make men partial to themselves and their friends; and [their] ill-nature, passion and revenge will carry them too far in punishing others; and hence nothing but confusion and disorder will follow; and that therefore God hath certainly appointed government to restrain the partiality and violence of men." Hobbes was more blunt; he stated that outside of society life was nothing but the war of all against all in which the life of man is poor, nasty, brutish, and short. Men therefore quit the state of nature voluntarily. Seeking the warmth and security of social organization, they learned to act in concert and to develop means of central direction, because, as Rousseau observed, men survive only "by coming together and pooling their strength in a way that will enable them to withstand any resistance exerted upon them from without."

The social contract theorists viewed the State as an act of voluntary participation, a view that in turn influenced their interpretation of the role of the ruling class. If the State is based on the free participation of the citizenry, then the citizens so assembled have chosen to be ruled. They have good reason to escape the chaos of the stateless society. Pursuant to this view, one should not too quickly condemn the concentration of political power which elitists hold to be a constant in history. It may be necessary to concentrate control in order to achieve such social benefits as security, protection, coordination, and cooperation. Neither should we hasten to condemn the privileges enjoyed by the rulers, because rewards are necessary to set rulers apart from the ruled and to attract the most talented persons to positions of rule.

Although today the social contract theory is viewed as a metaphor more than as a description of history, its message about rulers and ruled is by no means absent from contemporary political thinking. Thus, for example, Karl Wittfogel in his study of ancient China considers the initially cooperative exchange between farmer and state bureaucrat to have been a significant factor in the development of the state bureaucracy. Small-scale farmers were at the mercy of fluctuations in rainfall. But the more innovative among these farmers saw that the semiarid lands that they farmed did have nearby supplies of water, usually a central river or large lake. If such water were harnessed, and a permanent flow of water insured, agricultural productivity could greatly increase. This implied large-scale irrigation systems; eager to domesticate the arid lowlands, the farmers "are forced to invoke the organizational devices which—on the basis of premachine technology—offer the one chance of success; they must work in cooperation with their fellows and subordinate themselves to a directing authority."[8] The increased productivity brought about by a water-control system supports the managers and administrators necessary to expand and strengthen the State.

In conflict with the contract theory of the origin of the State is the view that *conquest* was the prime factor that transformed the "stateless" state of nature into the society organized into rulers and ruled. Proponents of this theory believe that the desire for increased power motivated village headmen to organize a militia and move aggressively against a neighboring village. The defeated village would be forced to pay a tribute to the victor, and perhaps was even incorporated into a political unit dominated by the headman of the aggressive tribe. One student of ancient Peru saw in this process the growth of integrated units under the leadership of chiefs, a step which logically progressed to the great empire of the Incas. Consider his description:

> As land shortages continued and became even more acute, so did warfare. Now, however, the competing units were no longer small villages but, often, large chiefdoms. From this point on, through the conquest of chiefdom by chiefdom, the size of political units increased at a progressively faster rate . . . an entire valley was eventually unified under the banner of its strongest chiefdom. The political unit thus formed was undoubtedly sufficiently centralized and complex to warrant being called a state. . . . Once valley-wide kingdoms emerged,

the next step was the formation of multivalley kingdoms through the conquest of weaker valleys by stronger ones. The culmination of this process was the conquest of all Peru by its most powerful state, and the formation of the single great empire.[9]

It seems certain that the citizens brought into such a State were not the voluntary participants metaphorically described by the contract theorists. They were heavily taxed and sometimes enslaved. The systems of tribute and control further extended the administrative apparatus of the State, because the rulers needed a bureaucracy to administer laws and collect taxes. It was the surplus food and, subsequently, other types of products extracted from conquered villages that sustained the ruling class. If there was a social contract, it was one forged by superior military strength and held together by coercion.

Fortunately, we do not have to trace the nuances of the contract versus conquest theories. We can be assured that the archeologist and historian will continue this debate, which is still far from being settled. We can be content simply to emphasize that social surplus plays the definitive role in the origin of the state no matter whether society is a product of voluntary participation or coercive participation. Social surplus leads to social stratification and permits a division of labor which results in a class that is free from the burdens of food collection. So freed, this class transforms itself into a ruling class. The rulers may be priests who govern by virtue of access to magical rites and ceremonies; they may be warriors who govern by virtue of military force; or they may be bureaucrats who govern by virtue of administering important social services such as the water supply. The rulers may be loved and admired by their subjects, or they may be hated and feared. But whatever the composition of the ruling class and whatever their relationship with the ruled, the division of society into rulers and ruled depends on the availability of a surplus.

Actually, the ambiguity of the historical evidence regarding social coercion versus social service can be turned to our advantage as we attempt to establish some general theoretical perspectives to guide our inquiry into American politics. Because we are not forced to choose between the two contrasting viewpoints, we can develop a perspective that mixes the two theories in a profitable manner. Such a mixture is suggested by the subtitle of our next section.

THE STATE IS A SOCIAL CONTRACT
BETWEEN UNEQUALS

Because the State in the most general sense benefits those who are ruled as well as those who rule, there is good reason for men to enter the social contract and to submit to some central direction. Because the social contract tends always to benefit some men (usually the rulers) more than other men, coercion and conquest are often necessary to establish and maintain the State.

Here, then, is a perspective that allows for the generalized benefits of the social contract and at the same time underscores the fact that these benefits are not equitably distributed. It is appropriate to insist that the social contract is between unequals because societies are arranged so that some men command and others obey. But it can also be insisted that the very fact that society exists is an indication that it is of general benefit. Men flounder and suffer outside society, and their lot can only improve when they join in collective action.

The axiom that titles this section, however, does not answer all of the questions about the function of the ruling class. It only poses in a fresh guise the paradoxical questions with which we began: Do elites exploit or do they serve? Are we to emphasize their privileges or their responsibilities? It is by now evident that contrasting interpretations of politics derive from how one chooses to answer these questions. Let us consider them in greater detail.[10]

Unequal Privileges: The Radical's Emphasis

That the State is a contract between unequals is readily admitted by the radical, and deplored as well. The rulers not only have greater powers than the ruled, which is true by definition, they also enjoy greater privileges. This is because a disproportionately large share of the social surplus produced in the society remains in the hands of the ruling class for their personal enjoyment and benefit. If craftsmen produce artifacts and ornaments, these status symbols become the possessions of the ruling class. If warriors venture forth to conquer and return with slaves and women, the slaves will serve in the fields and kitchens of the rulers and the women will be placed in their harems. If the productive labor of society is used to build palaces, temples, and monuments, these edifices will be inhabited by or dedicated to the members of the ruling class. It has been a constant fact of history that much more than an equal share of the social surplus is retained by the rulers for private pleasure.

To the radical, the distinguishing trait of rulers is their inclination to exploit. Having been granted (or having usurped) certain powers, the rulers seem unable to refrain from accumulating privileges. They do so through force, fraud, and a legitimating ideology. The lament of the radical is an ancient theme; listen to the prophet Micah:

> Hear this, you heads of the house of Jacob
>   and rulers of the house of Israel,
> who abhor justice
>   and pervert all equity,
> who build Zion with blood
>   and Jerusalem with wrong . . .
> Woe to those who devise wickedness
>   and work evil upon their beds!
> When the morning dawns they perform it,
>   because it is in the power of their hand.
> They covet fields and seize them;
>   and houses, and take them away;
> They oppress a man and his house,
>   a man and his inheritance.
> Therefore thus says the Lord:
>   Behold, against this family I am devising evil . . .

For Micah and his contemporaries and successors in the radical tradition, the State and its laws are the instruments of oppression. In the *Communist Manifesto,* Marx called the executive of the modern State nothing "but a committee for managing the common affairs of the whole bourgeoisie. . . ." From the radical viewpoint, rulers rule for their own benefit. Winstanley, a seventeenth-century leader of the English levelers, gave historical support to this viewpoint in his argument that the inequalities and injustices suffered by the English people had their origins in the Norman conquest.

> For what are all these binding and restraining laws that have been made from one age to another since that Conquest, and are still upheld by fury over the people? I say, what are they, but the cords, bands, manacles, and yokes that enslaved English, like Newgate prisoners, wear upon their hands and legs as they walk the streets;

by which those Norman oppressors and their successors from age to age have enslaved the poor people. . . .[11]

The radical perspective contains within it a theory of social change. The two unequal actors on the political stage stand in an antagonistic relationship to each other. Social change results from the conflict between them, especially from the energy released as the oppressed unite and challenge the exploiting rulers. Marxian theories of class conflict typify this point of view, as do the theories of other political analysts who view the conflict more in terms of authority relationships than in terms of economic ones.

There are actually two very different results which might derive from the conflict between exploiters and the exploited. And these differences are very important to our analysis. We can use Marx to illustrate one point of view and the American Declaration of Independence to illustrate the other.

The conflict between the oppressive bourgeoisie and the oppressed proletariat would, according to Marx, ultimately result in a classless society. The inequality between rulers and ruled stemmed from economic arrangements. Terminate these economic arrangements—specifically private ownership of the means of production—and the structural division between rulers and ruled would end. It would probably take a violent revolution to accomplish this, because everywhere the rulers tenaciously cling to their powers and privileges, but the aftermath would be well worth the struggle. History would move toward radical egalitarianism, a social community in which none would be more privileged than others. The long evolution of the State would end, ironically, in the State's demise.

Let us label this viewpoint the attack on the "structure of rule." This is the kernel of truth in the radical perspective: If rulers gain power and enjoy advantages by exploiting, the object of the exploited should be to eliminate all rulers, not just a particular set of rulers. Society must be restructured; it must be classless.

Contrast this doctrine with the Unanimous Declaration of Independence of the Thirteen United States of America, 4 July 1776.

We hold these truths to be self-evident, that all men are created equal, that they are endowed by their Creator with certain unalienable Rights, that among these are Life, Liberty, and the pursuit of Happiness . . .

That whenever any Form of Government becomes destructive of these ends, it is the Right of the People to alter or to abolish it, and to institute new Government . . .

But when a long train of abuses and usurpations, pursuing invariably the same Object evinces a design to reduce them under absolute Despotism, it is their right, it is their duty, to throw off such Government, and to provide new Guards for their future security.

Thus was proclaimed the "right of revolution," but the practical consequences of the words penned by Thomas Jefferson differ sharply from those of Karl Marx. The American Revolution was aimed at particular rulers and not the structure of rule. It was not to be followed by the "withering away of the State" but by new Guards.

We might label this view the attack on the "composition of the ruling class." This view as well as the Marxist view holds that rulers exploit and oppress, but the differences are more important than the similarities. For Jefferson and his colleagues it was not the "ruling class" in the abstract which was the villan, it was simply those obnoxious Englishmen, especially George III, who would not play by the rules of the game. It was not necessary to change these rules, only to change the rulers. This viewpoint has had a profound significance for American politics, because it effectively isolates American political thought from the more radical tradition which calls into question the very necessity of rulers. As we shall see, it allows for a drift toward the elitist viewpoint that social change is not the product of class tensions but rather results from differing opinions and ambitions within the ruling circles.

Unequal Responsibilities:
The Conservative's Emphasis

The conservative does not deny that the State is a contract between unequals, but he emphasizes not the inequality of privileges but the inequality of responsibilities. The rulers and the ruled make an unequal contribution to the general social order, with the former making much the greater contribution. This is an old idea, frequently expressed in creation myths. It is the elect who lead the people from darkness, chaos, or slavery into a new and better social order. This elect is then entrusted with the responsibility of preserving the moral and material gains thereby acquired. For example, consider this description of Mugabe, supreme ruler of the Ankole Kingdom (Western Uganda):

> Physical, magical, and religious powers were invested in the king's person. In song and in address he was called "lion," the fiercest and most courageous of animal cattle-raiders. He was called the "leading bull," for cattle increased through him by raid and gift. He was called the "territory of Ankole" for he had "eaten" the pastoral lands at his accession and defended them against aggression. He was called the "drum," for like the drum he maintained the unit of the men under his power. He was called the "moon," for through the moon he had power to drive away evil and bring fortune to the tribe.[12]

The conservative is not dismayed that rulers have many special privileges and enjoy advantages denied lesser men. These are the rewards for shouldering responsibilities on behalf of the entire society.

The ruler has two main types of responsibility: moral and material. Ibn Khaldûn, an Islamic philisopher of the fourteenth century, speaks to the first type of responsibility: "People cannot persist in a state of anarchy, and need a person to restrain them. He is their ruler. Royal authority is an institution that is natural to mankind."[13] Ibn Khaldûn is here anticipating a line of inquiry which, for modern sociology, is best expressed in the writings of Emile Durkheim. This French sociologist developed the theme that man cannot do without community and cannot do without the rules implied by community. The quest for company, for community, for social integration is part of human nature. Deny man these things and he loses a sense of direction and meaning. As succinctly stated by one scholar, "The disorder of the community means the disorder of the individual."[14] It is a short step from this comment to observing that man needs rulers: "Those who formulate and apply rules are the leaders of society, not merely because they rule it in a juridical sense, but because they preside over the inner order of man."[15] In short, if there must be rules, there must be rule inventors; if there must be guidance, there must be guidance givers. Thus do leaders provide a moral framework for society, a framework increasingly critical as society grows in complexity and scale. Those who provide this framework merit the powers and privileges they enjoy.

The responsibility for the moral integration of society is particularly evident in the public ceremonies which reaffirm the political beliefs by which men swear. Founding charters, creation myths, constitutions, sacred traditions, and the feats of past rulers express the origin, the growth, and the purpose of the political community. Political elites have responsibility for preserving these beliefs, and for teaching the community their significance. In this way, the solidarity and moral purpose of the society is continually affirmed. For example, the Zulu king is always approached with ceremonious salutations:

> What tradition and history was common to all the Zulu had to be told in the names of the Zulu kings and it was largely their common sentiment about the king and his predecessors which united all Zulu as members of the nation. At the great first-fruits ceremonies and in war-rites, the king was strengthened and cleansed in the name of the nation. He possessed certain objects, inherited from his ancestors, and the welfare of the country was held to depend on them. This ceremonial position of the king was backed by his ancestral spirits. They were supposed to care for the whole of Zululand, and in the interests of the nation the king had to appeal to them in drought, war, and at the planting and first-fruits seasons.[16]

The swearing in of a new President in twentieth-century America is less distant from the Zulu traditions than might at first be thought. Sacred objects (the flag, the Bible, the Constitution) play a prominent role; history and the heroes of history are called upon to sanctify the ceremony; the elect dedicates himself to the "truths we all hold dear" and pledges to protect the best that is America in the challenging days ahead. Myths, rituals, dogmas, sacred places and persons are typical accoutrements of lesser ceremonies such as the dedication of a public monument, the opening of a public building, the announcing of a new program, and simple public holidays.

In all of these rituals, the rulers are claiming to preserve those hard-earned values and victories of the past, and pledging to apply them to new conditions. They are protecting the political beliefs which men live by. For their willingness to assume such responsibilities, they are entitled to the powers and advantages of office. The pomp and circumstance that surround the rulers are necessary to symbolize to the people the integrity and dignity of the State. To strip the rulers of their eminent status would be to strip them of their significance, and society would be the sorrier for it.

Just as the moral well-being of the society depends on its rulers, so also does the material well-being. The rulers and the ruled are unequals in the sense that the elite have the responsibility for managing the society: They are the ones who get the trains to run on time! The conservative emphasizes that the rulers are indispensable in a complex society. Managing factories and transport systems, providing schools and hospitals, organizing armies and police forces require coordination and regulation, hence there must be coordinators and regulators. Because the material well-being of the populace depends on economic growth, social services, and social protection, the rulers who organize and direct their provision should be given the necessary powers to make things work and should be rewarded for their efforts.

The thesis that elites are necessary for the material well-being of the society can be substantiated by either of two different viewpoints about the masses. Most common is the assertion that the masses are incompetent and thus incapable of "acting in default of an initiative from without and from above." Elite theorist Robert Michels continues, "striking proof of the organic weakness of the mass is furnished by the way in which, when deprived of their leaders in time of action, they abandon the field of battle in disordered flight; they seem to have no power of instinctive reorganization, and are useless until new captains arise capable of replacing those that have been lost."[17] The conception that leaderless people are incompetent receives support from many quarters, including even some writers normally associated with the radical tradition. It was Lenin in *What Is to Be Done* who claimed that "without the 'dozen' tried and talented leaders (and talented men are not born by the hundred), professionally trained, schooled by long experience, and working in perfect harmony, no class in modern society is capable of conducting a determined struggle."[18] Lenin's influential political tract is still used today by communist parties as the justification for the vanguard role, a leadership concept which echoes Michel's pessimism.

In contrast to the view that the masses are incompetent is the proposition that men are rational *and therefore* organize themselves into hierarchies. The people are well aware that their material well-being is furthered by the actions and talents of the rulers, and thus they willingly defer to the judgments of those who command the society. The opportunity costs of an alternative arrangement would be prohibitive, although it is theoretically possible for social action to be organized on the basis of every member of society negotiating with every other member until agreement is reached. But rational men will not pay the costs of such an elaborate negotiating machinery, and prefer to delegate authority to a smaller group of talented and trusted leaders.

Whether you start from the premise that masses are incompetent or than men are rational, you arrive at the same conclusion. It takes leaders to make things go. Thus, there is a very pragmatic reason for a social contract between unequals: Differential responsibilities are assigned and it follows that there will be differential powers and privileges. Those powers must be unequal so that the society can be run efficiently while privileges must be unequal so that the most able will be attracted to the responsible positions.

The conservative sees the relationship between the rulers and ruled in terms not of privilege but of responsibility. The moral significance and material well-being of society rests on the shoulders of the elite. This view is part of a larger perspective which sees society as an "organism" in which each part is mutually interdependent with all other parts. John of Salisbury, a twelfth-century English bishop, stated the matter clearly. Society flourishes when "the higher members shield the lower, and the lower respond faithfully and fully in like measure to the just demands of their superiors, so that each and all are as it were members one of another by a sort of reciprocity, and each regards his own interest as best served by that which he knows to be most advantageous for the other."[19] In one guise or another, this proposition has had many able proponents throughout history, including not only theologians such as John of Salisbury but also political philosophers such as Edmund Burke, economists such as Adam Smith, sociologists such as Herbert Spencer, and modern-day social scientists of the functionalist school of thought.

For the conservative, society is not primarily the result of coercion and fraud. It is the result of reciprocity and mutual benefit. The rulers stand at the center of society and provide it with unification, coherence, and direction. Their powers and privileges should not be begrudged. High positions are not gained through force but by superior talent and hard work. Privileges are not stolen but are freely given as fair rewards for the responsibilities assumed. It would be an injustice to deny these rewards, and it would be impractical because how else would men of talent be attracted to positions of responsibility.

ELITE THEORY AND SOCIAL CHANGE

Elitists are sometimes criticized for having no theory of social change. It is true that in their view the interests of the status quo and the established elite are overwhelmingly advantaged in any struggle with new interests or a counter-elite. The clearest statement of this thesis is found in the classic study by Michels of pre-World War I Socialist Parties in Western Europe.[20] He observed the gradual drift of these parties, particularly the German Socialist Party, into the hands of conservative leaders. These leaders were skilled at thwarting any challenge to their powers. The powerful political machines they created virtually precluded their being ousted from office. Moreover, the leaderships had developed life styles and interests different from those of their followers. Generalizing from his investigation, Michels set forth one of the most famous theories of social science—the iron law of oligarchy. In its essentials, the "law" holds that all organizations come to be ruled by self-perpetuating elites with mass participation limited to ritualistically ratifying the actions of the oligarchy. Perhaps it is an overstatement to term this a "law"—which connotes an inflexible sequence of events without exception—but if one were to retitle Michel's discovery an "aluminum tendency" rather than an "iron law," it would be remarkable how often it would empirically describe the nature of organizations. Few exceptions to this theory can be found.

Why is this so? A cataloging of the advantages enjoyed within organizations by elites as compared to the advantages of the masses and prospective counter-elites will soon show why the "iron law" describes so many organizations. Those in control of an organization, for example, make use of such resources as its technical staff, publicity and communications machinery, financial resources, and manpower. They also have in their favor a superior knowledge of organization affairs and the opportunity to wrap themselves in the aura of the organization so that criticism of the leadership can be interpreted as an unpatriotic attack on the organization. Additional advantages of elites leading an organization are the important psychological advantages over rivals and potential counter-elites. Custom, the need felt by masses for tried-and-true leadership; the socialized reverence of the masses for extant leadership; and the appeals to experience, indispensibility, and accomplishments are frequently employed by such elites. The element of fear can also be employed by the incumbent elite. This includes both the appeal that dismissal of the leadership would discredit the organization to the outside world and undermine its bargaining position and also the appeal that counter-elites are insufficiently deferential to the accomplishments of the incumbents, and thus perhaps are "unpatriotic" or "traitorous." Intimidation and repression as tactics available to the established elite make the removal of the elite quite difficult.

Michels denies the political significance of any element outside of the ruling minorities. No political initiative comes from the public. The public is best understood as an atomized and fragmented mass, capable only of responding to the leadership of superior elements in society. Only the elite can transcend their own milieux and evolve a vision of a different society. The masses are trapped in their milieux, depending on the visions provided them by an elite.

From this it might be thought that elite theory cannot account for social and political change, and indeed this criticism has often been voiced. But it is misplaced criticism, because elite theorists have a definite explanation of change (which we shall evaluate later in the book). Because the important conflicts in society are not between classes but within the elite, the dynamic that accounts for social change is the constant struggle between a minority that holds power and another minority seeking power. It is in the process of elite circulation, or rather in blocked circulation, that we must seek one explanation for social change. Thus, Pareto has argued that when elites do not recruit the most able elements in society from outside their ranks and instead restrict entry to their ranks, they eventually become decadent and unable to cope with the tasks they must undertake. At the same time, the excluded talented elements form a counter-elite, organize the masses injured by the incompetence of the elite, and lead a revolution overthrowing the elite. Once this is done the new elite consolidates its power over the masses.

Certainly, one can argue that such events as the Russian Revolution of 1917 or the Cuban Revolution led by Fidel Castro are well-described by this view. Colonial revolutions, too, erupt when the colonizing elite refuses to recruit anyone but the most obsequious bootlickers among the natives into its ranks, compelling the best elements among the natives to form a counter-elite intent on revolt. Again, once in power, the way in which the Soviet and the Castro leadership consolidated their power over the masses illustrates the inevitability of elite rule after revolution.

It would, however, be foolhardy to assert that all social and political change can be described in this manner, and neither Mosca nor Pareto attempted to. Joseph Schumpeter, the great Austrian economist, has offered an alternative—or rather, a supplementary theory.[21] Although this theory, developed in his important essay *Social Classes,* is discussed in terms of classes, it is best conceived in terms of elites. According to Schumpeter—as adapted—elites' powers and positions in a national structure depend on the significance accorded their function. Thus, under feudalism, manorial lords were pre-eminent in national structure because of the importance of their military, agricultural, and other functions. But, as their decline shows, the continuing influence of an elite depends upon two factors: (1) the continuing significance of their special functions, and (2) the degree to which they successfully perform that function. Thus, changing economic conditions reduced the importance of the manorial lords, causing their relative decline, while capitalist elites gained power because of their enhanced function. Again, a political elite's failure to maintain economic prosperity when it is their announced or implicit task to do so will enable a counter-elite to mobilize and lead masses against them.

The preoccupation of Mosca and Pareto, in particular, with elite circulation reveals a further aspect of elite theory's conservatism. The basic challenge to society is not to reform itself but to keep from disintegrating. The social order is fragile indeed, and must continually be protected from the untutored passions of the masses. To unleash social energies, as the marxist revolutionaries have threatened to do, is sheer folly, because no one can know where this will lead. Indeed, a mob can destroy institutions and accomplishments painfully and slowly evolved over history. The elite theorists wished then for a moderate and paced circulation of elites, sufficient circulation to dampen the tendencies toward mass mobilization by frustrated counter-elites but not so much as to destroy the continuity and stability of society.

Perhaps elite theory's greatest value is that it provides an explanation for why political and social structures change so gradually, if at all. Most of history is not revolutions, but rather the day-in, day-out performance of important tasks by elites and the modest but significant changes in the composition of the ruling groups. When masses are occasionally aroused from their torpor, they are placated by elites granting symbolic benefits or moderate reforms. It is the extremely rare occasion in history that masses cannot be satisfied in this way. Then they are available for the mobilization by counter-elites, and severe breaks in historical continuity can occur. The Communist revolutions of this century are a case in point, as were the democratic revolutions of the eighteenth century.

DEMOCRATIC THOUGHT AND ELITE THEORY

The theory and the practice of democracy can be interpreted as a substantial modification of elite theory. Democratic thought, at least as shaped by two centuries of politics in the United States, accepts the elite thesis that there is always a division of political labor:

> There are some whose task it is to control the actions of others and issue commands, and others who have to allow themselves to be controlled and have to obey. Today as a hundred years ago there are governments, parliaments, and courts the members of which are entitled to make decisions that affect the lives of many citizens, and there are citizens who can protest or shift their vote but who have to abide by the law. Insofar as either of these relations can be described as one of authority, I would claim that relations of domination and subordination have persisted throughout the changes of the past century.[22]

Accepting the inevitability of a division of political labor has not for the democratic theorist meant accepting the many consequences seen by the elitist. Democratic politics is the gradual but certain chipping away of elitist implications of the division of society into rulers and ruled. Whether in the U.S. this chipping process has been very successful is the principal inquiry of most of this volume. At this point, we briefly introduce the inquiry by asking what it is that democratic institutions are supposed to do.

Stripped of flowery rhetoric, democratic theory reduces to the simple principle that *rulers are on probation.* This fact dramatically rearranges the power relationship between those who rule and those who are ruled. *Federalist Paper* no. 57 provides the background:

> Before the sentiments impressed on their minds by the mode of
> their elevation can be effaced by the exercise of power, [elected
> representatives] will be compelled to anticipate the moment when
> their power is to cease, when their exercise of it is to be reviewed,
> and when they must descend to the level from which they were
> raised; there forever to remain unless a faithful discharge of their
> trust shall have established their title to a renewal of it.

The composition of the ruling group is determined by a voting public,
and this leads to an equalization of the power differences between rulers
and ruled. Under the conditions of universal suffrage and competitive
elections, the balance of power shifts to the electorate, if only periodically. Because of this, what the rulers decide reflects a wider set of
preferences than just those of the (temporary) rulers. Men in power are
but transitory representatives of those who put them there. Thus the
most fascinating aspect of the democratic revolution concerns the
methods and implications of changing leaders, because this becomes the
key to an entirely new theory of the "ruling class."

The elitist points out that even though rulers are elected, they still
have all the advantages of the ruling class. For one thing, they are organized and the masses are disorganized. As Mosca puts it, "The domination of an organized minority, obeying a single impulse, over the
unorganized majority is inevitable. . . . A hundred men acting uniformly
in concert, with a common understanding, will triumph over a thousand
men who are not in accord, and can therefore be dealt with one by one."
Later Mosca explicitly challenges whether elections make much difference:

> The truth is that the representative *has himself elected* by the voters,
> and, if that phrase should seem too inflexible and too harsh to fit
> some cases, we might qualify it by saying that *his friends have him
> elected.* In elections, as in all other manifestations of social life, those
> who have the will and, especially, the moral, intellectual and material
> *means* to force their will upon others take the lead over the others
> and command them.[23]

Michels extends this analysis: Not only does organizational ability grant
power, the structure of complex society inevitably gives rise to an
organized and oligarchial minority.

The ruling class then retains its advantages despite the advances of democratic thinking. The rulers continue to siphon off an undue amount of the social surplus for personal benefit; they continue to make laws which reflect their own world views and which serve their special interests; and they continue to control the selection of the persons who will inherit their positions.

To this argument the democratic theorist in the U.S. answers along two lines. First, by the elitists' own admission there are internal power struggles within the ruling groups. A minority out of power will turn to the electorate, and thus deliberately involve the citizenry in deciding who should rule. This has enormous spillover effects. Opposition political movements grow, and the natural organizational advantages of the elites thereby diminish. Mass political parties and strong pressure groups add greatly to the political leverage of the individual voter. This is true even if these parties and pressure groups have their own internal oligarchies, because at least they present alternatives to the current rulers. In this connection, the significance of the First Amendment freedoms should be noted. It is an uncensored press, the right to associate and agitate, and freedom of expression which provide the foundation for political opposition. These freedoms are the organizational weapons that are used to fight the organizational advantages of the rulers.

Secondly, American politics has been organized with a view to the inherent tendencies of ruling classes. Rulers have themselves been *subject* to laws, as well as been given powers to make laws. As citizen-subjects, rulers are on an equal footing with nonrulers. Particularly ingenious in this regard is the elaborate division of powers internal to the government, the checks and balances which insure that no single group can arbitrarily usurp powers not expressly granted by the Constitution. According to *Federalist Paper* no. 51, the interior structure of government is so contrived "that its several constituent parts may, by their mutual relations, be the means of keeping each other in their proper place." The founding fathers were not indifferent to the potential for abuse by rulers. But the concentration of powers in too few hands and the arbitrary exercise of power could be checked by constitutional means, especially if these means avoided naive assumptions about human nature. Thus

ambition must be made to counteract ambition. The interest of the man must be connected with the constitutional rights of the place. It may be a reflection on human nature, that such devices should be necessary to control the abuses of government. But what is government itself, but the greatest of all reflections on human nature? If men were angels, no government would be necessary. If angels were to govern men, neither external nor internal controls on government would be necessary. In framing a government which is to be administered by men over men, the greatest difficulty lies in this: you must first enable the government to control the governed: and in the next place oblige it to control itself. A dependence on the people is, no doubt, the primary control on the government; but experience has taught mankind the necessity of auxiliary precautions.[24]

Constitutional democracy has not been designed to eliminate the division of political labor between rulers and ruled. It has been designed to provide an instrumentality whereby the public could select its own rulers and whereby the few with immense powers are accountable to the citizens whose lives they affect.

We do not intend to ask in this book whether the United States is a democracy, an exercise which would involve us in tedious and tendentious definitional logistics. We do intend to ask what perspective on democracy is provided by the elite theorists. This perforce will involve us in looking at how the basic promises of democracy have worked out in practice. And it will involve us in posing a general framework for asking what has happened and is likely to happen in this society.

Notes

1 Gaetano Mosca, *The Ruling Class* (New York: McGraw-Hill, 1939), p. 50. This work was initially published as *Elementi di Scienza Politica*, 1896. The version here cited was edited by Arthur Livingston and translated by Hanna D. Kahn.

2 This quotation is taken from *Les Systemes Socialistes*, initially published in 1902, and reproduced in Vilfredo Pareto, *Sociological Writings*, ed. S. E. Finer (London: Pall Mall Press, 1966), p. 134.

3 Translated from Alexandre Dumas fils, *Les Femmes qui tuent et les Femmes qui votent*, by Robert Michels and quoted in his *Political Parties: A Sociological Study of the Oligarchical Tendencies of Modern Democracy* (New York: Collier, 1962), p. 85. *Political Parties* was first published in Germany in 1911.

4 A useful study demonstrating many of the foregoing points is Robert M. Adams, *The Evolution of Urban Society* (Chicago: Aldine, 1966). See also V. Gordon Childe, *Social Evolution* (New York: Meridian, 1963). First published in 1951.

5 Renzo Sereno, *The Rulers: The Theory of the Ruling Class* (New York: Harper & Row, 1968), p. 117.

6 Childe, *Social Evolution,* p. 47

7 I. Schapera, "The Political Organization of the Ngwato of Buchuanaland Protectorate," in M. Fortes and E. E. Evans-Pritchard, eds., *African Political Systems* (London: Oxford University Press, 1940), p. 76.

8 Karl A. Wittfogel, *Oriental Despotism* (New Haven: Yale University Press, 1957), p. 18. Recent scholarship has pointed out that Wittfogel perhaps underestimates the strength of the rulers prior to the establishment of extensive irrigation systems and thus overestimates the extent to which hydraulic systems reflect voluntaristic action by individual farmers. The more likely interpretation is that the managers used an expanding water-control project to extend administrative control.

9 Robert L. Carneiro, "A Theory of the Origin of the State," *Science,* vol. 169, no. 3947 (August 21, 1970), pp. 735-736.

10 The following discussion reflects the influence of Gerhard E. Lenski, *Power and Privilege: A Theory of Social Stratification* (New York: McGraw-Hill, 1966), especially Chapter 1.

11 From Gerrard Winstanley, *Selections from His Works,* quoted in Lenski, *Power and Privilege,* p. 10.

12 K. Oberg, "The Kingdom of Ankole in Uganda," in Fortes and Evans-Pritchard, eds., *African Political Systems,* pp. 136-137.

13 Ibn Khaldûm, *The Muqaddimah,* trans. Franz Rosenthal (London: Routledge and Kegan Paul, vol. 1, p. 381.

14 Sereno, *The Rulers,* p. 130.

15 *Ibid.,* p. 131.

16 Max Gluckman, "The Kingdom of the Zulu of South Africa," in Fortes and Evans-Pritchard, eds., *African Political Systems,* p. 30.

17 Michels, *Political Parties,* p. 90.

18 V. Lenin, *What Is to Be Done;* reprinted in *Essential Works of Lenin,* Henry M. Christman, ed. (New York: Bantam, 1966), p. 145. *What Is to Be Done* was first published in 1902.

19 John of Salisbury, *The Stateman's Book,* quoted in Lenski, *Power and Privilege,* pp. 8-9.

20 Michels, *Political Parties, passim.*

21 Joseph Schumpeter, "Social Classes," in *Imperialism, Social Classes* (New York: Meridian, 1951).

22 Ralf Dahrendorf, *Class and Class Conflict in Industrial Society* (Stanford, Calif.: Stanford University Press, 1959), p. 71.

23 Mosca, *The Ruling Class,* pp. 53, 154.

24 *The Federalist Papers,* No. 51. These were a series of newspaper articles written in defense of the Constitution during the battle over ratification. The authors were Madison, Hamilton, and Jay, three ardent Federalists who had been involved in drafting the Constitution. There are many editions of *The Federalist Papers* available.

PART TWO

PERSPECTIVES ON AMERICAN SOCIETY

In this part, we shall show how the elite perspective draws together many of the diverse events in American history, and organizes them coherently. We, of course, do not intend to present a comprehensive history of the United States from an elite perspective, although such a task remains for some researcher to undertake. Rather, we wish to look at certain important events in the nation's history in order to graphically illustrate how the elite perspective compels us to look at the most important actors in our history, and thence at their interests.

When we view American history from this perspective, we see, initially, in the period of the founding and its aftermath, an elite of landed gentlemen dominating virtually every activity in the nation's life. Men such as James Madison and Thomas Jefferson were not only among the political elite, but they were, in addition, among the wealthiest people in land property, then the major source of wealth, and within the intellectual elite. They dominated virtually every facet of social life.

Nevertheless, the days of leadership of the land-owning elite came to an end. The leaders of our great business firms became influential before the Civil War, and their influence was vastly extended afterward. Their great enterprises altered the shape of every facet of American life changing the United States from an agricultural nation to the world's leading industrial power. We shall see in this part that at all stages in their history the business elite required that resources at the disposal of the political leadership be employed on their behalf. Using elite theory, we will explore in Chapter 3 the close but complex relationship between the political and industrial elite. In this way, then, we shall see the great value of elite theory in understanding the past and its relationship with the present.

CHAPTER 2
ELITES AND
AMERICAN HISTORY

American history is popularly portrayed in texts and politicians' speeches as if mass participation in important decisions through interest groups or "popular pressure" has been of major political significance. It is widely believed that "grass roots" social movements from abolitionists through conservationists, populists, progressives, and anti-Vietnam war crusaders have been responsible for significantly altering the course of American history when the major parties and institutions were unresponsive to the need for social and political change. Strangely, this conception of popular sovereignty in America is accepted through virtually the entire spectrum of American political opinion—from marxists on the left through liberals in the center to conservatives on the right—although each ideology accepts it for different reasons.

Despite the popularity of this interpretation of American history, many scholars who have studied the various periods in American history have reached quite different conclusions. This re-examination of American history (known as *revisionism*) is still taking place and many topics have not yet been reinvestigated under the careful eyes of revisionist historians and social scientists. However, enough studies have been made to cast considerable doubt on the conventional view of American history and to convince the reader that popular participation in political decision-making has usually been of minor importance. While politicians and other important political actors have frequently credited the masses for important policy changes, this has been entirely a symbolic act intended to reinforce and continue popular support and acquiescence in the political system.[1] Actually, most important policy changes have occurred in response to the demands and needs of important elites who have sought such changes for many reasons, including quite often the furthering of their economic interests. Of course, the political rhetoric accompanying these changes attributes them to "the people," "public opinion," "popular pressure," etc. These plus-words serve the dual function of continuing mass allegiance to the political system while at the same time maintaining mass apathy and disinterest in politics since masses are led to believe that their interests are being served.

Certainly, not all of American history can be characterized in this manner. From Shay's Rebellion through the ghetto violence of the 1960s, there have been periodic outbursts and short-lived popular movements which elites have had to take into account and either repress, assuage through symbolic benefits, or assuage through substantive benefits intended to appease the aggrieved group. But, these eruptions have been infrequent and short-lived as a viable force. Popular uprisings have been reactions to policy and have almost never pointed to or lead in the creation of new policy. Moreover, for the most part popular movements have had only a peripheral effect on American history; rather, as we shall see, from the founding period forward, American politics has been carried on in a "business as usual" manner by political and other elites.

It is, of course, beyond the scope of this work to write a comprehensive American history based on elite theory. Instead we shall examine several historical periods which in our view have had the greatest impact on the present. First we shall examine the founding period in which the Constitution was basically fashioned. Next we shall examine the Progressive Era, during which regulatory legislation ripened as an important public policy; the contemporary fruits of this period are patently visible as a multitude of regulatory agencies daily spew forth a plethora of decisions crucially affecting our lives. Finally, we shall examine the New Deal, during which modern economic policies were fashioned and the masses were allegedly given a greater share of power than they had ever had before.

THE FOUNDING PERIOD

During its founding period, America was divided quite clearly into three classes: the well-born or gentlemen, the middle, and the lower ranks.[2] To be a gentleman, wealth was essential since the rank demanded such attributes as fashionable dress, superior education, and the ability to patronize the arts. But from our perspective, the gentleman's most important attribute was his conception of political obligation; he viewed his right to rule exclusively on behalf of the entire population as natural and proper; any other arrangement was unthinkable and was regarded as "leveling," an appellation with the same stigmatic effect as the word "communist" during the era of Joseph McCarthy.

The men who gathered in Philadelphia in the spring and summer of 1787 were an elite overwhelmingly composed of the gentlemen class with substantial holdings in public debt; plantations; real estate; and manufacturing, shipping, and trading concerns. [3] Those few, like Alexander Hamilton, who participated in the Constitutional Convention but who did not themselves possess great wealth, were totally disposed to the views and values of the gentlemen elite and were recruited by the latter for important roles. Indeed, had people like Hamilton not been disposed to those values and beliefs, they would have been rejected by the gentlemen elite. Few, in fact, were as zealous in their defense of inequality and elite rule as was Hamilton, who dreaded granting any power to the masses.[4]

But of the Constitutional founders, Hamilton was hardly alone in his fear of popular participation in government. It was truly a unanimous sentiment among those present at the Constitutional Convention, no matter what their divisions were on other important questions. Indeed, Madison's notes of the Federal Convention of 1787, which form the main basis of our knowledge of what transpired at the Convention, are replete with evidence of the founders' fear of popular participation in government. For example, James Madison, who is viewed as one of the most democratic of the founders, asserted:

> An increase of population will of necessity increase the proportion of those who will labour under all the hardships of life, and secretly sigh for a more equal distribution of its blessings. These may in time outnumber those who are placed above the feelings of indigence. According to the equal laws of suffrage, the power will slide into the hands of the former. No agrarian attempts have yet been made in this country, but symptoms of a leveling spirit, as we have understood, have sufficiently appeared in certain quarters to give notice of the future danger. How is this danger to be guarded against on republican principles?[5]

Madison's answer throughout the debates was clear: The system of ·

checks and balances whereby minorities could prevent radical action against private property was the appropriate method. Thus, Madison stated that one of the principal functions of the Senate would be "the guardianship of property," while George Mason, who also was considered one of the most democratic of the delegates, accordingly suggested "the propriety of annexing to the office a qualification of property."[6]

Such sentiments were only mildly elitist compared to those of other delegates, however. For example, most delegates were opposed to popular election of the Chief Executive, and accordingly the "safer" method of election through electors was devised.[7] The delegates wished to restrict suffrage as much as possible without inviting another uprising like the War of Independence.[8] Unable to agree on the specific qualifications that would enable one to exercise the ballot, the delegates left the matter to each state to decide in the hope that most of the states would adopt their own highly restrictive standards. The possibility of sudden popular change was limited by the creation of a system of checks and balances. The major devices within this system were the presidential veto, the two-thirds vote of Congress required to override the veto, the difficult and cumbersome manner of amending the Constitution, and judicial review. And, indeed, it must be conceded that these Constitutional devices, especially judicial review, have prevented much proposed change during the course of American history.[10] Thus, the "dead hand" of the founding elite has acted, and continues to act, as a restraint on the wishes of more representative elites.

Of course, these attitudes of the founding elite do not mean that they were authoritarian or dictatorial. To the contrary, the debates and the subsequent Bill of Rights show that most of them were very concerned about the preservation of substantial individual liberty consistent with the preservation of the kind of society in which they believed. Rather they were concerned about who would make the important political decisions and about arranging a Constitution and governmental structure which would act as a restraint on social change. In both these respects, but especially in the latter, they have been notably successful. Elites have effectively made the decisions in American history, although the specific elites that dominated at any particular time have changed. The rule by an elite of gentlemen, which occurred after the founding period, was gradually replaced, after the Civil War, by a rising business elite that had major influence over many crucial governmental decisions. During this period, the Supreme Court interpreted the Constitution in a manner that permitted very little unwanted interference by the legislative and executive branches in the decision-making of corporate elites.[11] In addition, it was widely felt that the Senate, which the founders arranged to be appointed by state legislatures and not elected by the people, largely represented the needs of special interests and not the masses.[12] And, as we shall see, this elitist conception also very accurately describes the so-called Progressive Era, which historians have only recently correctly understood.

THE RISE OF CORPORATE AMERICA AND THE PROGRESSIVE ERA

After the Civil War, the United States underwent a rapid conversion from a rural agricultural nation to the world's leading industrial power. As the United States became urbanized, new institutions and methods came into being, and with these came new problems that demanded solution. The most important of the new institutions following in the wake of America's industrial revolution was, of course, the corporation which, in its pursuit of increasing sales and profits, adopted such novel methods as expanding distribution networks, technical innovation, mass production, and rational office management in the regular course of business. These together with other factors completely changed the shape and structure of the American political economy in the course of the 35 years between the end of the Civil War and the dawn of the twentieth century.

The growth of modern capitalism, contrary to the laissez-faire myths, has required intimate relationships between the corporate and the political elite. Most of the corporate elite have rejected objectionable government interference while at the same time enthusiastically accepting certain close government-economy relationships. That which changes, as we shall see, are the prevailing forms of the relationship between government and business (e.g., subsidy and regulation). Thus, even in the earliest stages of capitalism, businessmen relied on government to perform certain tasks. Consider only the common law (and later statutory law) of contracts, sales, negotiable instruments, and other commercial regulations which so occupy the courts. There is nothing in nature which requires the government to use its powers to settle such private disputes, but by so doing the state facilitates the proper functioning of the commercial system and assures businessmen that the obligations owed them will be enforced.

Again, during the very era in which the laissez-faire ideology was the conventional wisdom, political elites, at the behest of America's budding entrepreneurs, were engaged in massive subsidy programs to railroads and canal companies. Thus, up to 1871, a total of 100 million acres, then valued at approximately $500 million, had been granted to various railroads by the federal government. In connection with these grants, bribery and corruption were employed by the railroad barons with great frequency, while many, if not most, of the political elite of the nation succumbed.[13]

Subsidy and similar programs were but the first of several types of programs which American business elites called on government to undertake. The next stage, the era of regulation, which came to fruition in the so-called Progressive Era, provides a clear-cut test to determine whether elites or masses are largely responsible for social change. According to the conventional view of the Progressive Era, big business was engaging in a large number of practices inimical to the interests of the masses, especially farmers and consumers. Among other charges that have been made against industry of this era are: (1) that certain large firms were monopolizing ("trustifying") their respective industries with the attendant danger of charging monopoly prices to the consumer and destroying smaller competitors; (2) that greedy big business firms were busily depleting our natural resources without regard to the future; (3) that they were responsible for municipal corruption; (4) that railroads charged excessive rates to ship farm goods; and (5) that big business was totally indifferent to reasonable standards for food, drugs, and other products. The abuses became so patent, according to this theory, that muckrakers investigated them and brought them to the attention of reformers who organized social movements to combat the respective abuses. Ultimately, the reformers are supposed to have won victories over the trusts by securing the passage of such regulatory legislation as the Meat Inspection Act, the Clayton Act, and the Federal Trade Commission Act.[14]

Thus, to take but one example of the dynamic the conventional view envisions, meat and other food industries were viewed as utterly indifferent to decent health standards prior to the enactment of the Meat Inspection Act. Then the novelist Upton Sinclair investigated the operations of the Chicago packing plants and published his best-selling novel, *The Jungle,* which vividly exposed the horrendous conditions within the plants. The nation was so horrified by these dreadful conditions that popular pressure compelled Congress, over the vigorous opposition of the affected industries, to enact legislation designed to safeguard the consumer's health.

If this conventional description of the way in which such a typical piece of progressive regulatory legislation was enacted is correct, the era cannot be explained on the basis of elite theory, but, rather, must be interpreted along more conventional lines pursuant to which popular pressure and social movements initiated the sweeping changes in American political history.

But is elite theory inapplicable to the Progressive Era? Hardly. In fact recent evidence indicates that popular movements and pressure directed against "trusts" had very little to do with the enactment of regulatory legislation and that political and business elites, with occasional cooperation from other elites (often the new technological elite), were far more responsible for causing such laws to be passed. The reason business elites actively sought regulatory legislation were: (1) to meliorate competition and thus achieve a degree of stability which they could not obtain facing the hazards of hard competition, and (2) to assure the kind of rational, predictable government which could most effectively serve the needs of the business elite's firms. Let us look first at meat inspection legislation to see what recent research shows about its origins.

The "social movement" or "popular pressure" theories regarding meat inspection are undermined by evidence that leading businessmen and trade association executives were not only on record as being very much in favor of the legislation, but in the forefront of the fight for it. That is not to say that all meat-packing executives favored regulation, but most of the leading ones did. Upton Sinclair, the prime mover for regulation according to the conventional account, observed that "the Federal inspection of meat was, historically, established at the packers' request; . . . it is maintained and paid for by the people of the United States for the benefit of the packers."[15] Evidence supporting Sinclair's assertion

is persuasive. During the course of the 1906 hearings on meat inspec-
tions, representatives of the large meat-packing firms testified in favor
of the bill. Moreover, the leading spokesmen for the meat-packing industry publicly proclaimed the virtues of regulation. They sought in the
bill—and won—two important provisions: the principle that the government should absorb the entire inspection cost and that date-of-slaughter
labeling on meat should not be mandatory. The latter was sought because of possible public reluctance to eat older but perfectly good meat.

Why were the leaders of the major meat packers so in favor of a
strong inspection act? The principal reason was that in the 1880s most
of the large European nations had banned American meat because of
the low standards employed by some packers and had turned to Argen-
tina to supply the bulk of their needs. After the American-European
trade was restored, the large packers vigorously sought government
regulation so as not to be foreclosed from the lucrative export market.
Government regulation was the only effective way of assuring that *all* of
the members of the industry abided by the standards required to sell to
Europe. Voluntary agreements could easily be evaded with impunity by
the unscrupulous packer with the result that European barriers would
again be raised.[16]

In summary, then, meat-labeling legislation, the prototype of many
future statutes purporting to benefit the consumer, came about because
of the interrelated actions of an economic and a political elite. While the
public unquestionably benefitted from the implemented needs of the
big packers, it played no discernible role in bringing about the legislation
either through reforming or mass movements or through "popular pressure." But, as usual, the public was given credit for it, thus helping to
assure their allegiance to the system and their continued dormancy.

And notwithstanding the fact that consumer health and safety legislation bears such an obvious nexus to people's well-being, and hence
should arouse greater public response than other kinds of statutes, other
careful studies of health and safety regulation demonstrate the same
elitist dynamic illustrated by meat inspection. Let us examine both the
first Food and Drug Act (1906) and the Food and Drug Amendment
passed during the New Deal. The reason most of the large concerns supported such legislation was aptly described in the leading study of the
1938 Food and Drug Amendment: "Many prescription manufacturers

felt that their business might be increased if more restrictive practices were placed on the marketing of proprietary balms." Indeed, the leading drug manufacturers felt that the drug business as a whole was harmed when deceptive claims by quack medicine proprietors resulted in harm to consumers. Accordingly, the leaders of large pharmaceutical firms and trade associations actively sought regulation, and again no social movements or popular pressure played any significant part in the result.[17]

Conservation, too, provides another illustration of how elites—in this case, business, political, and scientific—were the principal actors in the formation of public policy. The reason for the demand of many large corporations for conservation is set forth in an admirable study of conservation legislation:

> . . . lumbermen . . . could no longer move on to virgin areas when they had exhausted their available timber. They now became more interested in using existing supplies more efficiently. . . . Wood consuming industries shared these concerns. Vehicle, box, and furniture manufacturers, for example, secured satisfactory supplies with increasing difficulty. If they could not obtain more reliable sources of lumber, they would be forced to curtail operations. . . . They became active in the American Forestry Association and swung their trade organizations behind the U.S. Forest service.[18]

Accordingly, business spokesmen joined with sympathetic applied scientists and engineers and with members of the political elite, most notably President Theodore Roosevelt, in sponsoring conservation legislation and other programs. In much the same way, the demands for sound federal policy for oil lands came from the oil prospectors, while the backing for other natural resource policies came from business and engineering leaders. Popular participation—or even interest—in the formulation or enactment of these programs was virtually nonexistent.[19]

Even municipal reform, long romanticized as the result of popular revulsion against corrupt municipal administrations and their connivances with "special interests," proves on examination to have an entirely different dynamic. Such new electoral techniques as the initiative, referendum, recall, and popular election of officials illustrate, in the conventional view, greater democratization and popular participation in municipal government. In fact, the principal impetus for municipal reform came not from middle- or working-class reform movements but from local business elites and the leaderships of the professional associations allied with and serving those business elites. The principal reason for this opposition to municipal corruption is, in the words of Leonard White, the great historian of public administration, that: "Businessmen finally acquire the conviction that the growth of their city is being seriously impaired by the failures of city officials to perform their duties."[20] Business concerns desired effective municipal management of such diverse infrastructural factors as flood control or traffic flow systems. Their objection was not to corruption *per se,* but rather to the very narrow interests of a political system in which words were the center of orientation. Under such a system, the metropolitan concerns of business leaders were being ignored in favor of narrow ward interests. Accordingly, reform associations financed and led by the local business elite sought to centralize urban governments and end the ward system through such devices as the city manager plan which was patterned on the operations of business firms.

The rhetoric employed by the reformers was, of course, framed in terms of the "public interest" or as being against "the machine" or "corruption" in order to gain popular acceptance for their program, but the central reforms themselves greatly centralized municipal decision-making and generally aided the downtown business community. Even such baggage of the reform ideology as the initiative, referendum, and recall were, as historian Samuel Hays acutely observed, ". . . only an occasional and often incidental process of decision-making. Far more important in continuous, sustained, day-to-day processes of government were those innovations which centralized decision-making in the hands of fewer and fewer people."[21] In many instances, it was not even necessary for the elite reformers to go to the electorate to secure the desired changes; their activities on the state level often induced the state legislature to change the form of municipal government without consulting the voters. Thus, on examination, municipal reforms, like other Progressive Era innovations, prove to be the result of the actions of business and political elites; social movements or popular pressure have almost no part in precipitating the change. In fact, labor organizations often opposed such change.

Of all the changes implemented during the Progressive Era, the one most misunderstood by the convential view is the regulatory legislation affecting business. According to the popular concept, big business was becoming even bigger after the turn of the twentieth century at the expense of smaller rivals. It accomplished this objective by engaging in various acts of "unfair competition" that were beyond the jurisdiction of the Sherman Antitrust Act. Accordingly, small business and popular forces, in fear of monopoly and its resultant effects, sought the enactment of regulatory legislation that would restrict the ability of large firms to engage in predatory practices. Big business vehemently objected to the enactment of such legislation, but was defeated by the popular coalition through the enactment of the Clayton and Federal Trade Commission Acts.[22]

This conventional explanation, like the others we have examined, does not hold up to careful scrutiny, however, in several respects. The first flaw in the conventional argument concerns the charge that big business was gaining at the expense of smaller rivals. In fact, the very reverse is true; there was a significant decline in the relative strength of the trusts from 1902 to 1914—and the sponsors of the 1914 legislation were aware of this decline. Even the much vaunted "Standard Oil Trust" had experienced marked declines in its market share prior to the 1911 decree entered against it, while the same deterioration of market position was suffered by market leaders in the automobile, agricultural implement, steel, copper, and other leading industries. In each of these industries, vigorous new firms entering on the basis of technological innovation or new consumer tastes were badly cutting into the markets of the older established firms.[23] One is compelled to ask what accounted for the proposals for new trade regulation legislation if there was no threat of monopoly and the political elite was aware of this as a result of Congressional debate and Bureau of Corporations' reports?

The answer was clearly not the inadequacy of the Sherman Act, which was perfectly capable of attacking monopoly, monopolization methods by large firms, and cartel practices such as price-fixing. The new legislation was aimed not at giant monopolies, but at the vigorous competitive methods employed by those firms beyond the reach of the Sherman Act because of their smaller size. Such firms' vigorous competition, if unchecked, could destabilize industries by means of such methods as price-cutting and exclusive dealing. And the function of the

Clayton and Federal Trade Commission Acts was to prevent instability by greatly restricting such modes of competition. The 1914 acts, then, were the antithesis of the Sherman Act which favored vigorous competition as a public policy.

Considering that the large established firms would benefit considerably from government regulation that would restrict competition, it is not surprising that big business leaders actively sought such legislation. For example, in 1908 Andrew Carnegie favored government regulation to solve the problem of fierce price competition in the steel industry, while in 1911 George W. Perkins, a J. P. Morgan & Co. partner and close associate of leading politicians, proposed the founding of a federal business court or commission to place limits on the legality of business action. The National Chamber of Commerce urged President Wilson to promulgate a strong federal trade commission bill, a position endorsed by steel industry executives as well as the leaders of major trade associations.[24]

The new trade regulation statutes were prepared by members of the political elite with, at all stages, the close collaboration of members of the business elite. In fact, a major substantive provision was prepared by an attorney who was at the time serving as a member of a special committee of the United States Chamber of Commerce devoted to trade regulation. Once again, neither "popular pressure" nor social movements played any significant part in the genesis of the new trade regulation statutes, although both the members of the business and political elites who prepared and shaped the new laws, just as in the prior cases of regulatory legislation we have examined, sought public acquiescence by asserting that the statutes were in the public interest.[25]

The last area of Progressive Era legislation that we shall examine is the regulation of the railroads. This was one of the few areas where a mass movement (the Grangers) contributed to the shaping of public policy. But, once again, the conventional account does not accurately assess the role of the general public. The conventional view states that railroads were exploiting farmers by charging them excessively high or discriminatory rates to ship their products to market. In the 1870s, the farmers became so aroused that they organized and led a social movement that pressed for state regulation of railroad rates. The Granger Movement, although short-lived, achieved its objective in many of the

Midwestern states over the bitter opposition of the railroads. However, there still remained the task of regulating the interstate rates and practices of railroads. Farmers' movements are credited, by the conventional view, with forcing the enactment of the series of statutes, from the Interstate Commerce Act of 1887 to the Mann-Elkins Act of 1910, that were designed to accomplish this purpose.[26]

Recent detailed studies, based on original papers of important participants which were unavailable at the time the conventional view was formulated, indicate a very different pattern of events from the one described above, one far more in keeping with what we have suggested characterized the other Progressive regulatory legislation. First, a study of the Granger laws in various states found that farmers generally did not support the Granger movement, but, rather, gave their allegiance to the Republican Party which:

> . . . spoke for the traditional mercantile and industrial interests of the separate states. The Granger laws were prepared by lawyers, usually with the help of merchants and shippers, and sometimes with the aid of railroad officials. Their agrarianism was an invention of their enemies.
>
> All the important Granger innovations—the strong commission, judicial review, and the classification of roads based on earnings— were concessions to the railroad interests.[27]

The recent findings, in short, show that the "Farmers' movement of the 1870s was not a major force in the shaping of this regulatory legislation."[28] Rather, the leaders in the battle were various local businessmen intent on avoiding rate discrimination relative to competitors selling to the same markets. Railroads, too, were not averse to state regulation on their terms since discrimination involved lowering a rate below what they felt should be their return. In a word, they would benefit considerably from being forbidden to discriminate in rates.

By 1880, many of the leaders of the railroad industry, in fact, became the leading proponents of federal railroad regulation rather than regulation by a plethora of state agencies. An examination of railroad executives' views in 1916 showed the vast majority favored and approved regulation. Again, rate regulation was favored because the railroads were thus precluded by law from engaging in rate wars or acceding to a shipper's demands for a discount. In fact, regulation brought more benefit to the railroads than merely shielding them from the hazards of competition, because the federal government undertook the responsibility of assuring railroads the right to charge a sufficiently high rate to make a profit. Thus, most of the leaders of the railroad industry worked for the enactment of each of the railroad regulatory statutes from 1887 onward. The content of the various federal railroad regulatory acts was shaped, however, not by the railroads alone, but also by various business leaders with diverse shipping interests. Farmer movements, like other popular movements, played a minor (if any) part in the creation of these statutes, while public pressure was, at best, manifested in a signature campaign organized by Pennsylvania oil producing leaders before the initial I.C.C. Act. Such "popular pressure" is, of course, a far cry from mass agitation or a protest movement and is little more than an instance of elite manipulation.[29]

These few examples are representative of how a considerable amount of regulatory legislation came to be enacted, not only during the Progressive Era, but in the years that followed. In these cases, elites were the principal actors, shaping and guiding the progress of the proposed policies from their inceptions through their enactments. The battles that transpired over these statutes and policies were struggles between the elites, and not masses who usually played a passive role—their acceptance purchased by pronouncements that the new reforms were in the "public interest" and that the masses' "popular pressure" was responsible for their enactments. While the ideologies supporting these pronouncements were very likely sincerely held by their spokesmen, the facts indicate otherwise, as we have seen. And although the "public" or "masses" might have benefitted from the administration of the statute, the law's biases are most clearly manifested in favor of the elites who sought the legislation. This is the clear message of the numerous "exposés" and investigations of the regulatory agencies which occur every few years and reach the identical conclusion that the agencies are serving special interests rather than the public interest.

THE NEW DEAL

There is little question but that the New Deal inagurated some enduring changes in the American political-economic landscape, but precisely what these changes are is a matter of some contention. Liberals maintain that for the first time the "common man" received a voice in national government and that the New Deal worked a great redistribution of wealth and income in favor of the poorer elements of American society. Conservatives, on the other hand, deplore what they consider to be the crushing of individual liberty as a result of the rapid growth of the State which began during the New Deal. Both of these views will be considered in our examination of the New Deal and in later chapters on the structure of power in post-World War II America.

If the liberals who urge that the New Deal marked the ascendancy to power of the "common man" are correct, we would expect that his representatives would use their power to redistribute wealth in his favor. However, this did not occur. Thus, in 1933, the year President Hoover left office and the New Deal was initiated, the wealthiest 1 percent of the adult population held 28.3 percent of personal sector wealth; in 1939, their holdings had increased to 30.6 percent. The comparable figures for the top 0.5 percent of the adult population were 25.2 percent of personally held wealth in 1933 increasing to 28 percent in 1939. Similarly, the top 1 percent of adults who held 65.9 percent of personal sector corporate stock in 1929 had increased its percentage held to 69 percent in 1939, the end of the New Deal. If we change our focus from individual to corporate wealth holding, we see the same result. In 1929, the 100 largest firms in manufacturing, mining, and distribution held 25.5 percent of all corporate assets, but in 1935 their holdings had risen to 28 percent.[30]

These figures should not be misinterpreted as necessarily proving that big business controlled or dominated the New Deal or that many New Dealers in their individual capacities did not wish to redistribute wealth; many clearly did. What the evidence challenges is the proposition that the New Deal was a "mass movement" of the underprivileged against big business. The first goal of such a movement in power would have been to redistribute wealth in its favor. This would be especially true if the movement were to blame "big business" wealth concentration for the Depression. The evidence, therefore, points to the conclusion that the New Deal was not a social movement, although it did clearly have to take into account and respond to a considerable amount of mass unrest, most of which was politically unfocused. But such mass unrest did not make the policy changes that occurred during the period; rather, unrest was one of several factors that elite policy-makers considered in making their important decisions.

The New Dealers were, in fact, a rather complicated political elite, antagonizing at times and pleasing at other times important sections of the business and labor leaderships. And, indeed, this is not surprising since there were diverse views within both the labor and business leaderships concerning the best way to deal with the Great Depression, the effects of which were not alleviated until the advent of World War II. Labor leaders, for example, disapproved of the selection of Frances Perkins as Secretary of Labor and disapproved of President Roosevelt's neutrality during the bloody Little Steel organizing strike of 1937, which the labor leadership lost.[31] In fact, by 1939, many in labor's leadership felt that "Congress was ignoring labor's demands and that Roosevelt was apathetic toward reform," a judgment supported by Roosevelt's general indifference to the enactment of the Wagner National Labor Relation Act.[32]

Nevertheless, the New Dealers did enact the Wagner Act and Roosevelt did sign the bill. One reason that the New Dealers supported the act was its probable effect in promoting industrial peace by regularizing management-labor relations so that bargaining between corporations and union elites would replace bitter strikes. Roosevelt asserted that the new act would provide a "*better* relationship between labor and management" and "an orderly procedure for determining who is entitled to represent the employees" at the bargaining table.[33] Thus, the Wagner Act was conceived as a way of preventing labor unrest from exploding and endangering the social system. It did this by legitimizing a labor elite whose ends would be economic bargaining within a legal framework and not radical action. In this sense, the New Dealers were a far more conservative force than those hard-nosed industrialists whose arrogance and high-handedness toward any organization of the working class *might* have driven workers into a social movement. And, indeed, many large industrialists, such as those at United States Steel, perceived things in the "New Deal" way and entered into collective bargaining arrangements with labor's elite.

Labor legislation, in fact, typifies the approach of the New Dealers to the problems they confronted generally. Faced with an intense depression and the bankruptcy of the economic system, they, in contrast to socialists and communists, sought the means to preserve the economic system and extant property relationships from the threat of incipient social movements. But it was obvious that to do so the system could not function as it had before; new experiments and techniques were needed to preserve the socioeconomic system. And this ceaseless searching for new means to preserve capitalism and restore prosperity to business is the key to the New Deal. In this relentless search, the New Deal had the support and participation of some of the business community and the bitter enmity of many others, the split reflecting the deep divisions within business leadership on how to deal with the Depression.

Even the Tennessee Valley Authority, the New Deal's boldest experiment involving state ownership and operation of a power system, should not be conceived of as an experiment in socialism, but, rather, as a means to develop the infrastructure of the Tennessee Valley and bring new industries to that region by providing them with cheap power. Of course, the New Dealers expected the inhabitants of the area also to reap the benefits of the program. But, in Roosevelt's words, "It was not initiated or organized for the purpose of selling electricity. That is a side function."[34]

Roosevelt's whole background and the pattern of his recruitment into Democratic Party leadership would lead one to conclude that he, and therefore the subordinates he recruited, would be intent on preserving the system. Roosevelt himself came from a distinguished, well-to-do family and had an extensive business background which included experience as a president of a trade association, vice-president of a surety bonding company, investor, president of an investment house, and director of an investment firm for banks.[35] His rise through the Democratic Party was entirely within regular channels, and in 1932 he was acceptable to the southern tories, big business contributors, and regular party leaders, whose support was necessary to successful nomination as a regular.[36]

Again, in 1936, Roosevelt drew an impressive amount of financial support from big businessmen, although, as usual, big business contributions to the Republican Party were far greater than those to the Democratic Party. But among the Democratic contributors to the Presidential campaign were executives, directors, or substantial shareholders of such giant firms as Cities Service Oil Company, American Tobacco

Company, General Motors, and International Telephone and Telegraph Company.[37] While such substantial big business support does not necessarily imply that the contributee will do specific favors for the narrow, specific interests of the donors, such large gifts do indicate that the donors are well-satisfied that the recipient will not act contrary to the donors' important interests by drastically shifting wealth or transforming the system of property relations or the basic ownership structure.

In fact, such businessmen felt that many New Deal reforms would strengthen the private enterprise system and bring prosperity. Accordingly, many businessmen formed a part of the New Deal elite in several respects. A study of the persons who occupied top government posts between 1933 and 1965 found that the principal occupation before appointment of 20 percent of these people during the Roosevelt Administrations was business, while 24 percent were lawyers (but there is no breakdown to determine the percentage of these lawyers who were connected with top corporate law firms). In contrast, only 10 percent of Roosevelt's top officeholders were educators, while only 6 percent were in the "other private" occupation category which would include much more than labor.[38] Thus, businessmen were well represented in the New Deal elite.

Businessmen outside of government as well as those within were active in evolving some of the most important New Deal programs. Social Security, for example, was developed and supported by some wealthy business leaders, several of whom served on the group that designed the Social Security scheme. And this is not surprising; the scheme is hardly radical; similar ones had been in effect in capitalist Germany since 1889, and in capitalist Britain since 1908. Social Security serves the economic system by bolstering demand during slack times. Moreover, unlike other forms of old-age and unemployment compensation, it requires the beneficiary to pay a large proportion of his own income while the portion that business pays is uniform and is easily passed on to the consumer. In brief, Social Security is very much like a form of compulsory insurance that is paid for largely by the beneficiaries. It is not, therefore, surprising to find that even most Republicans supported the bill. In contrast, a rival scheme (the Lundeen Bill), which was rejected by Congress and ignored by the President, would have paid for all forms of such compensation out of income and inheritance taxes, thus compelling the wealthy to foot much more of the costs.[39]

In summary, then, there was substantial public distress because of depression conditions which might have erupted and endangered the economic system. The New Dealers, with the support and aid of some of the big business elite and most of the labor elite, but with the opposition of much of big business leadership, developed a moderate scheme of Social Security, thus alleviating much of this diffuse distress. The moderate course taken by the New Deal elite was to be expected in view of the fact that the Administration recruited many persons from within the mainstream of American business and political life. These are recruitment channels heavily funded by financial and corporate leaders. In the process of enacting the legislation, elites led and made all of the decisions with masses supplying only a diffuse, silent unrest which was the impetus for a rapid solution to the enormous suffering occasioned by the poverty of the unemployed or the aged. But the solution of the New Deal was a far cry from the benefits offered by the Lundeen Bill, which masses might have sought had they been active rather than essentially outside the process that makes specific decisions.

Much the same process characterizes another monumental decision of the New Deal—the decision to use fiscal policy to regulate the economy. As we observed earlier in this chapter, the notion that there has been a period in American economic history when laissez-faire accurately described business-government relations is a fiction. Only the prevailing techniques by which government aided the business system have changed, and in the 1930s new techniques to end the Great Depression were desperately needed. New Deal economic policies to cope with the Depression evolved from, at first, cutting public works expenditures to employing such expenditures as a means of decreasing unemployment and, finally, to utilizing public works as a "pump priming" or "multiplier" device in 1938. Beardsley Ruml, a big businessman very involved in political problems, was most instrumental in channeling President Roosevelt's views to "pump priming." The President, after some initial resistance, justified his new commitment by observing that: "From our earliest days we have had a tradition of substantial government help to our system of private enterprise. . . . It is following tradition as well as necessity, if government strives to put idle money and idle men to work, to increase our public wealth . . . and to help our system of private enterprise to function."[40]

Again, neither mass "pressure" nor a "mass movement" was in any way responsible for the decision to employ a spending policy. Rather, the brilliant discoveries of an economist, John Maynard Keynes, had changed the thinking of some government officials and businessmen who suceeded in persuading the President. In the words of economist Seymour Harris, "He [Keynes] preached what has become a commonplace since he wrote; government should spend more and tax less in depression; and spend less and tax more in boom, These simple truths were discoveries of Keynes which had to be repeated hundreds of times before they made the required impression."[41] And this concept effected by a small elite has become a cardinal principle of American policy-makers.

SUMMARY

We have briefly examined three of the most important periods in American history in terms of their impact on the present, and have found the elite theory best explains their dynamics. The patterns of American history are best understood by closely examining the composition, recruitment, views, and values of small elite groups. It is beyond the scope of this book to develop further examples from these periods, or other periods, to further confirm this point. But it could be done. On the other hand, we do not assert that social movements or "popular pressure" have *never* been a major determinant of policy. Rather, we believe that those occasions are very rare and, as we shall see later, have been almost nonexistent in the period following World War II.

Notes

1 The concept of symbolism as a vehicle to tie masses to the political system is expounded in Murray Edelman, *The Symbolic Uses of Politics* (Urbana: University of Illinois Press, 1964).

2 The class structure of the period and its implications are discussed in great detail in the works of Jackson T. Main, principally *The Anti-Federalists* (Chapel Hill: University of North Carolina Press, 1961); and, for the earlier revolutionary period, in *The Social Structure of Revolutionary America* (Princeton, N.J.: Princeton University Press, 1965).

3 The evidence of this wealth is developed in Charles A. Beard, *An Economic Interpretation of the Constitution of the United States* (New York: Macmillan, 1913). The inferences drawn from the data by Beard have, however, been seriously questioned.

4   See, for example, Max Farrand, *The Records of the Federal Convention of 1787,* vol. 1 (New Haven: Yale University Press, 1911), pp. 424, 5.

5   Farrand, *The Records of the Federal Convention of 1787,* vol. 1, pp. 422, 423.

6   *Ibid.,* pp. 428, 462.

7   See, e.g., Farrand, *The Records of the Federal Convention of 1787,* vol. II, p. 57.

8   See Farrand, *The Records of the Federal Convention of 1787,* vol. II, p. 202.

9   It should be recalled that the founders explicitly rejected a Bill of Rights as unnecessary in the course of the founding debates.

10 An excellent, although now dated, study of how the judicial elite continually thwarted legislation is Louis Boudin, *Government by Judiciary* (New York: Russell & Russell, 1932; reprinted in 1968).

11 See, for details, Arthur Selwyn Miller, *The Supreme Court and American Capitalism* (New York: Free Press, 1968), pp. 50-62.

12 This mode of electing the Senate was changed by the Seventeenth Amendment in 1913.

    For a muckraking analysis of the Senate see David Graham Phillips, *The Treason of the Senate* (1906; reprinted New York: Monthly Review Press, 1953).

13 Robert Edward Riegel, *The Story of the Western Railroads* (New York: Macmillan, 1926), pp. 42, 43.

14 The best exposition of the conventional view is Harold U. Faulkner, *The Decline of Laissez-Faire* (New York: Holt, Rinehart and Winston, 1951).

15 Quoted in Gabriel Kolko, *The Triumph of Conservatism* (New York: Free Press, 1963), p. 103. In general, this account relies heavily on the facts and interpretation unearthed by Kolko.

16 *Ibid.,* pp. 98-108.

17 *Ibid.,* pp. 108-110; and Charles O. Jackson, *Food and Drug Legislation in the New Deal* (Princeton, N.J.: Princeton University Press, 1970). The quoted portion is from Jackson, p. 81.

18 Samuel P. Hays, *Conservation and the Gospel of Efficiency* (New York: Atheneum, 1959; reprinted in 1969), p. 31.

19 *Ibid.,* pp. 1-4, 88, 126, 138, 141.

20 Quoted in Samuel P. Hays, "The Politics of Reform in Municipal Government in the Progressive Era," *Pacific Northwest Quarterly* LV (October, 1964), 152.

21 *Ibid.,* p. 160.

22 Faulkner, *The Decline of Laissez-Faire,* pp. 175-186.

23 See Kolko, *The Triumph of Conservatism,* pp. 11-57; and Alan Stone, "The Politics of Trade Regulation." Unpublished Ph.D. dissertation, University of Chicago, 1971.

24 Kolko, *The Triumph of Conservatism,* pp. 173-175. Melvin I. Urofsky, *Big Steel and the Wilson Administration* (Columbus: Ohio State University Press, 1969), pp. 56-59. Louis Galambos, *Competition and Cooperation* (Baltimore: Johns Hopkins Press, 1966), p. 50.

25 Kolko, *The Triumph of Conservatism,* pp. 175, 326. Robert H. Weibe, *Businessmen and Reform* (Cambridge, Mass.: Harvard University Press, 1962), p. 138. Stone, "The Politics of Trade Regulation," part II, *passim.*

26 See Solon Justus Buck, *The Granger Movement* (Cambridge, Mass.: Harvard University Press, 1913; reprinted by University of Nebraska Press, N.D.), pp. 123-238.

27 George H. Miller, *Railroads and the Granger Laws* (Madison: University of Wisconsin Press, 1971), pp. 167, 168.

28 *Ibid.,* p. 196.

29 Gabriel Kolko, *Railroads and Regulation* (Princeton, N.J.: Princeton University Press, 1965), *passim.* Lee Benson, *Merchants, Farmers and Railroads* (Cambridge, Mass.: Harvard University Press, 1955), *passim.*

30 Robert J. Lampman, *The Share of Top Wealth Holders in National Wealth 1922-1956* (Princeton, N.J.: Princeton University Press, 1962), pp. 24-26, 209. Hearings Before the Subcommittee on Antitrust and Monopoly of the Senate Committee on the Judiciary, 88th Cong., 2d Sess. on *Economic Concentration,* part 1, p. 62.

31 C. K. McFarland, *Roosevelt, Lewis and the New Deal, 1933-1940* (Fort Worth: Texas Christian University Press, 1970), pp. 12, 13.

32 McFarland, *Roosevelt, Lewis and the New Deal,* p. 93. Paul K. Conkin, *The New Deal* (New York: Crowell, 1967).

33 Quoted in McFarland, *Roosevelt, Lewis and the New Deal,* p. 32. See also p. 21, 31.

34 Lester G. Seligman and Ernest E. Cornwell, eds., *New Deal Mosaic* (Eugene: University of Oregon Books, 1965), pp. 368, 369.

35 Daniel R. Fusfeld, *The Economic Thought of Franklin D. Roosevelt and the Origins of the New Deal* (New York: Columbia University Press, 1956), pp. 101-116.

36 For details, see Frank Friedel, *Franklin D. Roosevelt: The Triumph* (Boston: Little, Brown, 1956).

37 Ferdinand Lundberg, *America's 60 Families* (New York: The Vanguard Press, 1937), pp. 480, 481. For more recent data see G. William Domhoff, *Fat Cats and Democrats* (Englewood Cliffs, N. J.: Prentice-Hall, 1972).

38 David T. Stanley, Dean E. Mann, and Jameson W. Doig, *Men Who Govern* (Washington, D. C.: Brookings Institution, 1967), p. 132.

39 Broadus Mitchell, *The Depression Decade* (New York: Holt, Rinehart and Winston, 1947), pp. 310-313. G. William Domhoff, *The Higher Circles* (New York: Random House, 1970), pp. 207-218. Conkin, *The New Deal,* pp. 60-62. On the support of moderate business leaders for Social Security and other New Deal legislation, see Karl Schriftgiesser, *Business Comes of Age* (New York: Harper & Row, 1960).

40 Quoted in Herbert Stein, *The Fiscal Revolution in America* (Chicago: University of Chicago Press, 1969), p. 113. See generally pp. 109-114.

41 Seymour E. Harris, *John Maynard Keynes: Economist and Policy Maker* (New York: Scribner, 1955), p. 149.

CHAPTER 3
BUSINESS AND
GOVERNMENT

President Coolidge is better remembered for his aphorism that "the business of America is business" than for any of the public policies instituted during his administration. For, just like President Eisenhower's Secretary of Defense Charles Wilson's remark that what is good for General Motors is good for the country, the statement contains a great amount of truth. At the least, America's rise as a world power has in large part been connected with the rise of its industry and commerce. And, as we saw in the previous chapter, the leaders of American industry and commerce have at all times desired the intervention of the State to accomplish certain goals. Accordingly, business—or more accurately businesses, because we have not at this point shown any sense of cohesion in the business community—must seek to compel the State to act favorably to its interests.

But the fact that an institution is imposing and economically powerful does not *necessarily* indicate that its desires will be effected against competing interests. Aside from the problem of cohesion which we mentioned above, there is nothing that obviously demonstrates that there is an exact linear relationship between economic power and political power. Nor does it necessarily follow that the more economically powerful institutions dominate and control those—such as religious or entertainment institutions—that are economically much weaker. Yet, as we shall see, some theorists have implicitly assumed such dominating relationships to be given. Once this assumption is made, one need not examine whether, in fact, such diverse institutions as the military, the bureaucracy, or the scientific establishment have power and policies of their own, independent of the business community, or what occurs when there is a clash between the business community and another institution. The subservience of all other institutions to business is simply understood.

In this chapter, we shall examine some of the theories that purport to show that in American society a business elite dominates and controls virtually every other institution with few exceptions. Since the most renowned of such theories is marxism, we shall initially set forth the views of several writers who hold to this ideology. In critically examining these writers, the reader should not infer that our critique constitutes a broadside attack against marxism. We simply point out weaknesses in the analyses of some writers who label themselves marxists.

Marxism is only one of several theories that give analytical primacy to economic factors. While Marx has had great influence on almost everyone who has thought about questions of political power, many writers have been disinclined to accept all the tenets of marxism, and, instead, have selected only portions with which they feel analytically comfortable. We shall also examine in this chapter those writers who, though not themselves marxists, accept in some form or another the notion of an economically based ruling class whose power and influence exceed that of any other segment of the society.

FINANCE-CAPITAL CONTROL

The earliest book to examine American power from a marxist—or, more specifically, marxist-leninist—point of view is Anna Rochester's *Rulers of America.*[1] Her book attempts to prove the leninist thesis that finance capital, principally investment bankers, dominates and controls the major industrial corporations (pp. 103-120). But it also argues that finance-capital also controls the American political structure. It states that historically "the structure of government in the United States has always been shaped to prevent control by the masses"; the system of checks and balances was intentionally erected to prevent change sought by the masses (p. 122). Moreover, even if laws effecting change are passed in response to the popular will, "they must be administered by executives who not uncommonly sabotage the intent of the law. And if the law, even so, becomes too troublesome to the capitalists, they can carry it into court and have it declared unconstitutional" (p. 123). In a word, the system of checks and balances was designed to thwart social change and, in fact, operates in this manner. In the previous chapter, we saw that there is more than a grain of truth in this characterization of the system instituted by the founders.

Business's control of the political structure comes about, according to this work, not only because of the Constitution but also (and more importantly) because of business's control of the major political parties. Party machines, from the municipal to the federal level, "are tied in with the business interests" (p. 124). The principal means by which the finance capitalists control both political parties is by the contribution of campaign funds for which they receive as a *quid pro quo* legislation beneficial to either the capitalists as a class or groups within the class (pp. 125-127). Thus, for campaign contributions, the Roosevelt administration sought "the restoration of profits for the capitalist class through such measures as government credit to protect the financial structure, N.R.A. codes for maintaining prices and limiting production, and schemes to raise agricultural prices by reducing production" (p. 294).

Campaign contributions are, indeed, the key to big business control of politics, according to this theory. "Once the candidates are installed ...they render the political services expected of them" (p. 125). There is little doubt that generous gifts from people of great means are and have been an important—indeed crucial—source of campaign funds for both major parties.[2] For example, in 1952, 68 percent of Republican receipts from individual contributions and 63 percent of such Democratic receipts were in sums of more than $500.[3] But does this mean that the recipients of such sums must do the specific bidding of their contributors? Political scientist David Truman, for example, argues that the political obligations due because of campaign funds are highly ambiguous:

> Except where a donation is purely a matter of personal friendship, the central objective of contributions is access to the power of the elected official. Such access may mean merely the representation in legislative and executive circles, of a general point of view toward government policies, or it may mean an 'inside track' on lucrative contracts or jobs . . . [or] . . . merely a chance to argue a particular point of view or it may signify effective leverage for [or] against . . . action . . . [or] . . . it may indicate that the recipient is virtually the agent of the donor or merely that the latter has hopefully climbed aboard the bandwagon of an obvious winner . . . [or] . . . it may approximate extortion.[4]

The ambiguity for which Truman argues can only be sustained if we assume that the politician is in a haughty position relative to the prospective donor; the continual need of politicians to meet their mounting campaign costs would indicate, however, that it is the big donor who can afford to be haughty. Even so, it still does not necessarily follow that large donors expect or receive *specific* policy outputs from their political donees. Often, political office-seekers receive funds from conflicting business interests. For example, how is the aspiring officeholder to settle conflicts between importers and native manufacturers, dairy processors and oleomargarine manufacturers, or petroleum and coal producers? Clearly, he must maintain some degree of distance between himself and his contributors if he is not to alienate some contributors who will be displeased by at least some of his decisions. What seems reasonable is that big donors expect "a general outlook toward the role of government as a whole"[5] from their donees. Put negatively, big donors will not contribute to a candidate who holds views contrary to their deeply perceived beliefs, which include the sanctity of private property, the glories of the free enterprise system, etc. It is for this reason that the Socialist Labor Party and the Socialist Workers Party receive no contributions from big donors. To this extent, therefore, the system of party donation prevents anticapitalist viewpoints from being effectively presented to the electorate, and assures, in most instances, the election of persons favorable to capitalism. But this does not *necessarily* mean that officeholders respond to the specific wishes of big capitalist donors.

Perhaps campaign contributions do help explain why elected officials devote so much of their efforts to the use of government to promote a healthy business climate through fiscal and regulatory policies. Yet, at the same time, we shall also see public officials vote to trim lucrative oil depletion allowances or vote against an aircraft like the supersonic transport whose construction could result in generous profits to the contracting firms. Campaign contributions, contrary to the view espoused in *Rulers of America,* are a way of assuring a compatible relationship; they are usually not the means of creating a puppet.

Implicit in the conception of the nature of the American political system advanced in *Rulers of America* is the notion that business—or more accurately, big business—is usually unified and cohesive in its actions and interests. Specifically, this kind of marxist theory views the American political system as being controlled by a few banking groups, such as the Morgan group, the Mellon group, etc. (of which we shall have more to say later). Differences in businessmen's policy preferences are explained entirely in terms of the interests of the various financial-capitalist groups. Yet, even on the surface, this conception appears strained and unable to explain many of the patent splits within the business community. For example, the New Deal programs split the business community along ideological lines with each side adopting its different viewpoint because of their different conceptions of how to cure capitalism's economic illnesses. Again, the Vietnam war has seriously split the big business community. In these cases, there is no perceptible nexus between financial-group affiliation and an individual's specific policy preferences.

Nor, can the finance-capitalist theory explain the numerous battles within the business community between different industries and firms over issues as diverse as tariffs and other trade barriers, awards of television franchises, or government contracts for the supersonic transport. But notwithstanding these weaknesses, another marxist revived the finance-capital theory of control in a work published in 1957.[6] This work, *The Empire of High Finance,* was in many respects a marked advance over *Rulers of America.* The later date of publication compelled *The Empire of High Finance* to cope with phenomena like New Deal welfare legislation, post-World War II prosperity, and the cold war.

In contrast to the emphasis of *Rulers of America* on domestic policy, the later work focuses on foreign policy. This emphasis is justified because:

> Military business has become permanently important to many corporations, and to the big banks and insurance companies absorbing interest from the war swollen government debt. . . . With military business at the core of government, and foreign investment the source of extra profits for the plutocracy, control of foreign policy has become the pivot of the power struggle. Political rule by big business centers around the ominous issue of war and peace . . . [pp. 15, 16].

These and other business-government relations—for example, stock-piling, subsidies, the multiplicity of regulations, taxes, etc.—impinge on

business "at a thousand points" and require firms to regard business-
government relations as a major day-to-day matter (pp. 253, 256-267).
The Empire of High Finance refers to the interlocking relationships of
business and government as "state monopoly capitalism." Moreover, the
government itself, especially the executive branch, "is run mainly by the
leading lights of high finance, its chief manipulators and managers, all
men of great wealth and some having great fortunes." (pp. 254, 274).
There are three principal aspects of the political system: (1) The people
continue to exert pressure, (2) but ultimate control remains firmly in
the hands of high finance, and (3) political conflicts are reflections of
diverse interests among competing finance-capitalist groups (pp. 254,
255).

The Empire of High Finance observes that while elected officials are
usually not major capitalists—the American people mistrust and will not
vote for men of great wealth—the higher executive structure largely consists of "corporation lawyers doubling as government officials, career
government administrators linked to the financial oligarchy by social
and ideological ties; professional politicians defeated for office and
military men occupying civilian government posts" (pp. 275-276). These
high executive officials make the important decisions "sometimes with
the participation of the President, but often with his mere formal
approval" (p. 277). (This interesting assertion on Presidential decision-
making passivity will be discussed in the next chapter, where it is developed more fully.)

But why should a duly elected President appoint and defer to the
representatives of finance capital? Like *Rulers of America,* the later
work answers that

> The men of great wealth have an iron grip on the political parties, and
> can usually determine the presidential nominees, or at least make
> certain that they will be individuals amenable to big business domi-
> nation. This involves long-standing connections with the local politi-
> cal machines, control of publicity, media, and possession of the
> incomes needed to finance national campaigns . . . [p. 277].

But the later work adds complexities missing in the earlier one.

The different viewpoints espoused by different leaders are viewed as
reflections of the exact interests of the various financial groups dominating politics. For example, during the Truman Administration, the

investment banking firms of Brown Brothers, Harriman & Co., and Dillon, Read and Co. "had an unusual degree of influence," while Rockefeller interests were most influential during the Eisenhower Administration (pp. 287, 288). The work then traces specific personalities in the Truman and Eisenhower Administrations to particular industrial corporations and law firms allegedly associated with the different financial groups (pp. 287-292).

But how is such a theory to deal with the passage of welfare legislation? First, "Governments in America must still reckon with the labor movement, farmers, small business . . . on important occasions they have been forced to bend their sails to the winds of public opinion" (p. 292). Secondly, some laws that purport to be welfare legislation were actually intended as economic stabilizers to make the capitalist system operate more effectively (p. 255).

While the work largely confines its attention to the foreign policy area, it nevertheless draws the conclusion that financial oligarchs control all of government; no power distinctions are drawn with respect to different issue areas. But contrary to this assumption, it does not necessarily follow that what is true for foreign policy is true for other issue areas. Nor does it follow that finance capital controls the foreign policy area simply by showing, without further elaboration, that some important foreign policy officials in the Truman and Eisenhower Administrations had investment banking connections. One can infer a *general* pro-business orientation or ideological compatibility from the career backgrounds of officials, but, again, one cannot necessarily infer a specific policy orientation from an official's prior business connections. The high lateral mobility of top level business executives militates against the unproven conclusion of specific unalterable allegiances.

But whether one posits control of government by one or several financial groups, the central point of the marxist-leninist school that financial groups control industrial corporations and, in turn, control the government breaks down at the first link. Notwithstanding significant stock ownership in industrial corporations by financial corporations, individuals (excluding personal trusts) held more than three-quarters of all common stock in the period from 1939 through 1955.[7] While the holder of a small percentage of the outstanding shares may control a large corporation, this theory nowhere demonstrates that investment bankers do *in fact* control the major industrial corporations. One leading student of industrial organization concluded, after a review of the instances in which financial groups were shown to control industrial corporations, that such control is very rare.[8] Finally, the conduct of firms allegedly controlled by financial groups belies Perlo's theory. For example, if the Rockefeller group, as charged, controls the various Standard Oil Companies, how could one explain the fact that most of the Standard Oil Companies have invaded each other's principal marketing areas? Such conduct would be most irrational (and unlikely) if a single financial group controlled several competing firms.[9] The evidence, in a nutshell, strongly indicates the hollowness of the theory that a finance-capital elite controls either the government or most industrial corporations.

But, as we shall see, other theories that seek to locate exclusive control over government decision-making in an economic elite or in some important segment of the big business community equally fail to stand up to careful scrutiny. While such theories may shift their focus from finance capital to powerful economic families or peak associations, they also suffer the defect of viewing America's political decision-making elite too narrowly. Perhaps the most important of these concepts is the theory of family control, which we shall consider next.

THE THEORY OF CONTROL BY A FEW FAMILIES

The notion that a few great families control America's political destiny has had wide popularity since the rise of big business following the Civil War. Many politicians, eager to portray themselves as the "champion of the little man," have denounced the "malefactors of great wealth," who, it has been charged, have employed their great wealth to control the speaker's opponents, a condition which would presumably be remedied once the speaker was elected. Notwithstanding the popularity of the theory and its widespread acceptance, the theory did not receive a systematic exposition until the publication in 1937 of Ferdinand Lundberg's *America's 60 Families*.[10]

Despite its wealth of detail, Lundberg's work has a fairly simple thesis; the author seeks to demonstrate that 60 families dominate both American industry and government. A large portion of the book is devoted to tracing these families' alleged control of industry and finance, their interlocking through marriage, and their continuous association with each other. It finds that they usually intermarry and rarely marry outside their circle. Thus, the 60 families form a caste system (pp. 3-49). A large portion of the book purports to show that the 60 families have controlled the government from the post-Civil War period, in which they began accumulating their great wealth, through the period of the New Deal.

We shall not examine *America's 60 Families* review of government and business in the pre-New Deal period; the theories concerning the New Deal period apply with at least equal force to the earlier periods. The central conclusion about the New Deal's political character is that it "is not revolutionary nor radical in any sense; on the contrary it is conservative. Its mild tentative reformist coloration is but a necessary concession in the face of widespread unrest" (p. 448). Roosevelt was supported for election in 1932 and 1936 by some of the wealthiest families in America, notwithstanding his castigation of the rich (p. 449). Specifically, the New Deal was underwritten by wealthy individuals whose revenues derived largely from exploitation of retail markets—the light industries group (pp. 450, 479-483). This explains why New Deal economic reforms were all undertaken at the expense of heavy industry and the banks (p. 451). Although it is never explicitly discussed, it is clear that the author considers the principal means of controlling both major political parties to be the campaign contributions.

This theory of government and industrial control by 60 families has been vigorously criticized by elitists and pluralists alike. Among the former, Floyd Hunter and C. Wright Mills have leveled serious criticisms of the view that a few families control American government. Hunter found that these leaders acknowledged that there were members of socially prominent and wealthy families who were members of a "national power structure," but that this structure—according to the same leaders—contained many people who had no connection with the 60 families.[11] Mills's analysis of Lundberg is more systematic and thorough and is worth quoting extensively:

What Lundberg does is (1) generalize blood relations—sometimes cousinhood only—into power and financial cliques. We do not wish to confuse the two. In addition, we cannot go along with the list he has abstracted. . . . Of the so-called 60 families, there are 37 'families' represented by more than one member's tax payments. There are eight unrelated men included along with the Morgans; and there is another group of seven families forming his 38th 'family' (this is the 'Standard Oil Group'). . . . [i]f 'family' is to mean a blood tie there are many more than 60 families on his list; but the list is not even a full account of these families. Since only those paying a tax under the *family name* were included. Moreover there are a number of people . . . who paid much higher taxes in 1924 than many of the people named by Lundberg but who are not included in his listing of '60 families.'[12]

Even the notion that a few families control major corporations has been subjected to extensive criticism, although it is not possible to definitely refute this theory at the present time. Economist Robert J. Larner found, in 1966, on the basis of an examination of proxy statements and other business data, that management control and not wealthy family control was characteristic of most of the largest corporations.[13] It may be that Larner has underestimated the present extent of family control of large corporations, but, even so, there is no question but that the trend is very much in the direction of management control of corporations and that this style of ownership characterizes large-scale American industry. Since the "great families" control of large corporations is presumed to be the foundation stone of their control of government, the fact that the influence of these families on the business community is grossly overstated further weakens the theory of family control of government.

A later attempt by Lundberg to update and revive the family-control theory was similarly deficient.[14] Larner critically showed that, among other errors, Lundberg "assumes that the families alleged to control the largest corporations in 1939 still exercised control of these same corporations in 1964, even where the reports filed with the S.E.C. show no or insignificant stock holdings by these families."[15]

The family-control theory, like the other theories that attribute to a narrow interest group an all-embracing power over all governmental decisions, proves under scrutiny to be built on a foundation of quicksand. It does not factually show that "families" contain the most powerful or wealthiest people in America; it does not show internal cohesion among families and does not even attempt to show in any theoretical way how such "families" exercise control over politics. Indeed, even Lundberg, the family-control theory's foremost proponent, is forced to abandon it at crucial times. In sections of his discussion of the New Deal, he disregards the "60 families" conception to explain political decisions, and, instead, relies on an equally unconvincing argument that attempts to show that the New Deal was controlled by capitalists in the light goods industries. Finally, as Floyd Hunter argued, if the 60 families were so powerful, one could reasonably assume that community leaders with important contacts would have sensed their power. In fact, as his interviews demonstrated, community leaders were not aware of the existence of 60 dominating families, a fact that further compels us to reject this theory.

It is this sense of elusiveness—of the failure of informed people to perceive or sense the control and cohesion of the purportedly powerful group—which condemns not only the family-control theory, but all theories that seek to show that power is exercised by a narrowly based conspiratorial group. The burden of showing the power or control of a narrow, hidden elite is a heavy one, and the demonstrations have inevitably culminated in failure. One of the most interesting of such theories, however, is the one that finds dominating control or power in business peak associations. This theory was quite popular when German and Italian fascism and Japanese militarism were in their heyday and appeared to many observers to be the wave of the future. Closely associated with these forms of government were syndicates, associations containing representatives of industries. Nominally, these associations contained representatives of labor and capital, but, in fact, they were invariably dominated by big business representatives. Peak associations were comprised of the various industry associations or syndicates and among the most powerful and dominating institutions in the fascist countries. The theorist to which we now turn anticipated that peak associations would develop the same power in America.

PEAK ASSOCIATIONS

In a 1943 work, *Business as a System of Power,* Robert Brady brilliantly set forth the peak-association theory tracing the development of business power in Germany, Japan, France, Italy, Britain, and America.[16]

His conclusions, based principally upon the syndicates in fascist Italy and America's N.R.A. experience, were that peak associations exercise an increasing growth and influence. They act as the cohesive and collective will of big business, and have become inextricably interwoven with government. Brady assumed, without really showing why, that these were permanent trends. Business, he urged, must seek to dominate politics because of the rise of widespread "popular opposition, whose interests have been coming into conflict with those of organized business in a way which more and more challenges the traditional business view of the proper objectives and the responsibilities of economic leadership as such," and who consequently seek to control business politically (pp. 5, 6).

Brady contended that business cohesion was developing rapidly for four reasons. The first reason is the growth of peak associations which tend to act as centralized policy-makers for their constituencies. Second, certain business firms in each of the countries studied had grown enormously and had been increasing their share of total business assets. Third, the ties that bound these corporate giants together had been growing closer, and fourth, actual control of the major corporations had passed into the hands of self-perpetuating cliques (pp. 12, 13, 216-234).

The peak associations (in the United States, Brady views the National Association of Manufacturers as the most important one) and the various trade associations devote their energies and resources to such objectives as tariff protection (pp. 252, 253), legislation to dampen and prevent domestic competition (pp. 253, 254), governmental action to prevent business failure (p. 257), and governmental manipulatory policies to prevent business depressions (pp. 255, 256).

Finally, *Business as a System of Power* described, as follows, how the peak associations cope with their political problems. First, they establish popular organizations or gain control and dominate existing organizations "centered around the ideologies of the upper business and social hierarchies and controlled by the self-appointed and self-perpetuating . . . leaders from those ranks" (p. 317). Second, employers press for the establishment of a garrison state in which edicts replace laws, martial law replaces civil law, and the employer has authority in his firm similar to that which a general obtains in the army. Third, they bombard the populace with propaganda in which the employer is portrayed as a trustee and natural leader of the community. They also advance "the concept of a natural 'harmony' of interest between business and the public, business and the consumer, business and social and economic progress" (p. 318). Fourth, they engage in propaganda activities in which they envelop their own ideas in patriotism and attack opposing ideas as unpatriotic, foreign, and traitorous, while at the same time they mobilize the middle and professional classes into "patriotic" organizations; they purge schools of "unpatriotic" elements and generally engage in witch hunts while employing schools and other institutions to propagate their views (pp. 318 and 319). Fifth, they consolidate their supporters in a "solid interest conscious bloc" and form alliances "with any faction, movement, or party which has or may acquire popular following without disturbing the general social structure of command and subordination" (p. 319). The work concluded pessimistically by doubting whether, with all of this, America could escape becoming a totalitarian state dominated by peak associations like those in Germany, Italy, or Japan.

This nightmare has—fortunately—not become a reality, and it is clear that it vastly overrated the power and cohesion of the peak association. But even during the period of Brady's focus, the federal government consistently followed policies contrary to the wishes of the association that he felt was the leading business peak associations—the N.A.M. This does not mean, however, that peak associations cannot and do not wield great influence. Rather, Brady's principal error was that he failed to measure an organization's power or influence by some objective standard, such as success in getting its program implemented. If he had used such a yardstick, the weakness of the N.A.M. would have been transparent. Instead he concluded that the N.A.M. was powerful simply because of its membership roster, its reputation, and other subjective standards having no nexus with the organization's raison d'etre—implementation of its program.

Brady did not adequately grasp how organizational structure can limit political conduct. The N.A.M. is an organization composed of representatives of small, medium, and large businesses. Since virtually any firm may join the organization, it is, therefore, a relatively unwieldy organization for a big business elite to manipulate. Further, because there are many more medium-size and small firms than large ones, N.A.M. leadership has included representatives of medium-size and small manufacturers. It is, therefore, highly unlikely that N.A.M. is the "authentic" voice of big business, contrary to prevailing mythology. The unwarranted assumption that N.A.M. represents big business led pluralist Arnold M. Rose to make a different kind of mistake by erroneously concluding that big business has almost no political power.[17]

But the theory of peak associations may be, in part, retrievable using "success" criteria discussed above and looking a little more carefully at the various organizations composed of or controlled by big business leaders. A hint that such a closer scrutiny might shift focus to business organizations other than the N.A.M. is contained in Floyd Hunter's *Top Leadership U.S.A.* Hunter concluded, after interviewing many trade association officials and men "considered to be top policy-makers in the nation," that "many associations highly rated as powerful in political circles" are not indeed very powerful, but organizations like the Committee for Economic Development "were extremely important although relatively small. . . ."[18]

The hint that such organizations as the Committee for Economic Development (C.E.D.) are most influential in policy-making was taken up and developed by psychologist G. William Domhoff.

Why should organizations like C.E.D. play a role which the N.A.M. clearly does not? In part, the answer lies in the fact that the C.E.D. and similar organizations are elite clubs whose highly selective membership is recruited by invitation only, in contrast to the N.A.M., a far more democratic organization, which any manufacturer may join regardless of his size, his ideology, or any other factor.

In contrast to the N.A.M., such elite clubs as C.E.D. were organized from the top largely by members of the big business community with new memberships restricted to those invited by the extant membership. This form of organization can speak with considerably more unity than the peak associations which must accommodate diverse viewpoints. Unlike the peak associations, which must enroll any firm that fits the occupational category, an elite club will generally recruit to membership only those persons who subscribe to the organization's known views.[19] Finally, unlike the N.A.M., the leading elite clubs have been very sucessful in having their policy preferences implemented, as Domhoff observes.

Domhoff, in an essay published in 1969, argues that the answer to the question of how the big business leadership arrives at common policy preferences and makes its decisions known to political leaders lies chiefly in elite clubs, the most important ones of which include the C.E.D., the Council on Foreign Relations (C.F.R.), and the Foreign Policy Association (F.P.A.).[20] The incomes of elite clubs derive chiefly from the great corporations and the foundations (which are themselves dominated by the major corporations), and their membership rosters are dominated by corporate leaders. They have supplied many high officials to government. The C.F.R., for example, has supplied a large number of people for high-level foreign policy posts. John J. McCloy, who has held high-level government jobs and top corporate jobs, stated in connection with staffing the defense establishment during World War II: "Whenever we needed a man we thumbed through the roll of Council [C.F.R.] members and put through a call to New York" (pp. 28-32).

Elite clubs, Domhoff suggests, serve three principal purposes: (1) They are a talent pool and training ground for government service; (2) they sponsor education, discussion, and research, and invite government officials to participate in their sessions; and (3) they "size up" important leaders. Of the three functions, the second is most important because here members of the elite clubs plan how to achieve their objectives in foreign affairs (pp. 32-37).

There are additionally, he suggests, still other related institutions in which policy options are debated and decided and which supply personnel to the government's foreign policy branches such as think tanks (e.g., RAND Corporation) and special social science institutes financed by powerful elite-controlled foundations (pp. 37-41).

But two questions arise almost immediately in connection with Domhoff's description of elite clubs and related institutions: (1) Why must we assume that they represent business interests generally and not an aggregation of diverse, conflicting, or competing business interests; and (2) why should governmental leaders obey or even give serious consideration to the views of the elite clubs? Let us initially turn our attention to the first question, using the C.E.D. as an example in answering the question. To begin, C.E.D. includes top representatives of many of the largest corporations, including, in 1968, General Electric, General Motors, Westinghouse, Standard Oil (New Jersey), Socony-Mobil Oil

Company, I.B.M., Procter and Gamble, Ford, A.T.T., U.S. Steel, etc. These are the prototype of multinational corporations which manufacture an enormous number of different products in many different countries and in many areas of this country. Top officials of these firms must think in terms of the large units that they govern and weigh competing divisional and product manager claims. They must, like C.E.D. or foreign policy officials, think in macroscopic, rather than narrow, terms. C.E.D. and other elite clubs are, in this respect, the proper vehicle to express the interests of the great multinational corporations insofar as the members of these clubs have common objectives—and they certainly have common objectives in an economic environment promoting national economic growth, control of inflation, protection of foreign investment, etc. The C.E.D. and the other elite clubs are the arenas in which big business leaders discuss and resolve their differences on major policy matters. Ultimately, just as in their corporations and in the higher echelons of government, differences are resolved and a decision is made. If the organization is truly representative of the big business community, then this decision may be considered to be the overall sentiment of the business elite.

The second question, put in a slightly different form, asks whether government need be attentive to the pronouncements of such elite clubs. The answer is yes. Short of a change in the economic system, the health of multinational corporations such as I.B.M., I.T.T., Ford Motors, etc., must be a high-priority political item. If these large firms do badly, the effects on employment, wage levels, shareholder income, the economic well-being of supplier and distributor firms and their employees, shareholders, etc. are enormous.

It is therefore incumbent on government officials to arrange policies that will result in the maintenance of business confidence and encourage the large firms to invest, employ large numbers of people, and transact a considerable volume of business with supplier and customer firms. Large business firms will not manifest such confidence and engage in such affirmative policies unless the voice of business is carefully listened to, and its demands heeded. Government's failure to at least acknowledge the policy preferences of the large economic interests would shatter this business confidence and have disastrous results. As a result, what develops is such perceived mutuality of interest between high government officials and those elite clubs that are the authentic voice of big business that the latter's voice is extremely influential in the exercise of political power in the areas of business concern.

In this way, we can understand the role and nature of elite clubs without resorting to the notion of businessmen engaging in a surreptitious conspiracy to manipulate or dominate the government. The influence of these organizations arises naturally from the nature of their constituencies and the nature of the economic system. Thus, the erroneous theory of peak associations employed in *Business as a System of Power* can be transformed into a more fruitful conception of elite clubs that partially helps to explain the nature of the relationship between America's political directorate and the corporate elite. It does not explain the entire relationship by any means—we shall examine much more of that relationship in the next chapter—but this concept has brought us more insight than any of the other concepts we have examined to date. Its basic unit of analysis is organizations whose existence and purposes are already transparently visible and not abstract entities, such as "finance capitalists" or "60 families," whose cohesion is assumed rather than demonstrated.

Nevertheless we must remember that, even granting the advantages and cohesion of the elite clubs, there are other forces in American society, and we shall consider what happens when big business clashes with them. In addition, we must consider whether there are internal checks on the conduct of the management of large firms. Several theorists have considered these problems, and we shall next present the views of two important theorists (the economist pluralists), who have concluded that there are very imposing checks on big business in American society.

ECONOMIC PLURALISTS

This variant of pluralism is contained in the writings of lawyer Adolph A. Berle and economist John K. Galbraith. It starts with the recognition of the enormous power now vested in the hands of the directors and officers of the major corporations. Berle and Galbraith recognize that in the large oligopolistic industries competitive pricing has been replaced by noncollusive coordination in pricing and other competitive activities and the market is, therefore, no longer a check on the power wielded by the directors and officers of these major corporations. What then restrains their power? Galbraith answers that new restraints on private power "appeared not on the same side of the market but on the opposite side, not with competitors but with customers or suppliers. . . . I shall call [this] countervailing power."[21] According to him, the essential dynamic is that concentrated power on one side of the market usually begets concentrated power on the other side of the market. This process applies both to the selling and buying of goods and to the sale of labor. For example, one finds the strongest unions in those industries characterized by large firms. These are, of course, exceptions to countervailing power and it operates in different markets with varying effectiveness. An important qualification is that the restraint on market power is relatively ineffective during inflationary periods (pp. 112, 114-120, 128-130).

But in those instances when market conditions inhibit the exercise of countervailing power because of size disparity or other factors, the government checks the great agglomerations of power: "In fact the support of countervailing power has become in modern times perhaps the major domestic peacetime function of the federal government." Groups who suffer detriment as a result of countervailing power's failure to operate are the ones who seek government intervention. Of course, groups that seek to utilize government intervention on their behalf must organize to some extent: "Support to countervailing power is not endowed *ad hoc* by government. It must be sought." Since many groups have not successfully organized to seek government intervention, the government has not added to their strength (pp. 136, 146-150).

Adolph Berle's theory derives from a somewhat different perspective than Galbraith's. In a classic work published in 1932, Berle and economist Gardiner C. Means developed the theory that the beneficial ownership of large corporations was becoming separated from management so that shareowners did not manage their companies while managers, holding few shares, developed interests separate and apart from those of the owners.[22] While, as we observed earlier in this chapter, the precise extent to which managerial control characterizes the 200 or 500 largest corporations is subject to debate, there is no doubt but that Berle and Means pointed to what has clearly been the prevailing trend in American corporations.

From the many consequences that flow from the growth of manageri-
alism, there arises one question of overwhelming political importance:
What forces are to control the managers of these great corporations
whose economic decisions are of great moment to the public? Berle and
Means found that managers constitute a self-perpetuating elite whose
tight control of the resources of their respective corporations makes
stockholder fights to unseat them extremely costly, difficult, and
nearly always unsuccessful. Thus, we cannot rely on shareholders to
check corporate managers. Nor, it is generally acknowledged, can we
rely on competitors to check them, except within very broad limits;
when firms in most oligopolistic industries raise prices their rivals do
not cut prices in order to gain business at the former's expense. Rather,
as an extensive investigation by the Senate Subcommittee on Antitrust
and Monopoly (the Kefauver Committee) found, they frequently tend
to match the raised prices of industry leaders.

If not stockholders or competitors, what or who will check the
power of these managers? Galbraith's answer was that countervailing
power was the checking force, but Adolph Berle's answer was somewhat
different. According to him, the corporate rulers must continuously
solicit a "public consensus" to legitimate their actions. This accounts for
the vast "good will" output of corporate public relations departments.
In a word, they are always trying to assuage the public and interested
groups whose criticsim can result in serious harm to the firm. But who
in the name of "public consensus" will call into question corporate
actions? It is usually not other businesses, although there are, of course,
occasional instances when one firm or industry will expose another firm
or industry. But usually competing firms are wary of exposure of skele-
tons in their own closets. Of "greater force are the conclusions of careful
university professors, the reasoned opinions of specialists, the statements
of responsible journalists, and at times the solid pronouncements of
respected politicians. These are more likely to gain acceptance and influence events."[23] Once the experts arouse public opinion, the corporate
administrators will often respond, but if the corporation fails to respond, there will be a political intervention in economic affairs and, as a
rule, "these repeated political interventions compel the American system of economic administration to comply with the public consensus."[24]

What is one to say about Galbraith's and Berle's theories of checks on corporate power? Galbraith's theory carefully selects examples that fit into his theory. Yet there is much legislation that in fact is contrary to the notion of countervailing power. Galbraith himself cites the example of the Robinson-Patman Act which largely outlaws the right to charge different prices to different customers—the essence of bargaining and hence the essence of countervailing power. How can one be sure that the instances in which legislation restrains countervailing power do not outweigh the instances in which legislation promotes countervailing power? One would anticipate that unless the government is motivated by some unusual factor, it will probably help the stronger economic side rather than the weaker one. In any event, it certainly does not follow that political power will, if called upon to do so, cast itself in the balance on the side of the weaker economic unit. Secondly, the theory of countervailing power is inapplicable to many multisided situations. There are often several sides to an issue, and there is no theoretical reason why it is not possible for two sides to agree to oppress permanently the third. Is this not precisely the case when steel firms raise prices, the steel unions raise wages, and the public suffers the consequences? The Galbraith theory, in the final analysis, is neither a description of power in America nor even a sensible theoretical model of power.

Finally, even as an economic model, the theory of countervailing power is weak. The large food chains, mail order houses, and big department stores principally sell food, clothing, and furniture. Yet each of the industries selling to them is characterized by much smaller units than the retailers. Moreover, there are many labor markets in which workers are unorganized and no match for their employers.

Berle's reliance on intellectuals and honorable newsmen to counter the transgressions of corporations is also subject to considerable skepticism. Again, he starts with the unproven assumption that the State is a neutral umpire, and if a corporation's transgressions are revealed, government will pounce on that corporation for the benefit of the public. But even assuming *arguendo* that this conception of the State is correct, why should the public believe the diligent newsmen or intellectuals rather than the corporations which have superior public relations apparatuses? Again, since corporations are rather loath to reveal their internal operations, how is even the diligent investigator supposed to discover any but the most blatant corporate transgressions? One need only think of the great number of years in which the automobile manufacturers produced millions of unsafe vehicles before—finally—Ralph Nader came along and discovered a few of that industry's transgressions. One can only wonder at the many secrets hidden under the many corporate rugs which have never been discovered. In short, Berle's prescription is more a hope than an analysis.

The managements of great corporations are not, as economists Walter Adams and Horace Gray have observed, omnipotent.[25] They are to some extent restrained by interindustry competition, the possibility of a decisive technological breakthrough by a rival, limited competition by rivals and forces on the other side of the market, exposure, and government intervention. But far more impressive is the degree of unaccountability manifested by these managements in innumerable areas such as administered pricing, producing unsafe products, wasteful advertising and promotion policies, etc. There is, in short, little left to the Berle and Galbraith theories of restraints on corporate power except the occasional, infrequent instance in which such power is checked.

But how then are we to define the role and power of corporate executives if, on the one hand, we must reject the narrow-interest-group theories, and, on the other hand, the doctrines of Galbraith and Berle? One way is to define the corporate elite as but one segment of a larger elite. This approach, which was adopted by sociologist C. Wright Mills in his famous book *The Power Elite,* will be examined in the next chapter. But still another approach, in part reflected in our discussion of elite clubs, is to examine the political consequences of the economic setting. Put another way, what are the implications of the fact that the political system operates in tandem with a capitalist economic system? A recent study by political scientist Ralph Miliband, to which we shall now refer, examines this problem and reaches some interesting conclusions about the State in a society of large privately held corporations.[26]

CAPITALISM AND THE STATE

Ralph Miliband's *The State in Capitalist Society* purports to be a marxist description of the state system that prevails in all of the advanced capitalist democracies including the United States. The central thesis is that while the capitalist class does not govern, it effectively rules (p. 55). The capitalist class rules because of the State's commitment to the capitalist system, and because of the consequences that flow therefrom, some of which we have already discussed such as that political fortunes rise and fall with the health of the nation's business enterprises (pp. 83, 101). "And the crucial place which [capitalist] interests occupy in the life of their country has always caused governments to make their defense against foreign capitalist interests, and against the foreign States which protect them, a prime consideration in their conduct of external affairs." (p. 84).

The State serves capitalism in several other respects. Negatively, the State protects capitalism by repressing anticapitalists through such direct methods as outlawing anticapitalist parties, or harassing such parties, or electoral manipulation to legally prevent left-wing parties from being on the ballot,[27] or the use of repressive trials to quell left-wing dissenters and (more importantly) to frighten away other prospective dissenters. "Governments, in other words, are deeply concerned . . . that the 'democratic process' should operate within a framework in which left-wing dissent plays as weak a role as possible" [p. 83]. That all of the foregoing methods have at various times been employed in America is scarcely open to question. (But it should be noted that elites in all societies, in accordance with Michels's "iron law of oligarchy," employ such methods.)

The structure of bureaucracy also operates to maintain the status quo, and hence capitalism. Bureaucrats are specialists at sitting still and not effecting change and their ideological conservatism is not due to chance. Loyalty oaths and recruiting and advancement procedures for upper-level civil servants assure a "spectrum of thought of which strong conservatism forms one extreme and weak 'reformism' the other" (pp. 120-124). Further, government and business form cozy relationships as a result of the links between business sectors and the bureaucracies which are supposed to regulate them. Ambitions of civil servants to enter business and interchanging personnel are the principal facets of this relationship. Businessmen increasingly find their way into the State system and civil servants increasingly find their way into corporate life (pp. 124-127). Finally, if a maverick manages to filter through the recruitment process and loyalty oaths and avoids the symbiotic relationship between business and government, "there remains the vast weight of pressure which organized business is able to apply upon recalcitrant or hostile officials" (p. 128).[28] Thus, the capitalistic ambiance within which the civil service operates tends to produce a pro-capitalist bias within the bureaucracy.

The State and Capitalist Society seeks to show that capitalist dominance over key facets of social life tends to politically legitimate and support the business system. Essentially this is because money is the basic yardstick of power in a capitalist society. For example, capitalists dominate the means of communication (pp. 219-238). Again, capitalist advertising tends to associate not only products but the entire free enterprise system with socially approved values and norms, and, indeed, with happiness (pp. 216-218). Against these resources, anticapitalist forces are relatively helpless and their views are portrayed in the capitalist sources of communication as "irrelevant eccentricities, which serious and reasonable people may dismiss as of no consequence" (p. 238). Scoffing and ridicule are often far more effective ways of throttling anticapitalist thought than outright suppression.

Next, Miliband charges that the education system, from the lower grades to graduate schools, inculcates capitalist values in its students and confirms the class destiny and status of most students. At the lowest school levels lower-class students are given educations inferior to middle- and upper-class children, "And the very fact that some working-class children are able to surmount these handicaps serves to foster the notion that those who do not are themselves, because of their own unfitness, the architects of their own lowly fate,[29] and that their situation is of their own making" (p. 241). Again, witch hunts, loyalty oaths, and the attendant apparatus of fear deter recruitment of public school teachers with remotely controversial or "eccentric" points of view and deter the teaching of such views (p. 245).

Universities, which are heavily dependent on State and business financing, cannot afford to permit teaching which affronts capitalism. (A few "eccentrics" are, however, permitted to show that there is freedom of expression.) Further, academic personnel are increasingly employed as consultants by business and government, and such persons thereby have developed a community of interest with businessmen and government policies (p. 250). Next, *The State and Capitalist Society* observes that most schools are geared to supplying personnel for business needs; business schools and law schools are among the conspicuous examples of this process. Not only are such students taught management skills, but also "the ideology, values and purpose of capitalist enterprise" (p. 253). This is done not through a conspiracy, but because most teachers are themselves the products of this consensus in favor of capitalism (pp. 250-259). But even when teachers attack the status quo at universities, the economic and social system is not called into question; rather the emphasis is on how to solve such problems within the system's framework and not on socialist alternatives. Such safe controversy deflects "attention from the greatest of all 'problems' namely that here is a social order governed by the search for private profit" (p. 261).

The theory developed by Miliband purports to show why the State is *ruled* by capitalism, even if it is not *governed* by capitalists. It forcefully argues that the institutions of communication and socialization in a capitalist society favor the preservation of capitalism. Yet this theory leaves one somewhat dissatisfied. It tells us what will be excluded from consideration as State policy, but it tells us nothing about what the State will affirmatively do or which elites will govern the State. The theory persuasively shows the boundaries of state and viable political activity in a capitalist society. In a business society, the highest priority item of political actors is to assure the optimum performance of the business system. At the same time, the economic structure tends to enable those committed to the economic system to become members of the political elite. But this statement still does not explain much of what goes on within the political arena. What, for example, accounts for the presence of large numbers of men with a military background in important political and business roles? What accounts for the many battles, often very bitter, between various groups within the political elite? What accounts for the sometimes serious setbacks to important economic interests such as the banning of cigarette advertisements on television? What elites are responsible for the many kinds of policies that have no readily apparent connection with economic policy: foreign affairs, military policy, civil rights, health, education, etc.?

These questions suggest that American society may contain other elites who are as important as the business elite, and the business elite sometimes acts cohesively, while at other times there are conflicts within it. Again, the political leadership of the nation may have interests of its own above those of the business elite, or the State may be an umpire whose role is to resolve conflicts between the business elite and other elites. Several scholars, whose ideas we shall examine in the next chapters, have developed theories which seek to embrace some of these considerations instead of relying on the narrow notion that the busines elite controls all political decisions. These scholars can be grouped into two categories—elitists and pluralists—and their debate and differences will be explored in Part III.

Notes

1 Anna Rochester, *Rulers of America* (New York: International Publishers, 1936). Page references are to this edition.

2 Alexander Heard, *The Costs of Democracy* (abridged) (New York: Doubleday, 1962), pp. 46-49, 92-122.

   Congressional statements confirm the view herein. For example, Senator Charles Mathias of Maryland stated, "The bigger contributor is absolutely necessary the way the system has been working . . . unless you have big chunks of money, you couldn't make the commitments for various media contracts." *Washington Post* (March 12, 1970).

3 *Ibid.*, p. 47.

4 David B. Truman, *The Governmental Process* (New York: Knopf, 1951), pp. 309-310.

5 Arnold M. Rose, *The Power Structure* (New York: Oxford University Press, 1967), p. 461. See also pp. 370, 458-460.

6 Victor Perlo, *The Empire of High Finance* (New York: International Publishers, 1957).

7 John Lintner, "The Financing of Corporations," in Edward S. Mason, ed., *The Corporation in Modern Society* (New York: Atheneum, 1966), p. 194.

8 Joe S. Bain, *Industrial Organization* (New York: Wiley, 1959), pp. 101-103.

9 Paul A. Baran and Paul M. Sweezy, *Monopoly Capital* (New York: Monthly Review Press, 1966), pp. 17-20.

10 Ferdinand Lundberg, *America's 60 Families* (New York: Vanguard, 1937).

11 Floyd Hunter, *Top Leadership U.S.A.* (Chapel Hill: University of North Carolina Press, 1959), p. 65 especially and *passim.*

12 C. Wright Mills, *The Power Elite* (New York: Oxford University Press, 1956), p. 377.

13 See Robert J. Larner, *Management Control and the Large Corporation* (New York: Dunellen, 1970). See also the studies discussed therein, pp. 22-24.

14 Ferdinand Lundberg, *The Rich and the Super-Rich* (New York: Lyle Stuart, 1968).

15 Larner, *Management Control,* pp. 22, 23.

16 Robert A. Brady, *Business as a System of Power* (New York: Columbia University Press, 1943).

17 Rose, *The Power Structure,* p. 30.

18 Hunter, *Top Leadership U.S.A.,* pp. 32-36.

19 On the C.E.D. as an example of an elite club see Karl Schriftgiesser, *Business Comes of Age* (New York: Harper & Row, 1960); Karl Schriftgiesser, *Business and Public Policy* (Englewood Cliffs, N.J.: Prentice-Hall, 1967); and R. Joseph Monsen, Jr. and Mark W. Cannon, *The Makers of Public Policy* (New York: McGraw-Hill, 1965).

   On the N.A.M. see Richard W. Gable, "N.A.M.: Influential Lobby or Kiss of Death?" *Journal of Politics* (May 1953), pp. 254-273. Gable reports that between 1933 and 1946, 125 firms held 63 percent of all directorships; 88 percent of the executive committee memberships; 79 percent of finance committee memberships; and 52 percent of the major executive offices other than paid staff. Of these 125 firms, only 28 (22 percent) were among the 200 largest industrial corporations, and only 10 percent of them had assets of less than $10 million dollars. Thus, medium-size firms appear to have dominated the N.A.M. during that period (p. 259).

20 G. William Domhoff, "Who Made American Foreign Policy 1945-1963?" in David Horowitz, ed., *Corporations and the Cold War* (New York: Monthly Review Press, 1969), pp. 25-69.

21 John Kenneth Galbraith, *American Capitalism* (Boston: Houghton Mifflin, 1952), p. 111.

22 Adolph A. Berle, Jr., and Gardiner C. Means, *The Modern Corporation and Private Property* (New York: Macmillan, 1932).

23 Adolph A. Berle, Jr., *Power Without Property* (New York: Harcourt Brace Jovanovich, 1959), pp. 111-113.

24 *Ibid.,* p. 138.

25 Walter Adams and Horace M. Gray, *Monopoly in America* (New York: Macmillan, 1955), p. 20.

26 Ralph Miliband, *The State in Capitalist Society* (New York: Basic Books, 1969).

27 On the legal difficulties that third parties have encountered, see Note, "Legal Obstacles to Minority Party Success," *Yale Law Journal* 57, (1948), p. 1276.

28 Instances of such pressures are graphically described in Robert Engler, *The Politics of Oil* (New York: Macmillan, 1961), pp. 319-323; and Pendleton Herring, *Public Administration and the Public Interest* (New York: Russell & Russell, 1967), pp. 118-121.

29 That these are the values of American workingmen is suggested in Robert Lane, *Political Ideology* (New York: Free Press, 1962), pp. 57-81, 250-267.

A comprehensive examination of metropolitan fiscal characteristics concluded, with respect to allocation of expenditures for education, "The need is for the concentration of educational resources in the central cities. . . . Yet the present system distributes resources in exactly the opposite direction, less where the problems are most severe and more where the problems are relatively easy to cope with." Alan K. Campbell and Seymour Sacks, *Metropolitan America* (New York: Free Press, 1967), p. 181. The discrimination within metropolitan areas operates along class lines since the poor are concentrated in central cities and the more affluent outside the central cities.

PART THREE
THE "POWER-ELITE" DEBATE

Until the publication in 1956 of The Power Elite by C. Wright Mills, there was virtually no challenge to a prevailing orthodoxy among academic scholars that most important decisions in American political life were not made by a narrowly based elite. Rather the predominant current of thought, pluralism, held that power was diffusely spread and that numerous interest groups acting on behalf of their respective memberships were the principal actors in American political life. At the same time, usually outside the world of academic social sciences, other observers, generally of leftist persuasions, argued that American political life was dominated by a few big businessmen who manipulated political leaders. These latter studies were seldom well-documented and were usually convincing only to those who already held such views.

So the debate stood until Mills advanced his power-elite hypothesis, triggering a heated debate in both academic and nonacademic circles. The hypothesis was greeted with much controversy, and although the hypothesis gained some adherents, it was rejected by a far greater number of observers. And rejection was not limited to merely confirmed pluralists but embraced spokesmen of left, right, and center. Nevertheless, Mills's work raised the level of debate measurably.

In this part, we shall examine the arguments and evidence advanced by Mills, and then look at some of the criticisms leveled against the power-elite hypothesis. Finally, we shall set forth the position of pluralists and others who hold views similar to them.

CHAPTER 4
THE POWER-ELITE THESIS

THE THESIS STATED

C. Wright Mills was not only a highly regarded academic sociologist but is widely regarded as one of the intellectual precursors of the New Left movement of the 1960s. A man of the Left, he rejected both the conventional marxist ideology of the Old Left and the celebration of American capitalism which prevailed through the 1950s. He wrote books and articles on many subjects, but the work which, by far, has had the greatest impact on both scholars and laymen is *The Power Elite,* which purports to be an examination of the people who make what Mills terms the "important" decisions in America. As we mentioned previously, the power-elite theory has been much misunderstood by many commentators both as to method and content. Its methodology, especially, has often not been grasped by critics, and since methodology is central to an understanding of the book, yet was never explicitly described in it, we turn to it first.

Let us begin by examining the dangers of an approach shared by many elitists and pluralists—the decision-making approach. Pursuant to this method, formal interviews with decision-makers are conducted in order to find out why and how decisions were made. Under such circumstances, the interviewees' formal statements will, needless to say, indicate that they were dispassionate, listened carefully to all sides of an issue, were (possibly) subjected to some pressure from affected interests, but did not succumb to any blandishments. Further, all decisions, it will usually be reported, were made in public or within the framework of legitimate *in camera* proceedings. Theories are then built on the view that interviews and formal statements reveal how decisions are made and that secrecy does not exist. Unfortunately, men of great power do meet privately and make important decisions at meetings to which the public is not privy. Further, political leaders lie, distort, and often do not correctly perceive or understand what has transpired. If the sharp limitations of the decision-making approach are not yet apparent, consider only the raging debate about the actual purposes of one of the most momentous decisions of the twentieth century—the dropping of the atom bomb on Hiroshima in August 1945.

Was the bomb dropped in order to bully Russia? Or was it dropped out of military necessity? Historians and other scholars have pored through mountains of available documentation and have reached differing conclusions on the subject. And, indeed, on the basis of the evidence developed to date, the impartial reader may lean toward one view or another, but must be far from sure of which view is right. If so much controversy exists regarding the motives for one of the most important decisions of modern times, consider the decision-making method's defectiveness in relation to decisions that investigators have explored with considerably less thoroughness and about which less documentation is available. In short, while this approach clearly has value and should be employed in any serious discussion of political events, it has serious limitations.

Mills's methodology avoids the pitfalls of the decision-making approach, although he uses it in a subordinate way.

Mills's approach is to look at those institutions in America that notoriously and conspicuously exercise power with respect to certain issue areas. After identifying these institutions, he next asks who occupies the top positions and what are their common psychological and socioeconomic characteristics. He then seeks to show that, in the present era, the occupants of these command positions are interlocked, overlapped, and essentially share the same basic goals, although they do have differences.

Mills defined power in the following manner: "By the powerful we mean . . . those who are able to realize their will, even if others resist it. No one, accordingly, can be truly powerful unless he has access to the command of major institutions, for it is over these institutional means of power that the truly powerful are, in the first instance, powerful" (Power case, p. 9). Thus, power is the ability to effect decisions. It should be noted at this point that this definition, contrary to some distortions of it by Mills's critics, does not postulate that power can only be exercised when "others resist"; rather power can be exercised in the two alternative situations of resistance or passivity. The point is important because of Mills's contention that the mass of people are passive in the face of the power exercised by the power elite.

Mills developed the structure of American power in three dimensions: vertical, horizontal, and historical. Vertically, there are three levels; the power elite, the middle levels of power, and mass society. Mills observed that elite is an ambiguous term that has at least four sociological connotations. The first is in terms of institutional position and the social structure these institutions form; the second is in terms of the distribution of selected values (what people have); the third is in terms of membership in a clique-like set of people (what people belong to); the final conception is in terms of moral or psychological attributes (who they really are). Mills employs the concept of elite in the first sense—institutional position—and, once identifying the past and present incumbents of these institutional positions, he systematically fits the other conceptions of elite into place (p. 366).

Mills argues that American power relations have gone through four periods, and that we are now in a fifth period. In the first period, which lasted from the Revolution through the John Adams Administration, the social, economic, political, and military institutions were unifed in a transparent way: The individuals of each elite "moved easily from one role to another at the top of each of the major institutional orders" (p. 269). The second period, which lasted from the early nineteenth century until the Civil War, was characterized by "a political elite in charge of the new party system" and no small clique dominating either political or economic affairs (p. 271). In the third period, which began with the congressional elections of 1866 and lasted until the New Deal, corporate power became supreme. There was little governmental control of corporate power, but, on the other hand, there were vast raids on the public treasury by the corporate elite. The military were subordinate to the political, who, in turn, were subordinate to the economic elite (pp. 271-272). The fourth period—the New Deal—

did not reverse the political and economic relations of the third era, but it did create within the political arena, as well as in the corporate world itself, competing centers of power that challenged those of the corporate directors . . . the power of business was not replaced, but it was contested and supplemented . . . the New Deal as a system of power was essentially a balance of pressure groups and interest blocs [pp. 272, 273].

Finally, we reach the fifth period, which began with the onset of World War II, and with which the book is centrally concerned—the era of the power elite.

While Mills did not rely on a decision-making approach to support his findings about the fifth period, the vertical structure of power is defined in terms of the *kind* of decisions made. The top level—the power elite— consists of those men who decide questions of war and peace, slump and prosperity. Mills found three elite groups who made such decisions: the political directorate, top corporate executives and directors, and the high military. In addition, "The inner core of the power elite also includes men of the higher legal and financial type from the great law factories and investment firms, who are almost professional go-betweens of eco- nomic, political, and military affairs, and who thus act to unify the power elite" (p. 289).

The three groups at the top do not simply form an oligopoly of im- portant decision-makers. They interlock and overlap in four important respects. First, since the onset of World War II, and, especially since the beginning of the cold war, there has been a coincidence of objective in- terest among the three groups. The corporate interest in military pro- curement and, conversely, the military interest in assuring that its equipment programs are properly executed exemplify (but hardly ex- haust) the interrelations between the military and the corporate worlds. The multitude of economic relationships between the corporate and political directorates, and the fact that political decisions are framed in military terms (e.g., bombing North Vietnam, antiballistic missiles, etc.), coupled with the military's considerable autonomy and influence, com- plete the web. This does not mean, as Mills pointed out, that the three groups' interests always coincide or that there are not serious intragroup or intergroup divisions on specific policies (pp. 198 and 283): "But more powerful than these division are the internal discipline and the commu- nity of interests that bind the power elite together" (p. 283).

Second, the career patterns of the elite groups interlock; Mills traces numerous instances of those who interchange commanding roles at the top of one dominant institution for top roles in another.[1] Third, in many instances the origins, background, and educational patterns of group leaders coincide causing similar psychological orientations. Fourth, the members of different elites intimately associate with each other socially and in their business lives. Of course, the same factors that promote cohesion between the elite groups also promote intragroup cohesion and self-consciousness of their elite roles. In a word, "They accept one another, understand one another, marry one another, tend to work and to think if not together at least alike" (p. 11).

The principal mechanism by which the elite is perpetuated is the recruitment process. In order to advance up the ladder, it is necessary for one to prove his reliability to his superiors; "the rule is the co-optation of one's own kind by those who have taken over the command posts" (pp. 235, 348).

While the power elite make the "important decisions," Mills cautions that, in the process, they often must take into account other forces outside the elite, and sometimes must influence others (particularly Congressmen) to do their bidding. But, those outside the elite react rather than lead, and can only modify the broad policies that are made without consulting them. Organized labor is an example of such a reacting (or middle level) interest (p. 265). These interests "are concerned merely with their particular cut, with their particular area of vested interest" (p. 266).

Beneath the power elite, in a kind of political balance, lies the middle level of power. Decisions are made at this level which are not concerned with the questions of war and peace, slump and prosperity. Congress is the central institution at this level, but it also includes voluntary associations, interest groups, local governments and important local interests, organized labor, farmer organizations, etc. A balance of power exists among these institutions and organizations because "no one interest can impose its will or its terms upon others; or . . . any one interest can create a stalemate; or . . . in the course of time, first one and then another interest gets itself realized, in a kind of symmetrical taking of turns; or . . . policies are the results of compromise . . ." (p. 246). With the executive ascendancy in the middle third of the twentieth century, legislative action, local decisions, and the effects and pressures of special interest groups have been largely relegated to the middle levels of political power and usually involve special pleading for a narrow sectarian interest.

In part, the formation and strength of the power elite is dependent on the stalemate at the middle levels of power. But of greater consequence is the state of the populace which Mills describes as largely, although not yet entirely, a "mass society" (p. 302). It is a mass society because

At the opposite extremes, in a *mass,* (1) far fewer people express opinions than receive them; for the community of publics becomes an abstract collection of individuals who receive impressions from the mass media. (2) The communications that prevail are so organized that it is difficult or impossible for the individual to answer back immediately or with any effect. (3) The realization of opinion in action is controlled by authorities who organize and control the channels of such action. (4) The mass has no autonomy from institutions; on the contrary, agents of authorized institutions penetrate this mass, reducing any autonomy it may have in the formation of opinion by discussion [p. 304].

In contrast is a public society:

In a *public,* as we may understand the term, (1) virtually as many people express opinions as receive them. (2) Public communications are so organized that there is a chance immediately and effectively to answer back any opinion expressed in public. Opinion formed by such discussion (3) readily finds an outlet in effective action, even against—if necessary—the prevailing system of authority. And (4) authoritative institutions do not penetrate the public, which is thus more or less autonomous in its operations. When these conditions prevail, we have the working model of a community of publics, and this model fits closely the several assumptions of classic democratic theory [pp. 303-304].

Voluntary associations, a critical structural link in a public society, have declined in importance as a genuine public instrument because the citizen's link with these associations has grown more tenuous. Mills states:

Voluntary associations have become larger to the extent that they have become effective; and to just that extent they have become inaccessible to the individual who would shape by discussion the policies of the organization to which he belongs. Accordingly, along with older institutions, these voluntary associations have lost their grip on the individual. As more people are drawn into the political arena, these associations become mass in scale; and as the power of the individual becomes more dependent upon such mass associations, they are less accessible to the individual's influence [p. 307].

Thus, to the extent that America has become a mass society, it does not act as a check on the power elite. The mass tendencies are reinforced by other factors such as secrecy of key decisions, the complexity of many critical issues, the lack of true community in the metropolis, and the deficiencies of mass communications. Thus, to summarize the composition of modern American society:

At the top there has emerged an elite of power. The middle levels are a drifting set of stalemated, balancing forces: the middle does not link the bottom with the top. The bottom of this society is politically fragmented, and even as a passive fact, increasingly powerless. At the bottom there is emerging a mass society [p. 324].

Mills did not stop with this bleak description of American society; he was deeply disturbed by "the *higher* immorality which is a systematic feature of the American elite *and* an essential feature of the mass society" (p. 343). In essence, the higher immorality consisted of the deteriorated relevance of all codes and values, save one—money, the unambiguous criterion of success. Coupled with the general decline of values is the rise of celebrity criteria for making judgments and diverting mass attention from real problems. Since knowledge and wisdom are no longer regarded as prime values, "knowledge and power are not truly united inside the ruling circles" (p. 351). Knowledge and wisdom are not the keys to success in politics; rather, the keys are public relations and manipulation. Moreover, the public is not even informed of key political decisions, nor is debate conducted "in any intellectual form" (p. 355).

To Mills, then, the result is that as American power has become more centralized and has grown in scope, the holders of that power have grown less responsible to the citizenry and less talented in their capabilities. He pessimistically concluded:

America—a conservative country without any conservative ideology—appears now before the world a naked and arbitrary power, as, in the name of realism, its men of decision enforce their often crackpot definitions upon world reality. The second-rate mind is in command of the ponderously spoken platitude. In the liberal rhetoric, vagueness, and in the conservative mood, irrationality, are raised to principle. Public relations and the official secret, the trivializing campaign and the terrible fact clumsily accomplished, are replacing the reasoned debate of political ideas in the privately incorporated economy, the military ascendancy, and the political vacuum of modern America [pp. 360-361].

Such, in summary, is Mills's view of American society. Some of Mills's other points as well as amplifications of some of his foregoing views will be discussed in the next section. Whatever else it accomplished, *The Power Elite* raised the level of debate to a higher plane. Mills was the first major analyst of American society to draw distinctions between issue areas and to appreciate that different power relationships may accompany different issue areas, and he was the first writer on power in America to start his analysis from the central political institutions, thereby avoiding the pitfalls of either a "secret-control" theory or decision-making analysis.

Needless to say, a theory as unusual as this one provoked a considerable amount of criticism, some of it very able and perceptive, but some of which set up a straw man and proceeded to knock it down. The attacks on the power-elite theory came from both the right and the left and from some scholars not readily classifiable in any political camp. We shall examine some of the criticisms that best bring out the issues raised by Mills. The criticisms can be divided into several categories, each of which will be discussed separately.

THE ATTACK ON MILLSIAN ELITISM

A. Methodological
Pluralist political scientist Robert Dahl has cogently presented the methodological critique of *The Power Elite*. Initially, he suggests that, in order to determine whether Mills is correct or not, it is necessary to construct a model to test the power-elite hypothesis. If there is a power elite, it must be less than a majority in size and its preferences must on occasion prevail in the face of opposition. Moreover, a group must be cohesive to be a power elite; a high potential for control if a group acted in unity coupled with a low potential for unity would indicate

that the group was not a power elite. Dahl also points out that control is not influence and moreover it is wrong to generalize pervasive influence from influence or control in one area. He concludes by suggesting the following test to determine whether there is a power elite: You must show that (1) the proposed power elite is a well-defined cohesive group; (2) "there is a fair sample of cases involving key political decisions in which the preferences of the hypothetical ruling elite run counter to those of any other likely group that might be suggested"; and (3) the elite preferences usually prevail. Dahl argues that issues cannot be "key," and the test cannot be conducted if a small group dominates an indifferent mass.[2]

Dahl's test could, however, be rebutted by a Millsian. First, the elite that Mills describes not only has the potential to control or rule, it actually rules because elites are defined in terms of the institutional positions they occupy, and it is by virtue of the authority and coercion vested in these institutional roles that the elite rules. Thus, Mills's burden is not to show that his elites have converted potential control into actual rule, but rather that the elites are internally cohesive and together form *a* power elite rather than a diversity of elites.

Dahl's contention that there cannot be a ruling elite if the mass of people are indifferent to the decision because "the alternatives at stake can hardly be regarded as 'key political issues' "[3] is equally rebuttable. Dahl is, of course, free to choose his own definition of a "key issue," but certainly most people would agree that our major military and foreign policy actions are key; they are literally matters of life and death. Moreover, if we measure issue importance in terms of resource allocation, national defense expenditures have accounted for the greatest proportion of total federal expenditures in the postwar era.[4] Yet, so often, the decisions in these areas, fateful as they are, are made without debate or consultation, and as a matter of "patriotism" are then passively supported by the majority of people. To cite but a few of the numerous examples of the process, there are the Bay of Pigs invasion of Cuba, the bombing of North Vietnam and subsequent American invasion of Cambodia, the invasion of Santo Domingo, the 1954 overthrow of the Guatemalan government, Nixon's visit to China, and so forth.[5]

Another difficulty with Dahl's proposed test is that many issues are effectively excluded from the political arena. Are issues or views any the less "key" because they have been wholly excluded from the political arena? The answer is clearly no, if for no other reason than that repressed issues ultimately have a way of erupting to the surface as crises.[6]

Finally, Dahl proposes that "concrete decisions" must be "carefully examined" before we can conclude that there is a power elite. Unfortunately, as we observed in the last section, a "careful examination" of key decisions is often impossible to conduct because of secrecy and deceit in government. Thus, the details of some events may not be known until many years after the event has transpired. Consider, for example, the confusion surrounding the affair that led to the Tonkin Gulf Resolution[7] or the aforementioned controversy concerning the reasons for the dropping of the atomic bombs on Japan. A closely allied problem is unraveling the actual interests of the groups involved, or even determining who benefited most from the particular situation. For example, when the major steel producers withdrew their price increases in 1962 in the face of President Kennedy's objections, was their action due to an oral commitment by the President to press for investment tax credit legislation and regulations for shortened depreciation, both of which were most valuable to the steel producers, or was it due to adverse publicity? We just do not know, and because of our lack of knowledge, we do not know who was victorious in that situation. In summary, Dahl's decision-making critique of Mills must be rejected because it fails to embrace the *fait accompli* nature of many important decisions, and because the method Dahl suggests is highly unreliable.

The Power Elite is also criticized methodologically because the issues that the power elite allegedly decide are not clearly defined. It is further urged that the decisions that Mills uses as examples are, in modern governments, "rarely submitted to plebescites. Most modern governments give their executive branches unusual prerogatives to deal with situations considered relevant to national security."[8]

It will be recalled that Mills stated that the power elite decides "All the issues of war and peace . . . slump and poverty." Mills never amplified this definition, but gave as examples decisions such as participation in the Korean conflict, Hiroshima, etc. He selected these particular decisions principally because they were the obvious ones, but in the face of criticism, he never suggested some less dramatic foreign policy decisions or any domestic decision which would clarify what he meant.[9]

But Mills's failure in this respect does not mean that his definition of power-elite issues cannot be amplified, because he clearly gave us the outlines of what he had in mind. Certainly the notion of "issues of war and peace" is sufficiently clear. These are issues involving covert or overt, actual or implied military power. Issues of slump and prosperity would certainly include all manipulatory techniques employed by the federal government to affect aggregate levels of employment, price, and economic growth. Thus, fiscal and monetary policies intended to stablilize the business cycle would be included. To extend the definition one step further, we could say that it included a tariff decision such as the Trade Expansion Act of 1962 because of the tarriff's direct relationship to the balance-of-payments problem, which, in turn, is related to American military expenditures abroad and the maintenance of American bases and troops abroad. In fact, President Kennedy saw trade policy in almost Millsian terms: The worsening of America's balance of payments

> turned a new spotlight on the importance of increasing American exports to strengthen the international position of the dollar and prevent a steady drain of our gold reserves. To maintain our defense, assistance and other commitments abroad . . . we must achieve a reasonable equilibrium in our international accounts by offsetting these dollar outlays with dollar sales.[10]

The point is simply that Mills's skeletal definition is a sufficient guideline to enable one to decide which policies should be excluded and which should be included as important decisions in order to test his theories. An examination of the implications of each issue as perceived by corporate, political, and military elites should determine whether it is in Millsian terms an "important" issue. And, of course, depending on events, some issues which were at one time trivial can become important, while other issues can recede in importance. With this in mind, we shall now examine the substantive criticisms of Mills.

B. The Corporate Elite
We have already examined several theories that argued that the corporate elite or some component of it controls the policy-makers and policy-making of American national government. These theories overstated the pervasive power of big business leaders. Mills, who believed that corpo-

rate executives and related officials form but one part of the power elite, has been criticized by both the former group, who felt that he underestimated the power of the corporate elite, and by the pluralists, who concluded that he overstated the political power and influence of corporations and their officials. Pluralist Arnold Rose, for example, stated that since 1933 Democrats have won most elections, yet, "the majority of businessmen have strongly supported the Republican party. Businessmen have not only not dominated the political scene, but have shown an increasing sense of frustration and bitterness at being 'left out' in political decisions."[11] Moreover, Rose urges that, just because foreign policy advisors have business backgrounds, this does not prove that these people act to promote the interests of business; rather they seek to promote "their conception of the national interest in foreign affairs."[12] Another critic suggests that, in fact, because of numerous regulations and controls and the growth of "big government," there is relatively effective control of the business system by government.[13] Next, it is claimed that there is no cohesion in business and that there is "only one issue on which the top corporations would be united: tax policy. In almost all others, they divide. . . ."[14] Finally, it is urged that, even within the economy, no one business firm can significantly affect the economy (except through occasional instances of collusion), and hence "no one can be said to exercise power over the corporate economy," although collectively firms have a significant effect on the economy.[15]

The first of these contentions—that business is opposed to the Democratic Party—must be carefully scrutinized before we accept Rose's contention. Certainly, some extreme right-wing businessmen are bitterly opposed to the Democrats, but, in general, businessmen have generously contributed to the Democrats and have, in turn, been treated generously during that party's reign. Business has hardly suffered under the Democrats. First, in the area that, to business, is most significant, the New Deal effected no redistribution of wealth; in fact, concentration of wealth increased during that period. Further, since the end of World War II the share of personal sector wealth held by the most affluent 1 percent of adults increased from 23.3 percent in 1945 to 26 percent in 1956. The top 1 percent of adults similarly held 65.6 percent of stock in 1929 and 69 percent in 1939 (the end of the New Deal). After a decline in the war years, the share of the top 1 percent rose to 76 percent of corporate stock in 1953.[16]

If we change our focus from individual wealth to corporate wealth, we see the same trends. In 1929, the 100 largest firms in manufacturing, mining, and distribution held 25.5 percent of the assets of all such corporations; by 1935, their holdings jumped to 28 percent, and by 1958, after a wartime decline, they held 29.8 percent. In 1955, the 200 top nonfinancial companies directly owned 43 percent of the total assets of 435,000 nonfinancial corporations, and these corporations were controlled by fewer than 2,500 men.[17] These figures do not, of course, show that big business controls government but rather show that big business was not threatened by the Democrats, and had no reason to feel displeased with Democratic performance.

Next let us examine the claim that businessmen are frustrated because they are excluded from political decision-making. An examination of the facts will show that this is far from the case. A tabulation of top officials (assistant secretaries and special assistants to the secretaries up through the rank of secretary) of the State, Defense or War, Treasury, and Commerce Departments plus high officials in other executive-level agencies that deal with foreign policy indicated "that foreign policy decision-makers are in reality a highly mobile sector of the American corporate structure." Men who came from big business, investment, and large corporate law firms held 59.6 percent of these posts between 1944 and 1960.[18]

Another study of 1,041 persons who occupied top government posts between 1933 and 1965—many, if not most, of which cannot be deemed posts that involve "important decisions" in the Millsian sense—found that the principal occupation before appointment of 24 percent of these officials was business; 26 percent of the officials were lawyers; but there is no breakdown to determine the percentage of these lawyers who were connected with the top corporate law firms.

> The widespread impression that more federal political executives come from large businesses than small ones is correct. But the equally widespread impression that Eisenhower was the President who appointed the largest proportion of persons from large business is incorrect: President Kennedy chose the largest proportion, followed in order by Johnson, Truman, Eisenhower and Roosevelt.[19]

In a different study, it was shown that the National Security Council, the most active agency in creating foreign policy, and various presidentially appointed citizens' committees and task forces concerned with foreign policy were largely composed of business executives and corporation lawyers.[20] In short, the criticism of Mills that businessmen are frustrated because they have been omitted from governmental decision-making appears to be incorrect.

Next let us look at the argument that businessmen and corporate lawyers do not promote their financial interests, but rather they work for the national interest. This argument does not explain why their conceptions of the national interest are what they are. Different groups clearly have different conceptions. And unless one posits an enormous conspiracy of schizophrenic businessmen and corporation lawyers who really do not believe in the business system, one must assume that their conceptions of the public interest are consistent and compatible with the interests of the corporate system.

Indeed, the notion that corporate interest is perceived by such people as the equivalent of national interest is one of Mills's major points. As we observed in the previous chapter, the critical position of giant business firms in the economy coupled with the fact that public officials cannot permit significant economic disruption compels these public officials to equate the public good with the economic well-being of great corporations:

> Suppose . . . that financial crisis grips a concern such as General Motors, Du Pont, United States Steel or the Metropolitan Life Insurance Company. Here the impact would be felt economy-wide. The effects on workers, shareholders, creditors, suppliers and distributors of and tangent to the stricken organization would be intolerable. No government could stand idly by. What is more important, no government can ignore the possibility, no matter how remote, that such an incident can occur. Consciously or insensibly, its monetary and fiscal policies must increasingly be arranged with sufficient flexibility that at any time the federal government is in a position to bail out the private managers of large enterprises situated in key positions in the economy.[21]

The reader should bear in mind that we are talking about a small number of corporations when we speak of the firms whose actions can have substantial political impact. To illustrate the great importance of just a few firms, in 1953 the four largest corporations in each of the automobile, steel, chemical, and oil industries accounted for approximately 12 percent of net private domestic investment.[22]

Not only do the decisions of a few major corporations on the allocation of resources, rate of investment, wage and price policies, plant location, new product development, etc. have an enormous effect on politics, but, on the other hand, government cannot afford to institute policies that jeopardize "business confidence" for fear of deterring new investment and product development. A substantial drop in military procurement can also gravely affect business confidence and well-being.[23] In a word, there is great perceived mutuality of interest between the political elite and the large corporations and their executives in areas of great business concern.

Next, let us look at the contention that, since the growth of big government, business has been effectively regulated by government. First, a large number of studies indicate that in the regulatory field it is frequently the business interest which regulates the supposed regulators. Political scientist Grant McConnell, for example, has shown this to be true in enough instances to enable us to generalize the proposition.[24] But, additionally, the criticism misconceives the purpose of regulation. A great many regulatory and other laws were favored by big business leaders as effective means to aid the business system—as was shown in Chapter 2.

Now let us examine the charges that there is no cohesion within the business community, and that the only policy about which almost all businessmen agree is tax policy. Initially, let us recall that Mills never asserted that the power elite agreed on everything. Rather, he concluded that:

> Within the higher circles of the power elite, factions do exist; there are conflicts of policy; individual ambitions do clash. There are still enough divisions of importance within the Republican Party, and even between Republicans and Democrats, to make for different methods of operation. But more powerful than these divisions are the internal discipline and community of interests that bind the power elite together. . . .[25]

One can, without much difficulty, compile a list of big business communal interests including the sanctity of private property and the capitalist system of production, rejection of a socialist system of production, the sanctity of our system of constitutional government, government protection of American foreign investments, a preference for nonprice competition over price wars, etc.[26] Again, while there is substantial disagreement over what total defense expenditures should be or the efficacy of any particular defense system or whether a certain defense contractor is "cheating" the government, there is almost universal accord at the top levels of business about the need for an enormous defense budget. The reason for this consensus is the financial benefit derived by most of our large corporations from enormous defense spending; every major corporation does a substantial amount of defense business. Mills noted in this regard: "I think it obvious that war and the preparation for war as we know it is a perfectly marvelous way of solving and of ditching all sorts of problems confronted by the several members of the power elite, as well as by many other people."[27] In short, there is a wide consensus of views among corporate leaders, but within that framework there are differences in tactics, personality, and priorities. There are also bitter fights among would-be beneficiaries of programs, and between different industries. None of this, however, necessarily conflicts with Mills's central point on the consensus.

The final claim advanced against Mills's conception of the corporate elite is that while corporations collusively can combat governmental programs, individually they cannot. It is argued that they are therefore helpless against governmental decisions. But this argument ignores the enormous concentration of corporate power in just a few hands and overlooks the way in which that power can be used. An extensive quote will illustrate the concentration of power vested in the hands of but a few firms:

> In 1962 the five largest industrial corporations in the United States with combined assets in excess of $36 billion possessed over 12 percent of all assets used in manufacturing. The fifty largest corporations had over a third of all manufacturing assets. The 500 largest had well over two-thirds. . . . In the mid nineteen fifties, 28 corporations provided approximately 10 percent of all employment in manufacturing, mining and retail and wholesale trade. Twenty-three corporations provided 15 percent of all the employment in manufacturing. In the first half of the decade (June 1950-June 1956) a hundred firms received two-thirds by value of all defense contracts; ten firms received one-third. In 1960 four corporations accounted for an

estimated 22 percent of all industrial research and development expenditure. Three hundred and eighty-four corporations employing 5,000 or more workers accounted for 85 percent of these expenditures; 260,000 firms employing fewer than 1,000 accounted for only 7 percent.[28]

This enormous concentration of economic power has important consequences with respect to the possibility for coordination among firms. No longer is explicit collusion among firms necessary for a single firm to exercise great market power. The moves of one of the industrial leaders in an oligopolistic industry are often followed by other members of that industry. In the case of the steel industry, for example, U.S. Steel has often initiated price movements and has most frequently been followed in short order by other steel producers. The rapid dissemination of market information about big firms renders explicit collusion an unnecessary step.[29] Moreover, in nonpricing activities, explicit cooperation between firms is often legal. That a few large firms exercise great power was dramatically illustrated by the famous dispute between President Kennedy and the steel industry. The actions of an industry leader can be as effective as collusive activity among all industry members. Moreover, some firms are so powerful that their individual decisions can substantially affect the economy.

In summary, the facts do indicate both a community of interest between the political and economic elites, and a role interchangeability and overlapping among them. All of this occurs within the framework of a business society in which the proper functioning of that economic system is one of the prime functions of government. Moreover, it is a society in which the holders of great sums of money enjoy enormous advantages—political and otherwise—more so than the members of any other class. Money, as we have already observed, is the yardstick of the society and money makes its views known through elite clubs and other institutions as well as through its representatives in the political directorate. In this very complex sense, the corporate elite may be said to form part of the power elite.

C. The Military Elite

Even most of Mills's later supporters part company with him on the subject of an independent nonsubordinate role for the military. These critics observe that, unlike the military in many South American nations, the United States military have never played an independent political role, and have traditionally restricted their activities to the technical role for which they had been trained. Further, it is charged that Mills illogically adduces a long-term trend from the short-term military influence during the Eisenhower years. Then it is claimed that Mills ignores those frequent instances of rivalry between the military and other elites, while inordinately emphasizing the instances of their uniformity and ignoring the instances in which the President overrode the military.[30]

Domhoff, who largely agrees with the judgments in *The Power Elite*, states that even if, as Mills says, the United States has adopted a military definition of reality,

> it is because this was chosen by leading members of the corporate rich on the basis of their understanding of national goals and international events, not because it was somehow foisted on them by the military men they interact with at high level military 'colleges', promote and retire within the Department of Defense, and hire into large corporations upon retirement.

Pluralist Arnold Rose charges that the military enter high civilian posts only at the invitation of Congress and the Executive and their roles have been advisory and not decision-making.[31]

In a different vein, Mills's critics urge that in many instances civilians make important military decisions, and that civilians are often more militaristic than the military. For example, civilians and not the military are responsible for the development of counterinsurgency warfare. At other times, civilian and military functions become so inextricably interwoven that the practical distinction between the two becomes meaningless. Finally, the critics argue that there is no cohesion among the military. Not only are there interservice and intraservice rivalries, but there are enormous differences in viewpoints among generals, admirals, etc.[32]

Let us now examine these arguments. First, Mills never urged that there was perfect cohesion among the military or between the military and civilians. As with the corporate elite, within the military there are substantial differences within a common framework. Moreover, because of the nature of military discipline, once a decision is made, there must be rigid adherence to what is commanded, thereby effectively nullifying any previous lack of cohesion. Again, it is doubtful whether Mills would have quarrelled with the contentions that it is sometimes impossible to separate civilian and military functions or that civilians often take over what are essentially military functions. Indeed, these conceptions are incorporated in Mills's conception of the interlocking and overlapping of the three elites.

It may also be readily granted that because there is a military definition of reality, it does not follow that the definition of reality was foisted on civilian authority by the military. And it may readily be conceded that it is, indeed, the President who appoints military men to high civilian posts.

To understand Mills's view of the military it is necessary to begin with his conception of living in a "military neighborhood," by which he meant that, for the first time since shortly after the end of World War II, the United States has been and is open to a catastrophic military attack. Therefore, for the first time, America is subject to an emergency without a foreseeable end. Since any military decision or nondecision can bring catastrophe to the entire people, military decisions are necessarily political decisions of the highest order. In this sense, the military are involved in politics, even if they do not see it that way, simply by virtue of their "technical" decision-making.

Clearly, then, whoever makes such military decisions wields enormous power; and the question then arises as to whether the military are merely subordinate to civilians who exercise such power. Mills answers that the military do not play a subordinate role in two respects: They have come to possess (1) considerable autonomy and (2) "great influence among their political and economic colleagues." In what way do they derive this influence? Mills lists several methods: (1) Some military men have entered the high corporate and political realm; (2) others, while remaining soldiers, "have influenced by advice, information and judgments the decisions of men powerful in economic and political matters"; and (3) they have attempted to sway the general population. While direct assumption by the military of political roles has not been unimportant, of far greater consequence is the fact that "high military men have become accepted by other members of the political and economic elite, as well as by broad sectors of the public, as authorities on issues that go well beyond what has historically been considered the proper domain of the military."[33] Survival, in a word, has become so crucial a subject that any issue even remotely connected with it is deemed within the jurisdiction of the military. Finally, what cements the military to the industrial and the political elite are their mutual interests in a prosperous economy in which military expenditures play a large part—the "Military-Industrial Complex" notion.

Let us return to the first peg of military power—autonomy. Because of military secrecy, a general lack of information, and Congress's lack of skill in dealing with military matters, neither Congress nor the populace are able to review effectively what the military want. But is the Secretary of Defense or the President in a much better position? They must rely to a very large extent on the options which the Joint Chiefs of Staff present to them. And even Secretary MacNamara, widely considered the most resourceful Secretary of Defense, "never decided against a unanimous joint chiefs opinion."[34] It is not only on the question of what is needed for national defense (and offense) that the military exercise great autonomy, however; once America has committed itself to a military adventure—and these have not been rare—the problem becomes defined even more in military terms and the military make the key decisions. Thus, for example, in early 1965, the South Vietnamese government was in a state of near collapse. General Westmoreland stated that in the face of this collapse, "I had to make a decision and did. I chose a rapid build up of combat forces."[35] One can ask whether a President, the Congress, or a frightened public can afford not to usually follow the decisions of their military officers when the stakes are as high as they are and the consequences of error so great. The fights over the deployment of an A.B.M. system stand in marked contrast to the usual docile acceptance of every military decision; and, even in that case, the military elite largely got its way. Nor does showing that the military did not make many of the important policy decisions conflict with Mills's inclusion of the military in the elite. For what is important is the great number of fateful decisions that they do make, and this is a reflection of their autonomy.

The second aspect of military power—the great influence exerted by the military on their corporate and political colleagues—can hardly be denied. It is true that few military men have switched to political roles. Movement into corporations has been more significant. One study (1956) reports that more than half the retired generals who go into business become chairmen of the board, directors, presidents, vice-presidents, and managers. And in mid-1956, it was found that 261 generals were employed by the top 100 defense contractors. The 100 top defense contractors in 1963 included many of the largest industrial firms such as General Motors, General Electric, R.C.A., etc. [36] The community of interest is clear. Military business significantly pervades every sector of the American economy. The loss of business that would attend a substantial cutback in defense spending gives the business elite a significant reason to encourage high military expenditures.

It is also well known that the military have an extremely effective internal propaganda machine. But, probably of more importance is the power of the military within government. Through their friends in Congress whose districts are rewarded by the military, they can often exercise veto power over programs they dislike. [37]

In summary, the military do exercise substantial influence or power over some of the most important decisions of our time, and they do share a community of interest with economic and political elites and overlap significantly in the economic elite. Military power, in general, increases once a military commitment is made because their technical decisions become political decisions. For example, many of the important decisions made during the Vietnam war were made because the military decided they were necessary to "protect our boys." Further, the vastness of the military budget and the great scope and importance of military tasks converts what otherwise might be harmless discretionary decisions into matters of high policy. Finally, military power is greatly enhanced because of the secrecy and complexity of their operations, their ability to appeal to patriotism, and their even more frightful ability to argue that destruction and disaster will be the outcome if they are not given their way. In these respects, Mills was right in arguing that the widespread existence of a military neighborhood with a military definition of reality elevates the military elite to a high status.

D. The Political Elite

Mills here is accused of ignoring the roles of Congress, party, and interest groups on the one hand, and constitutional, cultural, and other restraints on action on the other hand. He is further accused of ignoring the considerable pressures on those in high places which delimit their actions.

Finally, there is the argument that it is the President, and not an elite, who has made the most important decisions, such as dropping atomic bombs or not intervening militarily in Indochina in 1954.

Let us begin by noting that Mills never denied that there are constitutional and cultural restraints on decision-making, "But it is also true, given the shape of major institutions in the United States today, that those at the top are more than privileged persons . . . they are also powerful with all the means of power now at their disposal."[38] One need not stop there, however, because in two respects constitutional and cultural restraints are trivial hindrances on the exercise of power. First, as America's experience showed during the Joseph McCarthy era, the usual response of government officials who knew better (or were presumed to know better) was to support McCarthy's efforts to destroy liberties. Free speech, the cultural and constitutional antidote to heinous government action, is always in a precarious position and often is effectively repressed. Second, as Mills observed, on numerous occasions, actions are undertaken without any regard to constitutional limitations or even elementary canons of veracity. In this regard, of the many instances of this practice, we need only note the Bay of Pigs invasion and the invasion of Santo Domingo or the many misleading statements made by executive leadership during the course of the Vietnam war.

Next, what of the pressures on those in high office and the importance in decision-making of Congress, party, etc.? First, we should recall that Mills's notion of power-elite decision-making applies only to "important" decisions. He readily conceded that below that level other factors have substantial impacts on decisions. Moreover, he noted on numerous occasions in *The Power Elite* that those outside the power elite must be accommodated or taken into account in important decision-making. But he observed that it is the power elite that initiates and gives shape to these decisions. After this is done, they may alter parts of a decision to assuage others.

Let us look at the Trade Expansion Act of 1962 as an example of this process. As far as it can be determined, the following sequence of events led to its enactment. Shortly after President Kennedy's election to office, George Ball (a Washington corporation lawyer with an extensive international clientele), Robert Schaetzel (a career State Department official), and Howard Petersen (a Philadelphia banker and member of C.E.D.'s Research and Policy Committee) prepared versions of a trade expansion bill. A campaign was organized around the bill and it ultimately passed Congress rather easily. After the general shape of the bill was developed by the aforementioned trio, various interests (including business groups seeking special protection and labor groups) sought to have it altered on the executive (and not Congressional) level. *Congressional Quarterly,* for example, quoted one informed observer: "People learned that they could do better by going downtown to the White House than by trying to get special amendments in the bill." The campaign for passage, which was staffed and run by big businessmen and the executive, tied the Trade Expansion Bill to U.S. military and economic commitment abroad, the "fight against communism," etc., so that it became very difficult for a Congressman or Senator to vote against the bill.[39] And this is precisely how Mills envisioned policy being made on the issues that concern the power elite.

Finally, we reach the argument that it is the President who makes decisions and not an elite. There are two crucial factors we must consider in this respect. First, a President is recruited and can only rise to consideration for this important post if his thinking is suitable to the economic interests whose financial support is required to subsidize his campaign. Second, before a President is nominated for election, he must prove through word and deed his deep and abiding commitment to the shared doctrines of extant party leadership (which is itself dependent on large financial contributions). Recruitment in this respect is an exclusion process whereby you eliminate those candidates with heterodox views. Thus, a President is a known quantity who was carefully selected to respond within a certain range of predictable ways. He may have certain options in any given situation, but these options are narrowly circumscribed.

The second consideration in connection with the thesis that the President, not an elite, makes the decisions is simply that a President usually depends to such an enormous extent on the recommendations of his advisors that they in effect make the decisions. In the area of foreign policy, the National Security Council (like the Joint Chiefs of Staff) is a principal advisory body, and, it has, since its inception, been dominated by people from the ranks of big business and related occupations. And the President does not invent policies; rather he depends on the recommendations of such advisory bodies as the N.S.C., who, as Mills noted, share a basic framework of beliefs in common, although they do disagree within the shared framework.[40]

There is, however, one set of institutions whose representatives have and still continue to play important roles in governmental decision-making. Foundations, "think tanks," and certain university programs supply personnel and advice to military, political, and business institutions. How are they recruited? First, there is the self-selection process—for who, usually, but a person committed to such work or at least not bothered by it would apply for such a job? Next, the "recruit" is screened for loyalty and competence. Then, during a trial work period, he is tested to determine his enthusiasm and skill at his job. His promotions depend on his continuing to pass these tests. This time-tested system of co-optation used in business, politics, and the military has been carried over into some of the new institutions. In the first instance, foundations are established by big business, "think tanks" by the military and business, and the social science research institutes (Stanford Research Institute, for example) by a combination of government and big business financing. Moreover, we should remember that during the 1950s higher education generally was purged of leftists; for example, in one survey of 165 colleges and universities, 102 reported instances of faculty members being fired for their political views. Coincidently, many universities began setting up special programs, such as Michigan State University's advisory program to the South Vietnamese government, which were intended to provide technicians and officials for government. In these ways a reliable pool of "scholars" are obtained for the power elite's purposes.[41] But, the major point is that these people are selected principally because of their adherence to the power elite's system, and not simply because of their skills in any neutral sense.

In summary, then, considerable evidence can be mustered to show the interlocking and overlapping relationship of the political elite with the other elites and the relative impotence of Congress and other middle-level institutions with respect to foreign affairs issues. But more analysis is required to determine the roles of other institutions with respect to the great fiscal and monetary issues. Certainly, the business elite's domination of the Treasury and Commerce Departments and the Federal

Reserve Board, coupled with the facts that fiscal policies largely originate in the executive branch and the Federal Reserve Board almost wholly controls monetary policy, indicates (but does not prove) that the power elite make these decisions in about the same way they made the 1962 tariff decision.

E. Mass Society

Another of the objections to *The Power Elite* which came from both the right and left concerned Mills's notion of mass society (which is different from what other scholars have in mind when they use the term). The reason marxists complained about this notion is made eminently clear by the following Mills' statement: "Marx was basically wrong. Look, it is obvious that the proletariat doesn't make history, no matter how much you want to stretch historical facts. At certain points in history it has been more active than at others, but clearly an elite has made and still makes world history. How anyone can deny this in the face of the modern power state is almost unbelievable."[42] Unbelievable or not, this conception was denied by both the marxists, who are committed to a theory of history in which the proletariat will overthrow capitalism, and the liberals, who believe that masses control a democracy.

On the best available evidence, however, the view that accords importance to public opinion in most foreign policy matters is mistaken. There is, of course, some organized public opinion on issues in which ethnic ties (e.g., American relations with Israel) are involved, and some organized intellectual opinion on other issues (e.g., American participation in the Vietnam war). There is, however, no broadly based cross-cultural organized opinion on foreign policy issues. And it is not even clear that public opinion is of much importance on issues involving ethnic ties. For example, while Jews vote predominately Democratic, President Truman, a Democratic President, imposed an arms embargo on Israel. On other foreign policy issues, there is no evidence that supports the view that public opinion is important. In many instances, for example, the people are presented with a *fait accompli* which they invariably ratify in overwhelming number. On other issues, in which secrecy or complexity is a factor, the prevailing attitude is that the administration has the facts and must know what it is doing. For example, in one major survey, 89.6 percent of the electorate indicated that they were confident that the government will do what is right.[43] (The extent of confidence might be changing but the results are the same.)

Even when large numbers of people become active in their opposition to a policy, the activity is often deflected or defused. For example, in May 1970, a combination of American troops invading Cambodia and the shooting of students at Kent State University by National Guardsmen triggered a nationwide protest by large numbers of college students across the country. Administrators and others channeled the spontaneous anger of the students into such "safe" activities as collecting signatures for petitions, conducting endless meetings, etc. When these demonstrations of discontent had subsided, nothing had changed except that the students had dissipated their energies and returned, like the remainder of non-elites, to a state of (begrudging) acquiescence in elite activities.

As this example illustrates, mass activity is infrequent and if it does occur there are many ways of channeling such activity. If this fails, elites can confer symbolic benefits or incremental tangible benefits to defuse the action.

Moreover, without having to answer the difficult question of to what degree has America become a mass society, it is possible to agree with Mills that many of the important decisions of our time have been made without the need for persuasion. One can also probably conclude that manipulation of the electorate is increasingly effective—although far more data is necessary to confirm this conclusion.

Finally, one can agree with David Truman that the extent to which one will express opinions, talk back, and join groups depends on the issue area.[44] In general, we can say that the degree to which people constitute a mass or a public with respect to an issue area depends on such factors as popular ignorance or knowledge of the issue area, complexity of the issue area, degree of secrecy about the issue area, perceived nexus between their creature comforts and the policy, degree of repression imposed on dissidents to the policy, and the extent of manipulation in that issue area. Using these criteria, it is clear that those areas most important to the power elite—foreign policy and complex monetary and fiscal policies—will be associated with far greater degrees of "massness" than most non-power-elite issues such as street crime.

ELITISM: AN EPILOGUE

Mills, more than any other of the elitist theorists, sought in *The Power Elite* to develop a comprehensive view of the structure of power in America. His analytical achievements were great and his critical independence laudatory. Nevertheless, there were some important deficiencies in his paradigm. Any comprehensive theory of power in America, whether elitist or pluralist, must come to grips with the following deficiencies or gaps in Mills's case.

First, there was no elaboration of what are the outer limits of disputes within the power elite and the causes of such disputes. Second, Mills too readily conceded a pluralist model on the middle levels of power. Yet, in some instances an institution on the middle level may have been "captured" by some affected interest. Third (and in this respect, Miliband's *The State in Capitalist Society* supplements Mills), the notion of the power elite was not related to the economic system. Fourth, Mills did not analyze many important institutions. In some instances, such as with foundations, institutes, "think tanks," and the like, this may be due to the fact that they had not yet blossomed. But what about such powerful institutions as the C.I.A. and F.B.I.? Fifth, his discussion of important domestic issues was sketchy at best; critically placed institutions like the Federal Reserve Board which an economic elite must control to properly run a system were not discussed; the subject of domestic policy still remains undeveloped in the Millsian framework.

Again, notwithstanding Mills's clear delineation of historical periods, he failed to see the significant extent to which the seeds of the power-elite period may have been planted in earlier eras. And here some of the important work being done by revisionist historians indicates a considerable continuity from the New Deal to the power-elite period.

He only briefly examined the independent role that laws may have in decision-making regardless of who the incumbent administrator is—whether elite or non-elite. For example, an administrator of an oil import quota program necessarily advances the interests of the domestic petroleum industry by faithfully administering the law. Again, for good or bad, the constitutional system deters social change and favors the *status quo.*

Mills's analysis locates the necessity of *an* elite in the nationalized and centralized conditions of American politics. He locates the composition of *the* elite in the immediate international and domestic conditions of post-World War II. His theory is sound up to this point. What is left out is the process by which the immediate conditions might change, and thereby set in motion elite circulation.

It is the next step which is missing. Can the conditions which give to the elite its particular composition change? If so, will the recruitment and consequent world view of the elite change? The answer to both questions, even within the Millsian framework, must be yes. The next step is the hardest one. What explains how the conditions, the larger social and political agenda, become transformed over time? If the United States is entering a period in which domestic issues such as environment, health care, social services, employment, and the like are edging aside the centrality of security and foreign affairs issues, then we will have a "new" elite. Thus the Rand Corporation is slowly transforming itself from a "think tank" on military strategy to a "think tank" on housing and transportation. Mills provides no handles by which we can figure out how the national agenda is changing, and why.

Factors which might explain elite circulation are discussed in a subsequent chapter. Here we conclude that Mills performs an important service in analyzing why there is likely to be a national power elite. The conditions for this have not substantially changed, only grown more significant with the passage of two decades. He performs a service also in showing how living in "a military neighborhood" practically dictates the composition of the elite. He falters only when it comes to explaining whether, and how, a nation might move from one neighborhood to another.

Such then is the current status of elitist thinking as applied to the American polity. And this picture of concentrated power is vigorously disputed by pluralists—in part, for reasons discussed earlier in connection with the critique of Millsian elitism. But, in addition to this adverse criticism, pluralists have advanced positive reasons favoring their own conception of diffuse power. We shall examine some of these theories in Chapter 5.

Notes

1 Mills's empirical work in this and other respects has been supported recently in G. William Domhoff, *Who Rules America?* (Englewood Cliffs, N.J.: Prentice-Hall, 1967); G. William Domhoff, "Who Made American Foreign Policy 1945-1963" in Horowitz, ed., *Corporations and the Cold War*; and Gabriel Kolko, *The Roots of American Foreign Policy* (Boston: Beacon Press, 1969).

2 Robert A. Dahl, "A Critique of the Ruling Elite Model," in G. William Domhoff and Hoyt B. Ballard, eds., *C. Wright Mills and the Power Elite* (Boston: Beacon Press, 1968), pp. 25-34.

3 *Ibid.,* p. 32.

4 See, for example, Francis M. Bator, *The Question of Government Spending* (New York: Macmillan, 1960), pp. 34, 38.

5 For a good review of many such operations see David Wise and Thomas B. Ross, *The Invisible Government* (New York: Random House, 1964).

6 Peter Bachrach and Morton Baratz, "Two Faces of Power," in William E. Connolly, ed., *The Bias of Pluralism* (New York: Atherton, 1969), p. 56. For a historical survey of popular disturbances in history see George Rudé, *The Crowd in History* (New York: Wiley, 1964).

7 Joseph Goulden, *Truth is the First Casualty* (New York: Rand-McNally, 1969).

8 Dennis H. Wrong, "Power in America," in Domhoff and Ballard, eds., *C. Wright Mills and the Power Elite,* p. 91.

9 C. Wright Mills, "Comment on Criticism," in Domhoff and Ballard, eds., *C. Wright Mills and the Power Elite,* pp. 239-241.

10 U.S. Congress. House of Representatives. Committee on Ways and Means. "Trade Expansion Act of 1962," Committee Print, 87th Cong., 2d Sess., p. 2.

11 Rose, *The Power Structure,* p. 34. See also Seymour Lipset, *Political Man* (New York: Doubleday, 1963), pp. xxxii, xxxiii.

12 *Ibid.,* p. 93.

13 Talcott Parsons, "The Distribution of Power in American Society," in Domhoff and Ballard, eds., *C. Wright Mills and the Power Elite,* pp. 75, 76.

14 Daniel Bell, "The Power Elite Reconsidered," in Domhoff and Ballard, eds., *C. Wright Mills and the Power Elite,* pp. 210, 211.

15 Robert Paul Wolff, *The Poverty of Liberalism* (Boston: Beacon Press, 1968), pp. 109, 110.

16 Lampman, *The Share of Top Wealth Holders in National Wealth 1922-1956,* pp. 24-26, 209.

17 U.S. Congress. Senate Committee on the Judiciary, Subcommittee on Antitrust and Monopoly. *Economic Concentration.* Hearings. 88th Cong., 2d Sess., part I, p. 62. See also Gabriel Kolko, *Wealth and Power in America* (New York: Praeger, 1962), pp. 56, 57. See also Don Villarejo, *Stock Ownership and the Control of Corporations* (Ann Arbor, Michigan: Radical Education Project, n.d.).

18 Kolko, *The Roots of American Foreign Policy,* p. 17. See also pp. 17-23, 140.

19 David T. Stanley, Dean E. Mann, and Jameson W. Doig, *Men Who Govern* (Washington, D.C.: The Brookings Institution, 1967), p. 37. See also pp. 31-53, 132-134.

20 G. William Domhoff, "Who Made American Foreign Policy, 1945-1963?" in Horowitz, ed., *Corporations and the Cold War*, pp. 41-48.

21 Morton S. Baratz, "Corporate Giants and the Power Structure," *Western Political Quarterly* (June 1956), p. 411.

22 *Ibid.*, p. 412.

23 Henry S. Kariel, *The Decline of Pluralism* (Stanford, Calif.: Stanford University Press, 1961), pp. 101, 168, 169.

24 Grant McConnell, *Private Power and American Democracy* (New York: Knopf, 1967), *passim.* Among the multitude of other studies illustrating this point are Phillip O. Foss, *The Politics of Grass* (Seattle: University of Washington Press, 1960); Walter Adams and Horace M. Gray, *Monopoly in America* (New York: Macmillan, 1955); Samuel P. Huntington, "The Marasmus of the I.C.C.," *Yale Law Journal* (April 1952), pp. 468-622; and Bernard Schwartz, *The Professor and the Commissions* (New York: Knopf, 1959).

25 Mills, *The Power Elite*, p. 283.

26 Marc Pilusik and Thomas Hayden, "Is there a Military-Industrial Complex which Prevents Peace?" in William E. Connolly, ed., *The Bias of Pluralism*, p. 146, and Floyd Hunter, *Top Leadership U.S.A.*, p. 216.

27 C. Wright Mills, "Comment on Criticism" in Domhoff and Ballard, eds., *C. Wright Mills and the Power Elite*, p. 241. And Charles E. Nathanson, "The Militarization of the American Economy" in Horowitz, ed., pp. 205-235.

28 John Kenneth Galbraith, *The New Industrial State* (Boston: Houghton Mifflin, 1967), pp. 74, 75.

29 Gardiner C. Means, *Pricing Power and the Public Interest* (New York: Harper & Row, 1962), pp. 16-45. And Joe S. Bain, pp. 276-278.

30 Suzanne Keller, *Beyond the Ruling Class*, pp. 108, 109. Talcott Parsons, "The Distribution of Power in American Society," in Domhoff and Ballard, eds., *C. Wright Mills and the Power Elite*, pp. 77-79.

31 G. William Domhoff, "Who Made American Foreign Policy, 1945-1963?" in Horowitz, ed., *Corporations and the Cold War*, p. 50. Domhoff, *Who Rules America*, pp. 257, 258. Also Arnold M. Rose, *The Power Structure*, p. 138.

32 Rose, *The Power Structure*, pp. 139, 147-151. Pilusik and Hayden, "Is there a Military-Industrial Complex which Prevents Peace?", pp. 127, 133-135.

33 Mills, *The Power Elite*, pp. 198, 205.

34 C. W. Borklund, *Men of the Pentagon* (New York: Praeger, 1966), p. 219.

35 Quoted in Richard J. Barnet, *Intervention and Revolution* (New York: World Publishing Co., 1968), p. 220.

36 Leonard Riessman, "Life Careers, Power and the Professions," *American Sociological Review* (April 1956), pp. 215-221. Also, Congressional Quarterly Service, *Congress and the Nation*, vol. I (Washington, D.C.: Congressional Quarterly, 1965), p. 1579. See also *Ibid.*, p. 1580, and Charles E. Nathanson,

"The Militarization of the American Economy," in Horowitz, ed., *Corporations and the Cold War,* pp. 205-233.

37 See J. W. Fulbright, *The Pentagon Propaganda Machine* (New York: Liveright, 1970); and John M. Swomley, Jr., *The Military Establishment* (Boston: Beacon Press, 1964), pp. 113-128; and Suzanne Keller, *Beyond the Ruling Class,* pp. 284, 285.

38 Mills, "Comment on Criticism," pp. 248, 249.

39 *1962 Congressional Quarterly Almanac* (Washington, D.C.: Government Printing Office, 1962), p. 250. Arthur M. Schlesinger, Jr., *A Thousand Days* (New York: Fawcett, 1965), pp. 771-775. *Business Week* (August 19, 1961), p. 99. *Business Week* (November 11, 1961), p. 27. *Business Week* (March 31, 1962), p. 77.

40 Richard J. Barnet, *The Economy of Death* (New York: Atheneum, 1969), p. 88. Domhoff, *Who Rules America?,* pp. 41-48. Richard J. Barnet and Marcus G. Raskin, *Washington Plans an Agressive War* (New York: Random House, 1971).

41 The following are some sources on this literature: James Ridgeway, *The Closed Corporation* (New York: Ballantine Books, 1968); Michael Parenti, *The Anti-Communist Impulse* (New York: Random House, 1970), p. 70; Warren Hinckle, "The University on the Make," *Ramparts* (April 1966), pp. 11-22; Sol Stern, "War Catalogue of Penn University," *Ramparts* (August 1966), pp. 32-40; Sol Stern, "The Defense Intellectuals," *Ramparts* (February 1967), pp. 31-37; David Horowitz and David Kolodney, "The Foundations," *Ramparts* (April 1969), pp. 38-48; and David Horowitz, "Billion Dollar Brains," *Ramparts* (May 1969), pp. 36-44.

42 Quoted in Saul Landau, "C. Wright Mills: The Last Six Months," *Ramparts* (August 1965), p. 48.

43 John P. Robinson, Jerrold G. Rusk, Kendra B. Head, *Measures of Political Attitudes* (Ann Arbor, Michigan: Institute for Social Research, University of Michigan, 1968), p. 177.

44 David B. Truman, *The Governmental Process,* p. 219.

45 G. William Domhoff, "The Power Elite and Its Critics," in Domhoff and Ballard, eds., *C. Wright Mills and the Power Elite,* p. 276.

CHAPTER 5
THE PLURALIST
THESIS

Pluralism is the prevailing orthodoxy in American political science; and yet, strangely, one cannot point to any work and say "there is the comprehensive statement of this theory" in the same way in which *The Power Elite* is the major elitist statement on American society. In part, the reason for this is that the term *pluralism* embraces several different theories with a common core. One stream, economic pluralism, was examined in Chapter 3, and even there we observed that there are several variants.

What then is the common ground which ties together the different philosophies called pluralism? Essentially, it is the conception that power, or the ability to make decisions, in American society is diffuse and that decisions are reached through bargaining. Thus, different people will be involved in health, scientific, labor, education, and other decisions. Moreover, different decisions affecting business will involve diverse industries and firms; there is almost no cohesion in business, or for that matter, in any other group. Because of this conception, pluralists do not believe that one can properly talk about an elite ruling the country or making the "important" decisions in it, although some pluralists do conceive of a multiplicity of elites each dominating diverse institutions or issue areas.

Now let us examine how pluralism and the power-elite hypothesis are different in some of their most fundamental characteristics. First, let us note that there may be a substantial degree of overlap between the two theories. Mills readily conceded (perhaps too readily) that on the "middle levels" of power pluralism is an adequate descriptive model, but he rejected pluralism as a model of decision-making in connection with "the major issues of peace and war . . . and the issues of slump and boom."[1] Again, he readily conceded the appropriateness of the pluralist model as it describes the power structures of local communities or interests and issues that are essentially local.[2] Thus, to Mills it is irrelevant whether the city of New Haven is best described by the pluralist model which Robert Dahl asserts in *Who Governs?* Further, Mills would concede that the petroleum and coal industries may fight over legislation that favors one or the other or that various communities and their respective business firms will fight fiercely over the location of specific public works projects. He would simply concede that pluralism describes these and similar situations and exclaim that he is talking about entirely different and much bigger matters—the "important" issues of war and peace, boom and bust. Mills would have said that the pluralists are describing only the middle levels of power and are disregarding the higher circles.

Another conception held jointly by elitist of the Millsian persuasion and most pluralists is that on the middle levels of power the relationships between political actors is characterized by bargaining processes. Such bargaining processes may take many forms among which are compromise of conflicting positions, logrolling, and alternating turns at victory. Thus, in the long struggle to obtain legislation providing a system of medical care for the aged, the two principal protagonists, organized labor and the organized medical profession, each received less than they desired when the final legislation (Medicare) was enacted. Again, each side secured allies by promising them support for policies unrelated to medical care in return for which the allies took their respective positions (logrolling). Finally, each side, at different times, secured victories and sustained defeats.

Pluralists see this model as generally describing the political process in America, while elitists of the Millsian persuasion see it as describing only a part of American politics, and, at that, not the most important part. But there are still others who do not see the pluralist model as describing important parts of the "middle levels of power," while, in other respects, these critics do accept important parts of the pluralist argument. Thus, the difference between the pluralist and Millsian positions is not simply antipathy. Rather, there are a number of different attitudes which may be held with respect to these issues, and even within the doctrinaire pluralist camp there are great differences in emphasis. Bearing this complexity in mind, let us examine some of the most important variants of pluralism beginning with group theory.

PLURALISM I: VETO GROUPS AND GROUP CONFLICT

Probably the clearest expostion of group theory is found in the first part of political scientist Earl Latham's *The Group Basis of Politics.*[3] He asserts that the chief social values cherished by individuals in society are realized through groups, which are defined as two or more interacting people. Groups are structures of power because they concentrate human resources for the achievement of given purposes. A State is also a group since it concentrates power for the achievement of given purposes. The State differs, however, from other groups in a very important respect: it is above other groups and establishes for them the norms of permissible behavior and enforces these norms. Within the bounds of behavior permitted by the State, groups seek to influence to their advantage the content of the rules, laws, administrative orders, and interpretations made by officials.

Each of the three branches of government can be conceived as a separate group with separate group functions. The legislature referees the group struggle and records the outcome of that struggle in a statute, while the executive and the judiciary police the rules won by the victorious group. Each of the three branches are internally divided into groups which, in turn, causes internal power struggles, various coalitions within agencies, and alliances with others outside the agency.

Groups serve as the great link between the State and the individuals for whom the groups exist to fulfill the individual's felt needs and values. Groups are organized for the two objects of expressing the needs and values of the members and giving the membership security and influence. They operate with varying mixtures of ideology and self-interest and seek to effect changes through: (1) strong internal organization which can concentrate power, and (2) the exercise of predominating influence when they encounter other groups.

This conception does not tell us the number of groups or whether the groups relate to each other collusively, cooperatively, or competitively. But Latham, whose central concern is the politics of economic groups, concluded with respect to economic power: "There are multiple centers of decision unstratified in any formal or systematic arrangement. There is no central leadership, no single group of administrative organs for planning and executing a unified policy, no master bureaucratic control for coordinating the motions of the myriad parts of the economy."[4]

A question raised by Latham's exposition of pluralism is why, if government is above other groups, should it placate those groups, even if the groups are powerful? Robert Dahl answers that active and legitimate groups make themselves heard "effectively," which means that "one or more officials are not only ready to listen to the noise, but expect to suffer in some significant way if they do not placate the group, its leaders, or its most vociferous members."[5] The governmental process is thus normally "the steady appeasement of relatively small groups" with bargaining among groups and between groups and leaders the basic component of the political process.

The group theorist's conception certainly has a powerful appeal when we examine the day-by-day, year-after-year work of Congress. Different interests are clearly involved in shaping highway-building legislation and housing grant authorizations or bank merger legislation. Some, indeed, argue that each of the numerous subjects on which Congress acts involves different interests with very little overlap among them. There are education interests, health interests, pipe line interests, welfare interests, etc.

But even if there is a diversity of group interests, is it not possible that some small number can dominate the rest and invariably, when interested, prevent the latter from achieving important ends?

David Riesman, who tackles this question, maintains that in contemporary American society no group has power, but that many groups have veto power to stop things inimical to their perceived interests. To a considerably lesser extent, he contends, each group has the power to initiate actions. The only people with power are those who can grant the demands of the veto groups.[6] America's national system is characterized far more by effective veto power than are smaller governmental units because "the smaller the constituency . . . the smaller the number of veto groups involved and the greater the chance that some one of them will be dominant."[7]

Riesman similarly concludes that the number of groups and other consequences depend on the scope of the issue:

Where an issue involves only two or three veto groups, themselves tiny minorities, the official or unofficial broker among the groups can be quite powerful—but only on that issue. However, where the issue involves the country as a whole, no individual or group leadership is likely to be very effective, because the entrenched veto groups cannot be budged.[8]

How does one prove such theories? Many pluralist writers make no attempt to do so, but one theorist, David Truman, employs a large number of legislative and executive branch examples in attempting to show how effectively group theory can explain the American political process. His findings are contained in *The Governmental Process.* Truman summarizes that "the work of one political interest group . . . results in a wavelike development of interest group activity; other groups are created to present different claims and to push opposing policies, and, in turn, still other groups grow up in response to these and so on."[9] Interest groups, after coming into being, soon discover that in order to obtain their objectives they must operate in the political field. This leads to the discovery that internal cohesion is necessary to operate successfully. They also discover that their fundamental problem is gaining access to those who make decisions, particularly the legislatures.

How does a group achieve success after it gains access? Internal cohesion is, as we have noted, very important. Public relations, which will create public support for one's position, is also important, as are mastery of the techniques of bargaining and logrolling. Groups also discover that they can derive advantages from access if they are able to exploit the legislators' local preoccupations.

In contrast to Mills's emphasis on the executive as the focus of important decisions, Truman conceives of the legislature as the principal place in which groups transact important business, while the President is primarily considered an umpire whose key role is effecting "continuous adjustment of the diverse interests in the nation, including not only the organized and limited interests but also the widely held interests and 'rules of the game' that are partly reflected in organized groups."[10] Although the President was elected through partisan support, his partiality among groups must be limited; he must be not only a great umpire, but a great compromiser. However, the many executive and administrative agencies below the President are subject to diverse group pressures.

One of Truman's major contributions to group theory is his concept of potential groups which purports to explain how the unorganized, such as ghetto blacks or agricultural laborers, are represented in the political process. He says: "In a sense one may think of the principal governmental leaders—legislative, executive and judicial—as the leaders of these unorganized groups. Part of the official's task is the regular representation of these potential groups in the actions of government." If officials fail to represent a potential group, alternative leaders may attempt to organize them. Thus the Black Panther Party and the United Farm Workers may be seen as attempts to organize such unorganized masses. But, in any event, the unorganized interests do have access of an "unconscious character" because the very possibility of their organization gives them influence on the President and Congress. The overlapping memberships and "rules of the game," which include fair dealing, the Bill of Rights formulations, and semiegalitarian notions of material welfare, also help to assure that the interests of unorganized "groups" are reflected in major institutions. Finally, Truman observes that "these unorganized interests are dominant with sufficient frequency in the behavior of enough important segments of the society."[11]

To summarize, then, the arguments of group theory, the prevailing trend in pluralism: Power is widely dispersed among various groups which represent diverse interests. Those interests that are unrepresented in groups are represented by the State, which ordinarily is an umpire, one of whose functions is to oversee the struggle between groups and set the rules for conflict among them. Finally, the groups tend to be in equilibrium in the sense that none continually dominate governmental decision-making and all are subject to veto by other groups.

There are, of course, many other aspects of pluralism as a descriptive theory, but, in sum, the foregoing characterizes its most essential points. Needless to say, the doctrine has been subject to criticism, some of which we shall now examine.

The Critique of Group Theory

It is clear that the most important test for pluralism would be the accuracy of elitism at the points where the two theories clash; and, of course, the opposite is equally true. Again, insofar as the pluralistic attack on Mills is cogent, this constitutes support of group theory, while the degree to which Mills's elitism withstands pluralist criticism reinforces belief in his theory. A judgment on this issue ultimately depends on the quality of the evidence that can be mustered in support of each of the theories.

A theme that has recurred at various points in our discussion of both pluralism and the power-elite hypothesis is the difficulty in generalizing about all or even a major part of the American political process on the basis of a limited number of empirical studies. The number of specific policy decisions made in America each day is enormous, and when these decisions are accumulated over a period of time, no study could begin to describe an adequate number of them to generalize satisfactorily. The methods of decision-making may vary within the various branches of the government. Perhaps the process by which the Interstate Commerce Commission decides to grant a railroad rate increase is quite different from the way in which Congress enacts medical care legislation or in which the Defense Department structures a proposed arms budget. Again, processes even within a single branch of government may change with time or with each new administration. What David Truman described in 1951 may have become obsolete in 1961.

Much of the group-theory literature fails to come to grips with these serious problems. Thus, Robert Dahl argued his views on the basis of studying political processes in the city of New Haven, Connecticut. Yet, is it justifiable to make sweeping generalizations about the American national political economy on this basis? Political scientist Earl Latham made his generalizations from the study of a single piece of proposed legislation of principal interest to the steel and cement industries which was defeated. Can even such a careful study as Latham's reasonably sustain such a broad interpretation? Even David Truman's study of many aspects of the political process employs examples that were chosen to fit a general argument more than to prove a generalized statement about the distribution of power in America.

Escaping from these problems is difficult indeed, but methods other than simply generalizing from case studies can minimize these problems. One of the most fruitful alternatives is to divide policy areas into hypothetical categories so that we can test whether there are strong correlations between kinds of policies and different power relationships. Thus, all economic subsidy policies *may* involve power struggles between different firms. Or perhaps we may find that only some kinds of economic

subsidy policies involve such relationships, and thus we can further re-
fine our categories.

One of the most interesting attempts to construct issue categories
and relate them to different power relationships was undertaken by
political scientist Theodore J. Lowi. He insightfully criticized the group
variant of pluralism for its failure to draw distinctions between kinds of
policies and their respective power implications.[12] His scheme hypothe-
sizes that there are three major kinds of policies: distributive, regulatory,
and redistributive. Distributive policies involve subsidy or patronage
policies typically associated with the nineteenth century. Such policies
would include river and harbor programs or defense procurement. In
such issues, battles are usually between individual units. Thus, two aircraft manufacturers will vie for the specific shape of a defense procurement bill and will exert influence within the Department of Defense to
obtain a specific contract.

Regulatory policies are defined in this scheme as rules or laws applicable to classes or groups of units. Thus, such policies would include I.C.C.
regulation of railroads of F.C.C. regulation of radio and television stations. It will be observed that these policies apply to classes of individual
units—railroads and radio and television stations. The specific decisions
based on these rules, however, work benefits and burdens on individual
firms. Lowi suggests that the power structure posited by pluralism applies to the enactment of regulatory statutes. Groups line up in favor
of and against the various statutes in this category. It should be recalled
here that Mills would not disagree with the Lowi theory that pluralism
governs this category of legislation since it would fall outside his category of "important" issues. And thus, the three different theories would
converge here and agree that the bargaining process between different
groups and their political protagonists applies in this area. We shall see
later, however, in our discussion of the "capture" theory, that at least
one important theorist thinks that too much has been conceded to pluralism, even in this category.

Finally, we reach Lowi's third category, redistributive policies, in
which neither he nor the Millsians would concede that the group-theory
model applies. These are the policies that operate not on groups or individuals, but on the social and economic environment, and which thus
affect the population as a whole or whole social classes or an aggregate

of persons equal in number to social classes. Policies concerning the general tax level, other fiscal policies, and monetary policies would be examples of this category. Since such policies would be classified by Mills as "important" (they have major impact on the problem of promoting economic growth and avoiding an economic bust), he would argue that a power elite basically makes such policies, whereas Lowi has urged that the battlelines over such policies form along broad ideological lines. Both would certainly claim that bargaining between groups has little effect on the way such policies are made or carried out.

Regardless of whether Lowi (or Mills for that matter) is wrong or right, the critical point is that categorization confronts the problem that different policy areas may have different policy relationships. The pluralist group theorists have not made any such distinctions, and thus have not convinced us that they can do more than (perhaps) describe a very small portion of the nature of the American political process.

But there are still other arguments about critical aspects of pluralism as an explanation of power, and these have been concisely summarized by William E. Connolly:

1. The prevailing system inhibits some segments of society from efficacious involvement in the balancing process while bestowing cumulative advantages upon other segments.
2. The process of interest aggregation ignores some concerns explicitly shared by many citizens because persistent, active, and legitimate "groups" fail to define these concerns as high priority interest. . . .
3. Many latent concerns—those which might well interest wide segments of society if they were publicly articulated as issues—are not identified or sharply defined by the prevailing system of issue formation.
4. The status quo biases in the prevailing system of issue formation and conflict-resolution discourage efforts within recognized channels to (a) increase "out" group involvement in the balancing process, (b) and (c) bring unorganized and unarticulated concerns to political arenas and (d) initiate reforms within organizations.[13]

As a result of intense scrutiny, even the group theorists' concept of interest and pressure groups has been placed in a different perspective. The pressure system, political scientist E. E. Schattschneider observes, has an upper-class bias and participation in such groups, even nonbusiness organizations, is related to upper social and economic status. Well over 90 percent of the people cannot get into the pressure-group system and such groups are, moreover, usually able to reach only a small segment of their constituencies (for example, only 6 percent of automobile drivers belong to the American Automobile Association). If in many instances the interests of the mobilized upper-class members of an interest group are in conflict with those of the lower-class members, the latter are clearly not represented.[14]

Next let us consider David Truman's notion of potential groups. Certainly, the potential of groups to impose high social costs upon dominant interests in society (through riots, etc.) is considered by politicians who must decide whether to make concessions or repress the "troublemakers." Concessions—which are often of just the symbolic variety—are, however, usually far less efficacious than a group actively making demands in a consistent and regular way or having politicians affirmatively attend to a group's needs as a matter of course.

But politicians' guesses about how to prevent the imposition of high social costs on dominant interests are just that—guesses. The calm of American politics is certainly not a reflection of the turbulence of our social life, as indicated not only by riots, protests, etc., but also by "high crime rates, numerous fads and crazes, and much inter-group tension."[15] Yet there is evidence that the kinds of people in high political office are often incapable of understanding these phenomena—even when they try. In sum, then, the concept of "potential groups" is far removed from the kind of influence available through other forms of political activity.

David Riesman offered his theory of "veto groups" without much evidence and it appears to be in conflict with the way in which many decisions are made in America. First, as we have noted before, many foreign policy decisions are made without reference to interest groups and, indeed, are often presented as *faits accomplis*. On the other hand, when there is an issue involving only two or three weak groups, very often nothing will get done. Everyone, for example, is for proper treatment of the insane and two or three groups are actively involved in the issue, yet not much is accomplished.

Finally, we should take note of one important theory which contends that the bargaining process between contending groups fails to characterize many, if not most, regulatory decisions. In this respect, the theory advanced by political scientist Grant McConnell is in conflict with both Lowi's and Mills's concession to the group theorists about regulation. Essentially, McConnell concluded, based upon a careful analysis of a multiplicity of regulatory case studies, that

> a substantial part of government in the United States has come under the influence or control of narrowly based and largely autonomous elites. These elites do not act cohesively with each other on many issues. They do not "rule" in the sense of commanding the entire nation. Quite the contrary, they tend to pursue a policy of noninvolvement in the large issues of statemanship, save where such issues touch their own particular concerns.[16]

For example, considerable evidence has been adduced to indicate that the Interstate Commerce Commission fell under the influence of the railroad industry so that its decisions and regulations consistently favor railroads over both competing modes of transportation and consumers. Again, the Civil Aeronautics Board consistently favored the regular airlines over nonscheduled or irregular airlines. As a third example, McConnell shows that the Department of Agriculture consistently favored certain large farming interests over other farming interests such as migrant workers.

To the extent that these examples are representative of agency-regulated relationships, it may be said that the agency has been "captured" by the regulated interest. Many theories have been advanced to show why such "capture" has taken place, but regardless of what the reason is, the evidence punctures the group theorists' conception that bargaining between groups characterizes the regulatory process. To the contrary, in numerous areas as diverse as transportation regulation, agricultural programs, and state boards of medical examiners, McConnell shows that the same capture pattern applies. But, it must not be assumed from what we have said that McConnell subscribes to the power-elite hypothesis because of his attack on the group theories of pluralism. He finds that numerous areas have come under the control of many different elites, but these elites do not act cohesively or over very wide areas of public policy. This theory, the multiple-elite hypothesis, thus combines group theory, in finding power to be very diffusely held, and elitism, in finding that each such area is dominated by a narrow elite. Since we defined pluralism in a very broad sense as the view that conceives that power in American society is widely held, we may consider the multiple-elite hypothesis as a variant of pluralism. We shall turn now to examine the multiple-elite hypothesis in greater detail as it is set forth in sociologist Suzanne Keller's *Beyond the Ruling Class.*

PLURALISM II: MULTIPLE ELITES

Simply stated, the multiple-elite hypothesis[17] is that, as modern industrial societies become more differentiated in their occupational and economic makeup, elites proliferate and their elite status is based on their attainment of professional skills. Not all elites are equally important, but one class of elites which is crucial for modern societies is the class of strategic elites, which is comprised of not only political, economic, and military leaders, but also members of the moral, cultural and scientific vanguard. Strategic elites are recruited on the basis of "individual motivation and capacity," unlike a ruling class which recruits on the basis of membership in certain families.

Elites in modern society proliferate because of four main processes: the growth of population, the growth of occupational specialization, the growth of bureaucracy, and the growth of moral diversity. The proliferation and partial autonomy of elites, their differences in composition, recruitment, and moral perspectives "decrease the likelihood of an omnipotent oligarchy. In addition these elites critically examine—and thereby check—each other's actions and decisions. Thus limited power leads to limited abuses" (pp. 65, 83, 273, 274).

In the United States, the elite that represents the public interest is the political elite consisting of the President, his Cabinet, Senators, and Representatives. The economic elite is only one of several elites and must compete with the others for the allocation of resources. Occasionally, one elite dominates another, but this is a rare exception, because no single elite in complex modern society can undertake or even designate the numerous social tasks to be performed by others. Moreover, no strategic elite is able to pre-empt moral leadership because each elite develops its own definitions of what constitutes "a just and right cause" within its own provenance. Each elite is subordinate in areas outside its specialty and none determines the patterns of selection and recruitment for the rest (pp. 96, 99, 125-127, 277).

This theory presents an interesting and useful notion of elites and their diversity in modern society. But curiously it does not produce a parallel concept of power. And this deficiency precludes the theory from answering some important questions. For example, what happens when various elites clash? All elites are not equal in power; in fact some (e.g., entertainment elites) have no power and can easily be restrained or restricted by other elites. For example, people in entertainment are largely at the mercy of the business world which controls the entertainment media. Occasionally, entertainers have been purged because of their views by the economic executives who run the media. Similarly, the political elite can ideologically purify the composition of other elites by such methods as exclusion of persons with "unwholesome" ideologies.

Thus, we can see that one strategic elite can sometimes determine the hierarchical structure of another elite. For example, persons who rise in and from educational elites often do so through structures created and manipulated by other elites; centers of international studies and other such institutions are created and financed by government, business, or both, and their staffing must be amenable to their sponsors.[18]

Now let us look at the notion that "skills and experience" are the chief requisites of advancement and recruitment into elites. One may properly speak of skill as the indispensible ingredient for the advancement of Albert Einstein and J. Robert Oppenheimer to the top of the scientific elite, but is that the proper word to apply to the accomplishments of politicians, a few of whom are semiliterate? Certainly, the use of the word "skill" in the context of the politician ignores the crucial factor of ideological compatibility with those already on top, which is so necessary for advancement in the political and business worlds. Moreover, also not considered is the factor of personality compatibility which is a necessity for advancement in the business world—and which is possibly even more important in the political world than in the business world. The crucial point is that as the pool of people with the requisite skills for performance at the top of an elite increases, personal outlooks and ideological factors become the important criteria for advancement.

Finally, the strategic-elite theory fails to appreciate that the other elites operate in the ambiance of the business world. There is little that is done by any of the elites for which business support and approval is not required. Educators, clergymen, and entertainers require for their continuous operation that commodity which only businessmen have in superfluity—money.

SUMMARY

Pluralism is, as we have seen, a term that is (or can be) used to describe a number of different theories that are based on the common concept that power is widely dispersed in the American political economy. Some of the pluralist theories conflict with others; examples of such theories are the group-conflict hypothesis, with its emphasis on the bargaining process, and the multiple-elite theory, with its conception of narrow elites dominating very limited areas. But, regardless of which pluralist theory we examine, the striking thing we find is their failure to confront the problem raised by the analysis provided by political scientist Theodore Lowi: Different kinds of political-economic activities may have very different kinds of power relationships.

When this is realized, we appreciate that the power-elite hypothesis and pluralism are not necessarily incompatible in very wide areas. Put another way, it may be possible to develop a theory of power in American society that in some areas accepts the pluralist findings and in other areas adopts the Millsian conclusions. Certainly, Mills's findings, which are based on an analysis of those who make the "important" decisions in American society, are not necessarily in conflict with McConnell's conclusions, which are based on cases of regulatory administration, when each study is restricted in its applicability to the kinds of situations actually examined. Nor, for that matter, are McConnell's findings about regulatory *administration* necessarily in conflict with Latham's conclusions about group conflict, which were based on the *enactment* of regulatory legislation. Perhaps reconciliation between many different views is possible on this basis. When we make such distinctions between kinds of policies and their power relationships, we may finally be able to develop a comprehensive model of power in America.

Notes

1   Mills, *The Power Elite,* p. 261.

2   In addition to *The Power Elite,* see Mills's comments in a letter to Dan Wakefield, a former student, in Dan Wakefield, "Taking It Big," *Atlantic Monthly* (October 1971), p. 69.

3   Earl Latham, *The Group Basis of Politics* (New York: Octagon Books, 1965), pp. 1-54.

4   *Ibid.,* pp. 26, 27.

5   Robert A. Dahl, *A Preface to Democratic Theory* (Chicago: University of Chicago Press, 1956), p. 145.

6   David Riesman, *The Lonely Crowd,* abridged ed. (New Haven, Conn.: Yale University Press, 1961), pp. 213-217.

7   *Ibid.,* p. 215.

8   *Ibid.,* p. 222.

9   Truman, *The Governmental Process,* p. 79.

10   *Ibid.,* p. 399.

11   *Ibid.,* p. 515.

12   Theodore J. Lowi, "American Business, Public Policy, Case Studies, and Political Theory," *World Politics* (July 1964), pp. 677-715, esp. pp. 690-713. See also Pilusik and Hayden, "Is there a Military-Industrial Complex which Prevents Peace?", p. 152.

13   William E. Connolly, "The Challenge to Pluralist Theory," in William E. Connolly, ed., *The Bias of Pluralism,* pp. 18, 19. See also Robert Paul Wolff, "Beyond Tolerance," in Robert Paul Wolff, Barrington Moore, Jr., and Herbert Marcuse, eds., *A Critique of Pure Tolerance* (Boston: Beacon Press, 1965), pp. 40-52.

14   E. E. Schattschneider, *The Semi-Soverign People* (New York: Holt, Rinehart and Winston, 1960), pp. 28, 29, 31-33, 38-41.

15   Jack L. Walker, "A Critique of the Elitist Theory of Democracy," in Charles A. McCoy and John Playford, eds., *Apolitical Politics* (New York: Crowell, 1967), p. 209.

16   Grant McConnell, *Private Power and American Democracy,* p. 339.

17   Suzanne Keller, *Beyond the Ruling Class.*

18   See James B. Ridgeway, *The Closed Corporation, passim.*

PART FOUR

ELITES AND
AMERICAN DEMOCRACY

The concept of political elites presents special problems to democratic societies. There is the initial difficulty encountered on the philosophical level: how to reconcile the fact of elite rule with the normative tradition stressing self-government, popular sovereignty, and related democratic values. Then there are the practical, institutional difficulties: how to devise political institutions which insure that elites govern in accord with preferences and needs of the broader population. In the United States, theorists have been busy on both counts, with some of the most elaborate and creative thinking being that of the "founding fathers." At least since the Constitution and its bolstering propaganda, the *Federalist Papers, American* thinkers have busied themselves searching for a political theory which encompasses the facts of elite rule and yet gives due protection to the promises and practices of democratic governance.

We cannot review democratic theory in detail (and, of course, there are many, many variations on a theme), but two points of conjunction between elite theory and democratic theory merit attention. In reconciling the democratic tradition to the concept of rule by the few, theorists have stressed the question of how the elite are chosen. It is said that despite the concentration of power in a few hands a nation is democratic if its power-holders are chosen by the larger population that they govern. Thus, the democratic theorist lavishes attention on political parties and elections, because these have become the institutional arrangements for assuring democratic recruitment. Closely related to a concern with recruitment is the theoretical emphasis on political representation, and especially on holding the elite accountable for their policies and actions. It is said that despite elite rule a nation is democratic if those who govern represent the preferences of the entire population; this happy arrangement occurs, according to many theorists, because failing to be responsive results in punishments of various sorts; among the more important of these deprivations are losing office, customers, or popularity.

The next three chapters review theories and facts which bear on the recruitment and removal of elites in American society and which bear on the effectiveness of the institutions designed to promote elite responsiveness and accountability. This review places elite theory in the broader context of democratic politics in the U.S., and asks how successfully the promises of democracy have been realized in the face of immense concentrations of power by the managers of the political economy.

CHAPTER 6
THE RECRUITMENT
OF
POLITICAL ELITES

The number of persons who provide day-by-day direction to the political-economic life of the United States are few in proportion to the total population. This is a common enough feature of all societies regardless of whether they are chosen by and accountable to the broader citizenry.

> In all assemblies and groups and organized bodies of men, from a nation down to a committee of a club, direction and decisions rest in the hands of a small percentage, less and less in proportion to the larger size of the body, till in a great population it becomes an infinitesimally small proportion of the whole number. This is and always has been true of all forms of government, though in different degrees.[1]

Although America is a nation of more than 200 million people, no more than a few thousand play a direct role in governing the society and no more than several hundred occupy the critical command posts in the national political economy. An even smaller proportion of the total population directly governs nations such as India, with its 550 million citizens, or China, with its three-quarters of a billion citizens.

Of long-standing fascination is the formation and composition of governing groups. How do citizens move into and out of the top circles? What social interests and political viewpoints dominate within governing groups? What criteria guard entry? What kinds of actions or errors of judgment typically result in the downfall of individual leaders or in the collapse of entire ruling groups? Inquiry into questions such as these is generally organized under two headings: the recruitment of political

131

elites and the circulation of political elites. We borrow this terminology in this and the following chapter.

In using the term "political elite," we do not imply that the members of this elite are all powerful. The decisions they make may regularly reflect the preferences of the broad public as those preferences have been expressed through the democratic channels of elections, individual petitioning, and organized pressure. The amount of power in the hands of the elite is a matter for analysis, not definition. Neither do we imply that the political elite is a cohesive group and like-minded on all major issues. For example, the political elite of the United States includes leaders of the political party that is temporarily out of power—the "loyal opposition." And it includes persons who aspire to top positions in the political economy and who would not be grieved to see incumbents pushed aside. Conflicting career ambitions necessarily lessen the cohesion of any elite group. Just as the "power" of the elites is an issue for empirical investigation, so is the "cohesion" of the elites.

What is assumed in our analysis is the presence of an elite. The power to influence political, social, economic, religious, artistic, and educational events is not equally distributed across the entire society. Some citizens have enormously more powers than do other citizens. Following C. Wright Mills, we say that the national political elite are the men who direct the large banking and industrial institutions, who occupy the strategic positions in the huge governmental machinery and in the military establishment, who, in short, can by their personal decisions affect in direct and important respects the livelihood and lives of the rest of the population. The elite stand at the apex of the power hierarchies which reach from the average voter to the National Security Council, from the foot soldier to the Joint Chiefs of Staff, from the switchboard operator to the Board of Directors of American Telephone and Telegraph.

Because this book is about politics, we are primarily interested in political elites, although we do not assume that all or even the most important political elites are those who hold formal governmental office. For reasons made clear in the previous part, the polity and economy cannot be easily separated, and our reserach interest would be more accurately defined by the term "political-economic elites." This phrase is a bit awkward, however, and we shall use the more common form of "political elites."

CRITERIA OF ELITE RECRUITMENT

In nearly all societies of the world throughout much of human history, the recruitment of political elites was simple. It was determined by biological reproduction. The political elite literally reproduced themselves. Just as wealth and social status (as well as their absence) were passed from one generation to the next, so also were political offices and prerogatives. Thus, persons remained in the order, upper or lower, in which they were born. To study political elites was to investigate the ruling families. The system of hereditary elites did not preclude dynastic quarrels and palace revolutions, which could sometimes be very vicious, but this system did effectively preclude recruitment into the elite circles of any except the very few born at or near the top.

Perhaps the greatest contribution of the democratic revolution was to sever officeholding from blood line. Democracy, except in certain radical formulations, does not deny an elite, but it urges that the qualifications for this elite be talent, accomplishment, and achievement, rather than birth and blood line.

We shall see, however, that in a democracy recruitment is by no means completely open. There are in the United States powerful and wealthy families whose favored sons have repeatedly found their way into elite circles—Adamses, Roosevelts, Tafts, Kennedys are dramatic examples in politics, as are the Mellons, Rockefellers, and Fords in economic affairs. But to stress biological reproduction would give us a very distorted view of elite recruitment. The routes into high positions are varied and depend on a great many factors other than birthright. We thus need a more complex model than one borrowed from the days of hereditary rulers if we are to probe into the patterns of elite recruitment in the United States.

UNEQUAL, BUT NOT FIXED CHANCES

We begin with the simple observation that some individuals have a greater opportunity to reach an elite position than do others. Life-chances are unequally distributed across the population. But to this comment, we must add the observation that one's chances of reaching elite positions are never completely determined. Although a person may start his life with disadvantages, these handicaps, with the possible exception of mental deficiencies, can under certain conditions be overcome.

A simple exercise illustrates the principle of "unequal but not fixed chances." If we had a list including every 20-year-old citizen in the U.S., we could study it and make predictions about which few on the list would reach top positions in 30 or 40 years. Indeed, if we actually traced the careers of this age-cohort over the next decades, we could describe in great and rich detail the processes which select a few for top positions, a few more for peripheral positions, and relegate the great majority into the residual category, the general public. Although no one has attempted such a study, enough is known about recruitment processes that fairly accurate statements can be made about what type of persons are likely to reach the highest positions.

Say that our list includes the following:

The son of a corporation lawyer whose firm has its head offices in Washington, D.C. The 20-year-old son has graduated from Princeton, with honors, and recently been admitted to Harvard Law School. While at Princeton he was active in reformist political movements, including antiwar campaigns. He was elected editor of the campus newspaper, from which position he editorialized against those who try to bring about political reform by attacking the system.

The son of a black, auto-worker in Detroit. This 20-year-old is currently chairman of the Afro-American Association at a large state university. He stands a good chance of being elected student union president in his senior year. Although he favors radical changes in educational policy, he has managed to work effectively with university administrators and has even impressed conservative members of the state legislature with the articulateness and forcefulness of his arguments.

A longshoreman in San Francisco; he is the son of a union official, is keenly interested in union affairs, and already has been chosen secretary of his local. His formal education is limited to community college, but he is an effective organizer and popular with fellow-workers.

He has campaigned actively for local candidates of the Democratic Party, and is regarded as a comer in local party circles.

A farm worker who graduated from Jerseyville High School, but decided against further education in order to take over part of his father's farm. He was a football hero in the community and largely because of this became president of his senior class. Some members of the local Elks Club are urging him to join, an invitation he likely will accept because he has some interest in running for the town council.

If we were to estimate the chances of these four persons reaching the national political elite three decades hence, certainly we would rank their chances in the order in which they are listed. Perhaps we would give the Princeton graduate a score of .01, that is, for every 100 persons with approximately his characteristics 1 would end up in the political elite. To the black activist, we might give a score of .001; for every 1000 blacks who demonstrate his talents, 1 might find his way into the governing circles. To the budding labor leader, we might give a score of .0001, indicating that his chances are 1 in 10,000 of reaching a position of national prominence. And to the local athlete, we would, being generous, give a score of .00001, suggesting that for every 100,000 in his situation 1 person might move along the political ladder into the national governing elite. (If this seems too generous, recall that Lyndon Johnson's first serious job was teaching school in Texas.)

An interesting factor about this exercise is how sharply we could change the probabilities by altering a seemingly minor trait of any of the four persons. Suppose that the black undergraduate led a violent demonstration against university officials; his chances of being moved along the channels leading to an elite position would suffer. If the young union leader's father is California's representative to the National Committee of the Democratic Party, the son's opportunities for a political career leading to national importance surely would increase. And if the farm worker declines to join the Elks, preferring to spend his evenings watching television, his score would drop to the point where it would be difficult to assign.

Speculating about the chances of different 20-year-olds reaching the top positions of society illustrates the basic principle of elite recruitment in a democracy. We see first that opportunities are not equal.

Family background, social status, sex, race, formal education, political connections, and viewpoint operate to advantage some greatly and to disadvantage others greatly. The most persistent finding in studies of political recruitment is that opportunities to reach the positions of immense power and responsibility are not evenly distributed in the society, but tend to cluster according to an identifiable set of social and political traits. The exercise also shows, however, that chances are not fixed, not at birth and not even by age 20. No matter how we describe a 20-year-old, we could never assign him a score of 1.00. Family prestige, wealth, and political connections greatly facilitate entry into the governing elite, but they can never insure it.

It is unfortunate that critics and defenders of democracy take turns stressing these two facts, the critics complaining that there are not equal opportunities to reach elite positions and the defenders countering that recruitment is relatively open to ambition and talent. Because neither is the complete picture, an emphasis on one versus the other only distorts analysis of elite recruitment. The movement of men into and out of the most powerful positions in society depends on the allocation of life-chances, but also on ambition and changing political circumstances and conditions.

ELITE RECRUITMENT AND THE CLASS BIAS

The tiny group, consisting primarily of men, that directs the political economy of the United States is overwhelmingly recruited from the wealthier families of society. Few persons reach elite positions in political and economic life unless they are born to wealth, acquire it fairly early in life, or at least have access to it. This is most true of the owners and managers of the immense financial and industrial properties of the society, but it is generally true also of elected and appointed government officials. If men aspire to high elected office, but are of modest means, it will be necessary for them to have access to the wealthy who finance political campaigns. In excess of $300 million was spent on the 1968 Presidential campaign alone (including primaries), with even such minor candidates as Senator Eugene McCarthy and Governor George Wallace spending approximately $10 million apiece. High appointed officials need not have wealth, or access to wealth, to head a major executive agency, but for reasons noted below these men are almost always recruited from the wealthier class in society.

Vulgar marxist propaganda is overly simplistic when it claims that the two or three hundred wealthiest families, the multimillionaires, somehow control American society. It is not wrong, however, to claim that the wealthiest strata of the population supply a very disproportionate number of those recruited into the elite. Top positions are nearly always held by men from prosperous business or professional families, or by men who themselves have become leading businessmen and professionals.

If we were to rank the adult population into five equal size groups according to wealth, and then calculate the proportion of the elite drawn from each quintile, the result would approximate what is shown in the following figure. The wealthiest one-fifth of the American families contribute about nine of every ten of the elite of the political economy; the next wealthiest contribute most of the remainder; and there may be a scattering recruited from the wage-earning, working class.

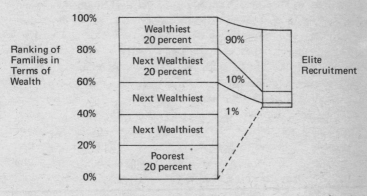

Class Bias in Recruitment of the Elite

Not only is the governing group generally drawn from the wealthier strata, it is unrepresentative in terms of race, education, religion, nativity, and occupation. If you aspire to political-elite status it is advantageous to be white, well-educated, Protestant (and, more specifically, of Episcopalian or Presbyterian upbringing), native-born and preferably of British or Northern European extraction, and successful in a prestigious occupation. A person lacking one or even more of these traits might still reach elite circles—Supreme Court Justice Thurgood Marshall is black, Lyndon B. Johnson attended a teacher's college, John F. Kennedy was neither a Protestant nor of "acceptable" lineage, and Harry S. Truman began as a Kansas City haberdasher. But the fewer of these advantaging traits you have, the lower your chances of ending up among the elite. Notable exceptions notwithstanding, the "better-off" in society dominate the channels that lead to elite positions.

To record this fact is not to provide an explanation for it. Before attempting an explanation, we should remember a simple rule of politics. The best predictor of the amount of power and responsibility a person has is the amount he recently had. Men do not become Presidents who yesterday were state legislators or small-town mayors. Since the end of World War II, the men who reached the Presidency were either Vice-Presidents (three cases), or, in the case of Eisenhower, a five-star General, Supreme Allied Commander in Europe, and popular war hero, or, in the case of Kennedy, an articulate U.S. Senator who happened also to be from an extremely wealthy family. Similarly, in the business world, the stepping stone to the corporation presidency is a senior vice-presidency not a junior accountant position. This rule of politics, or career ascent generally, works at less dramatic levels as well. Sometimes it is even institutionalized, as with the seniority system in Congress, but usually it is the natural outcome of political processes.

We can generalize this process in a way that will provide a context for explaining the close association between ascent into elite circles and membership in the wealthier classes of society. The political elite are chosen from a distinct subset of the general population. We might characterize this subset as a plateau which one must reach before one can be a candidate for an elite position. The point can be simply diagrammed:

An elite position must be achieved, but the plateau from which it can be most easily achieved constitutes a cluster of ascribed positions. To be well-born, wealthy, well-educated, in a prestigious occupation, and beneficiary of establishment connections is to be located among the "not so average citizens." The first rung on the ladder leading to the elite is, for some, provided by birth. For most persons, the social strata of their birth is a considerable distance from elite status. It is not impossible to reach the all-important plateau, but it takes tremendous effort, specialized talent, and not a little bit of luck. We might add, in words penned by Mosca, that "at all places at all times the best luck, or the worst, is often to be born the child of one's father and one's mother."[2] The idea that the plateau from which a few rise to elite positions is heavily populated with the rich and only sparsely populated by the not so rich is well-expressed in another passage from Mosca: "The rich invariably have a considerably shorter road to travel than the poor, to say nothing of the fact that the stretch of the road that the rich are spared is often the roughest and most difficult."[3]

What, in effect, we have identified is the "bourgeois principle" that power and status should be congruent in society. If in a capitalist society social status is measured in terms of occupational prestige and the accumulation of wealth, it seems natural to many citizens that those with prestige and wealth should be heavily represented among the powerful. There would be something "unnatural" about elevating into elite status men and women of humble origin and modest accomplishments. It does not surprise us that the wealthy are set apart, and elevated, in our culture; they are seen to be and act as if they are different from the middle-class salariate and the working-class wage-earner, to say nothing of the 25 million Americans living below the poverty line. In the capitalistic culture which has evolved in this society since the industrial revolution, it is assumed that wealth means importance, accomplishment, and achievement. And the universality of this belief helps to make it so. This goes far in explaining the close fit between the social stratification system and the hierarchy of power and influence. Three further factors help cement this close fit.

Self-assertion, Self-elimination. Robert Dahl, in his account of New Haven, Connecticut, makes a telling point as he explains how the prestigious, establishment families managed to rule New Haven for the first half-century of its history:

The elite seems to have possessed that most indispensable of all characteristics in a dominant group—the sense, shared not only by themselves but by the populace, that their claim to govern was legitimate. If the best families regarded public life as a prerogative, they must also have looked upon it as an honorable career. . . .

A man born of humbler origins than these patrician families "must have regarded it as an act of unusual boldness, if not downright arrogance, to stand for public office."[4]

What Dahl records about New Haven of more than a century ago is not without its contemporary analogies. Persons assert themselves very differently depending on their status in the society. Some behave as if they should be giving orders and making decisions; others behave as if they should be receiving orders and allowing others to make the decisions. Thus do people differ in whether they assert themselves or eliminate themselves from the competition for elite positions. Patterns of self-assertion and self-elimination do not correspond perfectly with social status, but the correspondence is always positive and generally rather strong.

Consider two of the 20-year-olds described a few pages back. The Princeton graduate belongs to a social group that historically has supplied a disproportionate share of the political elite. He himself is launched on a career that has in the past taken others into the highest circles. His family, his family's friends, his father's business associates, as well as his peers from Princeton or Harvard would not consider it unusual at all if he announced that he was thinking in terms of a political career, or that he intended to advance in the hierarchy of corporation management. The farm boy with a high school education is located in a very different milieu. It would be unusual if he considered himself a possible recruit into the elite groups. He has few models to emulate, no contacts to put him into the right channels, and little reason to think of himself as potentially wealthy or powerful. His sense of what life holds precludes attention to a career line which eventuates in elite status. Such a self-image is realistic, just as is the self-image of the Princeton graduate. What this realism tells us is that patterns of self-elimination and self-selection cannot be separated from the historical advantages that accrue to certain social groups, and which become part of the cultural values they all carry.

The Electorate Chooses. Electoral support of political candidates from the wealthy class, as well as electorate tolerance of political appointees from among the wealthy, is a second factor leading to class bias in elite recruitment. The average citizen views those whom he respects for nonpolitical accomplishments as meriting support in the political sphere as well. A successful business or military or civic career identifies one as eligible for high office. Past accomplishment is accepted as an indicator of future accomplishment. And because the wealthy, well-educated holder of a prestigious occupation has "achieved" and has "demonstrated leadership," he is eligible for political-elite status. Thus, George Romney transfers an image as a successful automobile executive to the political arena, wins the governorship of Michigan, tries for the Presidency, and winds up in the cabinet.

What seems to underlie the granting of support by the electorate has been described as follows. The average citizen is uncomfortable when asked to elevate others to positions of great authority deliberately. The very act of electing someone to govern implies a sharp inequality between voter and political elite. However, if the candidate also possesses traits highly valued in society—wealth, status, intellect, skills—then selecting him to govern is less challenging. In American society where "getting ahead" is a core value, the voter grants the right to rule in terms of whether a person has demonstrated that he can "get ahead," and the voter measures this in terms of wealth and similar indicia of achievement. In this manner, social prestige legitimates political authority.[5]

The Helping Hand. The correspondence between social status and access to elite groups depends on more than patterns of self-assertion and self-elimination or the kinds of criteria employed by voters in supporting political candidates. Movement into the highest circles is affected by evaluations of persons in superior positions. Even when stress is placed on objective considerations for granting promotions and sponsoring careers, there is no way to avoid the influence of judgments by those at the top of the career ladders. It is extremely difficult to establish objective measures of "managerial ability" or "Presidential timber." Talent, writes C. Wright Mills, "no matter how defined, must be discovered by one's talented superiors." In another context, he notes in connection with ascent into top managerial positions: "One often hears that practical experience is what counts, but this is very short-sighted, for those on top control the chances to have practical experience of the sort that would be counted for the higher tasks of sound judgment and careful maneuver."[6] We accept as axiomatic that ascent into the political elite can never be entirely independent of the helping hand of those already in the higher positions.

Persons who have some control over the pathways to membership in the political elite tend naturally to favor persons of similar ideology, status, and background. We later shall note the political implications of this, but for the present we shall simply emphasize that this further biases the socioeconomic criteria in selection processes. The social prejudice applied from the top need not be a blatant attempt to exclude the socially undesirables. Indeed, it seldom will be. It is the less sinister but equally consequential by-product of the way in which critical career positions are filled. Men look to familiar faces and established circles when choosing their associates, or they promote from among the many talented young a few who thereby move into the highest circles. When the position is strictly appointive, those who are already established apply the appropriate social or religious or racial criteria with ease. When the office demands professional training, either the criteria are applied at an earlier stage, when young people are recruited into the key training programs, or they are applied when the "best suited" person is chosen from among the many qualified to assume an important position, a judgment which often implies consideration of breeding, style, manners, and social contacts. Class distinctions can influence nomination for elective offices as well as appointment to lucrative apprenticeship positions. But the need for broad social representation to insure electoral success can work against this class bias, and, of course, certain politicians can battle against class bias by winning impressive electoral victories. Thus, John F. Kennedy proved that a Catholic could win Presidential primaries even in traditionally anti-Catholic states.

In summary, no conspiracy theory is needed to explain the self-perpetuation of dominant social groups. Persons are attracted to careers by friends and associates, and since the people with whom you associate are usually similar in social status, there is a continuous process whereby upper classes supply most of the recruits for the higher positions and the lower classes supply the recruits for the other positions. That the top corporate and political positions are not immune to an "old boy network" has been well-documented. Moreover, those already in established positions who are seeking new talent are sensitive to past achievement, and especially to achievement in endeavors they best understand. Nothing more effectively demonstrates achievement than the accumulation of wealth or the attainment of top management positions in large corporations or success at running a giant university. The connection between achievement and elite recruitment is particularly important for our understanding of American politics; we shall discuss it in more detail.

AN ELITE OF ACHIEVEMENT

Evidence about the social origins and social composition of elites has led some observers to conclude that *who you are* is the definitive criteria for entry into elite circles. This conclusion is wrong. Although who you are can provide significant advantages, it does not guarantee a place among the powerful. The elite who direct the political economy of this society are a subset of the wealthy class, along with a sprinkling of those who arrive by other routes. What we must understand is which minority from among the wealthy is most likely to be recruited into the most powerful positions.

To answer this question, we must devote much more attention to achievement, and less to ascriptive advantages. The criteria for entry into elite circles are *what you achieve* more than who you are. To be sure, America's higher society has its idle rich—the jet-setters who ski at St. Mortiz, race horses at Del Mar, and sail in the Bahamas—but these persons are not among the powerful, although they sometimes mix with the powerful on social occasions. That the men who manage giant corporations, who direct military operations, and who hold the command posts in the government might from time to time engage in the leisure activities of the jet-setters does not indicate that jet-setters belong to the political elite or that the political elite are idle men.

We stress an elite of achievement not to deny the close association between wealth and power, but to put this association in its proper context. Persons who reach elite positions will have demonstrated ability to manage, to direct, to command. It is in this sense that achievement is the final arbiter of elite recruitment. Of course, not just any achievement qualifies one for recruitment. It is better to be a success at running

General Motors than to be a success at selling worn-out General Motors products on the used car lot, although the latter may involve greater perserverance and harder work than the former. It is better to be an innovative dean of a prestigious business school than an innovative teacher in the school where the dean sends his young children, although teaching a room full of eight-year-olds may require more innovation than overseeing a business school. It is better to be the popular vote-getting Mayor of New York City than the popular vote-getting Mayor of Oshkosh, although it may take more magnetism to turn out the vote in Oshkosh than in New York. It is better to be the victorious division commander than the daring platoon sergeant, although more military leadership may be exercised by the latter than the former.

It is not, then, achievement considered as some abstract value but very specific achievements in certain spheres of activity which propel one ever closer to the political elite. This again suggests why the better-off contribute so disproportionately to the elite groups. The wealthy or well-born have the initial advantages that provide the education and contacts necessary to gain positions in which talent and ability can be demonstrated on a grand scale. The used car salesman may be as skilled, as personable, and as hard-working as the president of General Motors, but he was born into the working class, not the upper classes; he attended a local junior college, not Harvard Business School; his friends also sell used cars, rather than direct corporations that manufacture them; he votes from time to time, but does not contribute thousands of dollars to political candidates. When the list is compiled of possible appointees to the Cabinet or possible candidates for the ambassadorship, it seems never to include the skilled, personable, hard-working used car salesman, but almost always includes the head of the company whose cars he sells.

Being able to display your talents on a grand scale is a requirement for elite recruitment. It marks you as a person who can make the critical institutions of American society work. What, indeed, is governing but the ability to manage successfully the super-institutions of the American political economy. The men who can direct the Federal Reserve Board are selected from the top bankers and business economists of the country; the men who can manage the Pentagon are selected from the top militarists and industrialists; the men who can manage the Justice Department are selected from the largest, most successful law firms; the men who are nominated for the Presidency are selected from the governors of the large and important states. If, as it happens, these persons come from the wealthier classes, and began life with high status, or soon acquired it, this does not prove that they are men of no achievement.

If the wealthy and prestigious of society have a platform on which to display their achievements, they have an additional advantage as well. They are successful in those activities that correspond closely to what is most esteemed in society. The head of a giant corporation or the talented lawyer, much more than the successful entertainer, intellectual, or athlete, claims that that in which he excels is critical to the well-being of the whole society. The claim is not idle, certainly not in a nation which puts heavy store in the efficient working of a capitalist economy.

Thus, although success is weighed in every sphere of social activity, not all the spheres are viewed as equally important. We fete the "mother of the year," but her glory lasts for but a few hours and certainly is not readily transferred into a claim to political-elite status. And we acknowledge the leading ground gainer in professional football or the top box-office attraction on Broadway, but as regards access to elite status such achievements pale in significance when measured against those of the military hero or the leading industrialist in the electronics field.

Those who aspire to the political elite are advised to be achievers, but not only achievers. In the first place, their achievement should be spread out on a huge canvas so that it is clearly visible to those who count; in the second place, their efforts are best spent in spheres of activity that already are highly esteemed in the society. Persons who start life with wealth are advantaged over other "achievers" in both respects.

To these general observations about the elite of achievement, we can append a brief note about the "political personality." Much nonsense has been written about this topic, as if there were an identifiable cluster of psychological traits which are requisite for reaching elite positions. Such arguments are not persuasive in view of the enormous range of "personality types" who have occupied high positions. Even such loose hypotheses as the notion that the elite are distinguished by "a deep deference need" or a "drive for power" are doubtful; very self-effacing persons have reached high positions, and even ambition itself is not an absolute requisite.

We eschew psychological theorizing except to point out that men must be willing to lead, to command, to assume responsibility and give directions if they are to reach the posts that serve as stepping stones into the elite. Although the ambitious are more likely to reach these posts than the indifferent, it is not always necessary to be driven by the wish to reach the top. It is only necessary to be willing and capable of doing what men at the top do. This, perhaps, is the wisdom captured in President Truman's memorable phrase, "If you can't stand the heat, get out of the kitchen." The climb to the top, whether resulting from ambition, co-optation, or fortuitous circumstances, breeds in persons a willingness to make hard decisions, and to pass judgment on the decisions and abilities of others.

A CAUTION AGAINST HASTY CONCLUSIONS

We have now given considerable attention to the correspondence between wealth and power in U.S. politics, or, more precisely, to the fact that higher social groups are distinctly advantaged in the processes of elite recruitment. It would not do, however, to conclude that the governors are simply an executive committee for the wealthy classes. The relationship between power and wealth is too complex to be so easily disposed of. The evidence of these last few pages takes note that wealth and social status define in large measure the pools from which the elite are recruited, but the evidence, thus far, is silent on whether the elite govern on behalf of the upper classes. Mills is surely correct to stress that:

> The fact that members of the power elite come from near the top of the nation's class and status levels does not mean that they are necessarily "representative" of the top levels only. And if they were, as social types, representative of a cross-section of the population, that would not mean that a balanced democracy of interest and power would automatically be the going political fact. We cannot infer the direction of policy merely from the social origins and careers of policy-makers.[7]

The dangers in deducing policy solely from considerations of the social compostion of the elite groups can be seen in three comments. First, although the wealthiest one-fifth of the population produce the overwhelming majority of the elite, not all wealthy citizens or holders of prestigious occupations join the select circles. The elite are a very much smaller group than 20 percent of the adult population. We must know other things about the criteria of admission before connecting recruitment and policy direction. And it may well be that admission, among other things, requires a deliberate effort on the part of the recruit to consider the interests of social groups *other than* his own. It is doubtful that a political elite wholly indifferent to claims of the middle and working classes would long withstand electoral defeats and consumer protests.

Second, it is necessary to distinguish social origin from social status. Present status can be a product of mobility as well as birth. And although nearly all political elites are among the "important" before they enter the elite circles, it does not follow that they were born to wealth or powerful families. There is no political ruling class based on hereditary wealth in the U.S. There are always some among the elite who began their lives in modest circumstances, and who acquired their wealth as they made their political career. Of the last five Presidents, only one, President Kennedy, was born into great wealth. Even routes into top corporate positions do not completely deny ascent by those whose social origins are less than noticeable. Marriage is one means of upward mobility, but so also is an important technological discovery or sheer talent at financial manipulation.

It is important to realize that the routes into the political elite are more diversified than the composition of the established elite. Of course, this does not mean that those whose humble origins acquaint them with the concerns and needs of the lower classes recall those concerns and needs several decades later when they reach top positions. The self-made man is often callous toward those who "prove" by their poverty that they deserve to lose in the great American race where the fit survive and the fittest command. The poor have no greater enemy than the self-righteous who by talent, luck, or corruption have climbed the ladder to success.

Third, and certainly the most important cautionary observation, the dominant values held by the elite can change sharply even though recruitment patterns from the wealthier classes remain constant. Since the late 1930s, American foreign policy has shifted from pro-Soviet feeling to virulent anticommunism to accommodationism, yet in the aggregate the social origins of the chief foreign policy-makers have scarcely changed.

Consider an even more telling example. Notwithstanding great differences in their economic systems, the U.S.S.R., Tanzania, South Africa, and Britain *all* have elites drawn primarily, if not exclusively, from the better-educated, wealthier, well-born, and higher status groups in society. Moreover, the social policies of these states diverge in many significant respects. Thus, whether we make comparisons over time or across cultures, we learn that the social policies of elites can vary enormously while the patterns of elite recruitment hardly vary at all. It would not do to infer policy directly from the social origins or economic accomplishments of the elite recruits.

CODES OF POLITICAL CONDUCT

The elite are men of achievement, but the accomplishments they proudly cultivate are easier to come by for those of status and wealth than for those lacking such advantages. The elite also are men able and willing to manage large enterprises and direct the efforts of many less powerful citizens, but the leadership traits they display are more easily developed if one is born to or acquires upper-class advantages. These observations help us to steer a middle course between those who insist that elite recruitment is "open" in American society and those who insist that it is "closed." Recruitment is open in the sense that one has to achieve to acquire it; it is closed in the sense that the relevant achievements are far more accessible to those born with wealth and family connection.

Now we come to a second aspect of elite recruitment, one that involves political beliefs rather than social traits. Some commentators insist that the elite are a cohesive group, sharing approximately the same political views. Others insist that the elite are deeply divided within their own ranks about appropriate public policy, and that these divisions are what allow a measure of popular control as the electorate chooses among the competing elites. Whether one sees the elite as cohesive or competitive will largely influence one's view of American politics. We have already provided some evidence on this question, and we shall return to it in the following chapters. At this point, we only consider how the methods of recruitment may affect the elite's cohesiveness. The evidence forces us again to steer a middle course between the position that the elite are a cohesive group as regards their political beliefs and the position that they are deeply divided amongst themselves.

Differences Within the Elite. Political beliefs generally refer to policy views or to broad ideological orientations: What is a person's stand on school integration, nuclear stockpiling, trade with China, revenue sharing with cities, technical aid to Africa, consumer protection laws, the Arab-Israeli conflict? We often apply the terms "liberal" and "conservative" to reference a cluster of such policy views, although these terms are vague and seldom can describe the entire package of policy views held by any given individual.

Within limits, a great variety of political views find their way into the governing circles. Persons seek and accept elite positions in order to promote many different public and private interests. The electorate chooses from among candidates who differ markedly in what they propose about foreign policy, economic controls, social welfare, treatment of criminals, etc. It is a cliché, and one which confuses rather than clarifies, to claim that everyone or even a sizeable majority of the elite share the same general viewpoint on public policies. It is true, however, that for a period of time the members of a key group may converge on the same position in a specific arena of policy, as the Vietnam policy of the 1960s well illustrates. But even on Vietnam there was dissension within the elite, even within the small circle of military and foreign policy advisors, and certainly within the broader circle including Congress, leading media persons (the "opinion-formulators"), and the business sector.

Of course, not just any viewpoint can be held on any issue. The "broad limits" within which policy views are acceptable effectively eliminate the far left and the far right from elite circles. No man is likely to reach the political elite if his views include nationalization of private property, inheritance taxes which disallow any wealth being passed along from parent to child, or total State responsibility for health care. Neither is a man likely to reach the political elite if his views include no regulation of industry, a return to slavery, or nuclear bombing of Communist China. To eliminate radical policy views, on the left and the right, is not to say that what remains represents consensus. Many factors provide for a range of political opinions and policy proposals *within* the elite.

Foremost among these factors is two-party politics. On many consequential policy questions, the center of gravity of the Republican Party differs substantially from the center of gravity of the Democratic Party. Moreover, within each of the two parties there is a "liberal wing" and a "conservative wing." It would be foolish political analysis to try and force Senator Barry Goldwater and Governor Ronald Reagan, on the one hand, and Senators Jacob Javits and Clifford Case, on the other, into the same political camp by insisting that their policy differences account for little.

Something resembling a "two-party" system also exists in the world of corporate power:

> In the higher circles of business and its associates, there has long been a tension, for example, between the "old guard" or practical conservatives and the "business liberals," or sophisticated conservatives. What the old guard represents is the outlook, if not always the intelligent interests, of the more narrow economic concerns. What the business liberals represent is the outlook and the interests of the newer propertied class as a whole. They are "sophisticated" because they are more flexible in adjusting to such political facts of life as the New Deal and big labor, because they have taken over and used the dominant liberal rhetoric for their own purposes. . . .[8]

This passage, written in the 1950s, needs only minor revision to be applicable to the 1970s; today we witness business differences in policy areas such as minority hiring and training, consumer protections, and environmental policies. There are corporations which aggressively hire minorities and establish special training programs, which conform to the fair advertising codes of the F.T.C., and which deploy some profits to clean rather than foul the air and water. There are other corporations which are more laggard on such matters. Debates on "corporate responsibility" are not absent in trade association conventions and in leading business journals, and one hears much of enlightened versus unenlightened management.

With respect to the dispute over whether the elite are a unified, similar thinking group or a competitive, noncohesive group, we can draw an initial conclusion. By a substantial margin, internal policy differences rather than internal policy agreements characterize the political-economic elite. The recruitment process filters out only those whose views are "bizarre": the rabid racist, the nineteenth-century laissez-faire capitalist, the serious socialist, etc. But having filtered out these odd viewpoints, the recruitment process allows many different viewpoints to find their way into the ruling circles, being carried there by the progressive and the conservative corporation chiefs, the hawkish and more dovish militarists, the many varieties of Republicans and Democrats.

Are we then to conclude that all the evidence verifies the opinion of those who consider the elite to be internally divided, a conglomerate of cliques squabbling amongst themselves in such a way that their power is nullified and the public can retain popular control? This would be a hasty conclusion. In important respects, the elite do have a unified outlook, but this outlook we prefer to describe under the label of "codes of political conduct" rather than "policy positions." To adhere to the code of appropriate political conduct, one must adopt an acceptable stance on each of these three issues: (1) How should political decisions be made? (2) What core values from the American tradition must be preserved regardless of the whims of public opinion? (3) How should the political and corporate institutions in one's domain be protected? Elite recruitment in the U.S. precludes persons whose conduct and outlook is "inappropriate" with respect to these three matters. More than that, the processes of recruitment help shape and give operating substance to the conduct and outlook of the elite.

Making Political-Economic Decisions. The acceptable way to conduct matters of state is negotiation among the leaders, and in this way the elite are linked together by a process of bargaining and compromising. No matter how dissimilar are views toward policy questions, there can be agreement on the appropriate way to reach decisions. This is the kernel of truth in the aphorism "reasonable men can agree to differ"; the "differ" refers to policy views but the "agree" refers to the manner of adjusting differences. The processes of recruiting into corporate and political management positions place a high premium on this type of reasonableness. Recruiting persons who agree about how to reach decisions has one consequence effectively described by a British social scientist:

> Whilst each specialized elite concerns itself primarily with defending its own interests against other elites, there grows up at the same time an attitude towards the process of decision-making—particularly at the national level—which is shared by otherwise rival elites. The elites

come to be committed to a process of decision-making *in which only they participate.*[9]

The decision circles are limited, and entry criteria are partially established by those already belonging to these circles.

This does not deny the real differences of opinion within the elite, nor does it deny elite competition which is so widely touted as the guarantor of democracy, but it does introduce a substantial modification. Major aspects of this modification will be saved for the final chapters, but two subsidiary points can be recorded here.

First, there is the danger to democracy that the elites accept only each other as being among those "who count." Mills seems to have had this in mind when he wrote that

the higher members of the military, economic, and political orders are able readily to take over one another's point of view, always in a sympathetic way, and often in a knowledgeable way as well. They define each other as among those who count, and who, accordingly, must be taken into account. Each of them as a member of the power elite comes to incorporate into his own integrity, his own honor, his own conscience, the viewpoint, the expectations, the values of others.[10]

Second, and directly related to the first point, as members of the elite take each other into account, they pay correspondingly less attention to the non-elite. Thus one politician has described his task as "the ability to reach decisions, to solve problems without being unduly influenced by the feelings of persons who are committed or paid, or who for lack of information or ability are incapable of reaching a decision."[11] The procedure of decision-making reflected in this sentiment leaves little room for the "committed" or "uninformed" public, let alone for seeking out public opinion or mobilizing non-elites into the decision process. If decision-making is a matter of inter-elite negotiations, the public is more likely to be tolerated than involved, perhaps represented but not consulted.

Elite recruitment more or less requires acceptance of the principle that horizontal communication among the elite rather than vertical communication between elite and non-elite is the primary mode of making decisions. The gulf between "us" and "them" is the gulf between those few with immense powers and complicated responsibilities and those many whose lives depend on how those powers and responsibilities are discharged, not a gulf between Republican and Democratic leaders or between Ford and G.M. executives.

We risk sounding repetitious and again emphasize that common understanding about *how* and *with whom* to conduct matters of State does not imply consensus about what the specific policies should be. It only implies agreement about the process of hammering out these policies. Contrasting viewpoints and conflicting ambitions are never absent within an elite, but the differences never extend to disagreements over the rules of the game and the team of players.

Preserving Core Values. Certain values are so central to the American experience that no person need aspire to top positions unless he holds and, better yet, symbolizes these values. We noted that acts of achievement play a part in forming the elite; we can now add that the value of achievement performs a similar function. Unless he takes an oath to achievement in word as well as deed, no man is marked as on his way to elite circles. The American dream is hard work and upward mobility, values frequently if loosely described as the Protestant Ethic (an ethic by no means limited to those of Protestant persuasion). If this ethic is today under assault from the counterculture movement, it is far too early to proclaim it dead. At least the present generation of elites and those now in positions to succeed them will pronounce the values of achievement as vigorously as their careers demonstrate them. Do not expect to find among the elite any who have soured on the "Great American Dream."

If achievement and accomplishment are sacred symbols, so also are the democratic doctrines and principles. Whatever their private views and whatever their behaviors, the elite unanimously proclaim our way of government as the best. More than vague symbols and phrases are at stake. There is a specific, serious commitment to the principles of democracy as the elite understand them—to the importance of separation of powers, to the First Amendment freedoms, to the sanctity of elections.

It, of course, is evident that these values are violated often; Presidents deliberately disguising intentions in Vietnam in order to render the Congress impotent, the Justice Department and the F.B.I. in their dubious

treatment of political dissidents, and national Democratic leaders over-
looking (perhaps encouraging) questionable ballot counting in Chicago,
are but a few examples. But, in this regard, the elite are no different
from the citizen who cherishes universal suffrage but neglects to vote,
from the worker who supports his liberal leadership but blocks training
programs for blacks, or from the businessman who swears by the principles of free enterprise while engaging in price-fixing arrangements.

The gap between professed values and actual behavior is universal,
not a unique property of political elites in America. And although the
gap is a serious issue for political analysis, it would be a mistake to concentrate only on how the elite fail to act in terms of professed principles. Insight into the politics of any society is provided by attention to
the specific principles that are being slighted. Thus, in the United States,
the political elite are measured against the principle of competitive elections, not one-party politics; the principle of freedom of expression, not
press censorship; the principle of religious tolerance, not religious con-
formity; the principle of racial equality, not apartheid. If the elite slight,
as they often do, the values of competitive elections, free expression,
tolerance and equality, then we investigate the conditions under which
these and not some other values are being violated.

The immediate task, however, is to underscore that the code of political conduct includes verbal dedication to core political, social, and economic values in the American tradition. Elite recruitment is predicated
on professing and symbolizing these values. Shoved aside are aspirants
to elite positions who fail to take these values seriously. That is, a corporation executive may continue to trade with South Africa, but he must
show some sign of hostility toward its racism. And he may promote
trade with the Soviet Union, but he must also express hostility toward
its communism. Neither apartheid nor communism are tolerable elite
values within the bounds established by patterns of recruitment.

Protecting the Institutions. The elite are of one mind when it comes
to protecting rulership and the institutions of rule. However varied the
career lines of the elite and however different their policy views, the
elite are in general agreement about the merit of a division of political
labor in which a few have wide powers and the many have negligible
powers. This belief is compatible with democratic selection procedures,
because it makes no assumption as to how the few are chosen; it is com-

patible with changes in the composition of the elite, because it makes no assumption as to the merits of any social strata dominating recruitment; it is compatible with liberal or conservative policies, because it makes no assumption regarding the overall trend of domestic or foreign policy. The belief in the very institution of rulership stands above concern with techniques of elite recruitment or with interests represented among the elite. It is a commitment to the structure of power and not to particular personalities or policies.

The commitment to an effective division of political labor shades imperceptibly into an overriding concern with law and order. Although this slogan came to refer to differences in policy positions regarding Vietnam and racial justice during the 1960s, the law and order phrase has much broader reference than any given political issue. Law and order refers to the regular channels of doing political business, especially to those channels through which the non-elites deal with elites. From the perspective of the rulers, whether in government office or corporations or the military, there is only one way to institute political reform, and that is according to the general framework which gives center place to elections and petitioning. To protect law and order from black militants, "peaceniks," or "ecofreaks" is not a matter of racial justice, war, or the environment; it is a matter involving the structure of rule prevailing in the United States. Of course, the "regular channels" generally concentrate power at the top and spread popular control very thinly at the bottom, but this, from the elite perspective, is simply the fact of political life.

The elite and aspirants to elite status are in accord about such matters. You do not reach the top or even get close unless you are committed to the notion that there is a top and bottom. That those who manage the society feel protective about the institutions they manage is natural and understandable. In part, they are protecting the institutions and values to which they have devoted enormous energies and commitments. And, to be sure, they are protecting the ways of conducting political business which have put them in charge.

But beyond parochial career concerns and self-serving interests, the protectionism of the elite springs from a deep and undoubtedly sincere belief that without law and order there is no hope for any of the values and interests which animate sections of the American public, no hope for racial justice or lasting peace or clean air. This is the significance of another phrase generated by the politics of the 1960s, the well-known injunction "work within the system." Political dissidents, whether of the left, right, or middle, can throw the rascals out, but not destroy the system; they can petition and demonstrate and complain, but not abolish the system which permits petitioning, demonstrations, and complaints; they can renounce acquisitiveness, but not destroy the system which allows others to acquire. In short, to work within the system is to accept the facts of power distribution within the society. Those with power are subject to certain pressures from the non-elite, and even subject in some cases to eviction from powerful positions. But to strip the positions themselves of the authority and force necessary to maintain law and order is to risk the destruction of all political values.

This refrain is frequent in elite circles, and it is certainly not limited to American political elites. It is a constant of history that rulers deploy their forces more vigorously to protect their respective systems than even to protect their own position. And, of course, elites are seldom at odds with the large majority of the population in their desire to protect law and order. Although the motivation for wanting to preserve the system may be different at different levels of the power hierarchy, the concern for law and order extends well below the level of the elites.

Certainly it would be misleading to assume that large numbers of American citizens side with assaults on the basic institutions and rules of society. This was illustrated in a city election in Berkeley, California, in 1971. A politically radical slate of candidates and a very outspoken black mayoralty candidate sought positions on the Berkeley city council, and won. In the same election, the voters from all segments of the community were rejecting a proposal to split the Berkeley police force and bring it under community control, with a different division for the black areas, for the university area, and for the predominantly white, middle-class areas. Thus the electorate which dramatically changed the composition of the governing council resoundingly defeated a proposal (by a two-to-one vote) which would alter the source of controls of the major means of protecting law and order.

CONCLUSIONS

A review of the evidence on elite recruitment shows that social origin and social status establish general eligibility for elite positions, but that a person must demonstrate achievement, on a grand scale, before he actually enters the elite circle. The evidence also suggests that social origin, status, and achievement do not guarantee entry, because not only who you are and what you achieve but *what you believe* operate as screening and selecting devices. This does not mean that the elite are a cohesive or conspiratorial group. Quite the opposite is true; their ranks are often split wide open by serious and lasting divisions of opinion over public policy. Major differences within the elite are aired openly, primarily through the election process but also in the mass media. Still, not just any conduct or outlook is compatible with elite recruitment. Those who reach the highest positions in the American political economy have learned the appropriate way of working with fellow power-holders, have come to some agreement about how best to treat non-elites, have adopted the "sacred" political-social values of the American tradition, and have willingly taken a fiercely protectionist stance toward the institutions of law and order. Rivalry never extends to a challenge of the rules and ways of rulership itself.

In sharing a common social origin, similar recruitment experiences, parallel economic and political responsibilities, and general outlook, perhaps the members of the elite resemble a family. The family is not always an agreeable or unified unit. Very often it is characterized by squabbles, quarrels, and rivalries, deriving both from differences in temperament and from competing ambitions. But its cohesiveness overrides such differences. It is a family also in the sense that it reproduces itself politically (not, to be sure, biologically). Each upcoming generation of new managers and power-holders is nurtured in the common perspectives about their role in American society. This indoctrination occurs without their disavowing a variety of opinions on immediate issues of the day. The strength of the American political system can be located in the variety of policy views accommodated within the acceptable code of political conduct. Thus, President John Kennedy and his younger brothers held policy views well to the left of father Joseph, but they nevertheless were his political as well as biological offspring. Their energetic and successful political lives were directed toward preserving the American structure of rule and the codes of political conduct by which the elite live.

The idea of political reproduction suggests why the family of elites comes quickly together when threatened from the "outside." Quarrels and competing ambitions are put aside when law and order is at stake, because if the institutions that preserve order and the structures that divide political responsibilities (very unevenly) go, so do the elites. Individual family members may come and go, but the social order that allows for the continual emergence of new elites must be protected.

We have in this chapter come full circle. We began by remarking that the democratic revolution brought to a sharp end the ancient practice of elites biologically reproducing themselves. Now we learn that a form of political reproduction has replaced this ancient practice. The more modern forms of elite recruitment and reproduction share with the ancient forms a tendency to perpetuate rule by the few. The point we wish to stress has been very well-stated by George Orwell, where he discusses the Communist Party in *1984*. His account is equally applicable to the elite which control the American political economy.

> The Party is not a class in the old sense of the word. It does not aim at transmitting power to its own children, as such; and if there were no other way of keeping the ablest people at the top, it would be perfectly prepared to recruit an entire new generation from the ranks of the proletariat. In the crucial years, the fact that the Party was not a hereditary body did a great deal to neutralize opposition. . . . The essence of oligarchical rule is not father-to-son inheritance, but the persistence of a certain world-view and a certain way of life, imposed by the dead upon the living. A ruling group is a ruling group so long as it can nominate its successors. The Party is not concerned with perpetuating its blood but with perpetuating itself. Who wields power is not important, provided that the hierarchical structure remains always the same.[12]

Notes

1 James Bryce, *Modern Democracies* (New York: Macmillan, 1924), p. 542.

2 Mosca, *The Ruling Class*, p. 456.

3 *Ibid.,* p. 58.

4 Dahl, *Who Governs?,* p. 17.

5 The point is elaborated in an unpublished paper by Sidney Verba; it is re-viewed in Kenneth Prewitt, *The Recruitment of Political Leaders* (Indian-apolis: Bobbs-Merrill, 1970), p. 30.

6 Mills, *The Power Elite,* p. 140, 141.

7 *Ibid.,* pp. 279-280. A study which updates *The Power Elite* comes close to making exactly the error which Mills warns against. G. William Domhoff, in his *Who Rules America?,* sought to show that a social upper class dominates the power elite. But even if true (and it is only partially true), this does not answer whether the upper class is politically cohesive or simply a collection of statistically similar people. It is doubtful that an "upper class" acted cohe-sively to recruit such non-upper class people as Harry Truman, Lyndon John-son, Richard Nixon, Spiro Agnew, or George McGovern. If Domhoff fails to show class cohesion, he also fails to demonstrate that social background corre-lates with political viewpoint in any direct sense. Our belief is that specific recruitment patterns are more significant in channeling the outlooks of elites than are social origin factors. Proving the upper-class origins of the elite tells us much less than will systematic evidence on career patterns and ideological screening. The overrepresentation of a social upper class no doubt gives some common tone and style to the elite circles, but it does not begin to explain what is politically critical about those circles.

8 *Ibid.,* p. 122.

9 Geraint Parry, *Political Elites* (New York: Praeger, 1969), p. 91, italics added.

10 Mills, *The Power Elite,* p. 283.

11 The quotation comes from an interview of local politicians conducted by one of the authors. The relevant study, though not the quotation itself, is Prewitt, *The Recruitment of Political Leaders.*

12 George Orwell, *1984* (New York: Harcourt Brace Jovanovich, 1949), pp. 210-211.

CHAPTER 7
THE CIRCULATION OF POLITICAL ELITES

Pareto is responsible for the title of this chapter, although his Italian contemporary, Mosca, should receive credit for many of the insights suggested by the phrase. "Circulation of elites" is a catchy phrase which perhaps explains its frequent use in political commentary over the past half-century. But its simplicity of sound is deceptive. The circulation of elites is an exceedingly complex social phenomenon. It will be necessary to stray somewhat from our attention to American politics to insure that we understand this phenomenon. The detour into the writings of Pareto and Mosca will, however, prove valuable. It provides a vocabulary and a perspective which can be turned to advantage in exploring further the composition and structure of the ruling groups in America.

THE CHARACTER OF ELITE CIRCULATION

Pareto and Mosca define elite circulation in somewhat different ways. For Pareto, circulation is the ascent of talented individuals from the lower classes into elite positions accompanied by the descent into political oblivion of decadent and incompetent individuals who were lucky enough to be born into the upper classes. Mosca devotes less attention to the upward and downward mobility of individuals. He stresses how new social groups and interests come to prominence as well as how established groups lose their powers.

We will begin our study with Pareto. Pareto's famous definition of elites views them as "superior persons." The elite are those who excel in

any of the many human endeavors that catch the imagination of mankind. Here is how Pareto develops his argument:

> Let us assume that in every branch of human activity each individual
> is given an index which stands as a sign of his capacity, very much the
> way grades are given in the various subjects in examinations at school.
> The highest type of lawyer, for instance, will be given 10. The man
> who does not get a client will be given 1—reserving zero for the man
> who is an out-and-out idiot. To the man who has made his millions—
> honestly or dishonestly as the case may be—we will give 10. To the
> man who has earned his thousands we will give 6; to such as just man-
> age to keep out of the poor-house, 1, keeping zero for those who get
> in. . . . To a clever rascal who knows how to fool people and still keep
> clear of the penitentiary, we will give 8, 9, or 10, according to the
> number of geese he has plucked and the amount of money he has
> been able to get out of them. To the sneak-thief who snatches a
> piece of silver from a restaurant table and runs away into the arms of
> a policeman, we shall give 1. . . . For the chess-players we can get
> very precise indices, noting what matches, and how many, they have
> won. And so on for all branches of human activity.[1]

This definition leads Pareto into a statistical, even mechanical, identification of the elite; they simply are "those who have the highest
indices in their branch of activity."[2] By this logic whoever has political
power, that is, whoever has excelled in the political battles for control
of society, is among the political elite. But Pareto immediately encoun-
ters difficulties in applying this conception in sociological inquiry. It is
evident that some who rule are ill-equipped to do so; and some who are
prevented from ruling are clearly able. Pareto's initial simple classification of elite and non-elite turns out, on closer inspection, to be a four-
part classification:

1. Those who are politically able, and who rule.
2. Those who are not politically able, but nevertheless rule.
3. Those who have ability in political respects, but are prevented
   from ruling.
4. Those who are not politically able, and who do not rule.[3]

The first group presents no difficulties. They fall neatly into Pareto's
initial conception, because they are an elite by virtue of superior posi-

tion and superior talent. And the last group presents no difficulties; they are truly the mass, who have neither power nor the ability to exercise it.

It is the relationship between the second and the third group that is of political interest. Herein is the dynamic that sets the cycle of elite circulation in motion, or, at least, should set it in motion. Elite circulation is the falling from power of individuals or, more accurately, families, who, by reason of incompetence, do not belong in the ruling class; while at the same time the most talented and able members of lower classes are moving into high positions. Effective elite circulation keeps categories two and three in the above list to an absolute minimum.

Pareto is concerned that this circulation of elites not be impeded. If upward and downward mobility is blocked, social equilibrium is threatened. This, of course, happens in two ways. If downward mobility is blocked, the proportion of inferior persons within the ruling group increases, until finally society is so poorly managed that social decay begins. And if upward mobility is blocked, there will be an accumulation of superior persons among the non-elite, until finally these persons will forment social rebellion in order to claim their just place among the leaders. Pareto particulary feared aristocracies for this reason. Because aristocracies bequeath privileges and powers to offspring, they endanger the society, both by harboring in their midst ineffectual elites and by denying ascent to talented persons who appear among the non-elite. One of Pareto's oft-quoted phrases is his observation that history is the graveyard of aristocracies.

Thus the interest of Pareto in elite circulation is, at bottom, a concern for social stability more than social justice. This is one of the reasons that we classify Pareto among the conservatives. He viewed society as fragile and was preoccupied with how to protect it. A political radical, in contrast, is more likely to view society as unjust and be preoccupied with how to reform it. It is interesting, however, that either perspective can lead to a concern with elite circulation. What we today include under the labels "equality of opportunity" and "upward mobility" are very similar to Pareto's conception of elite circulation. These phenomena are equally important to conservatives and radicals; they are important to the former because equal opportunity and mobility can be a means of stabilizing society and they are significant to the latter because these processes can be the means of correcting social injustices.

Gaetano Mosca also viewed political life from the perspective of elite circulation. But his emphasis was broader than that of Pareto. Circulation of elites is more than the surfacing of talented individuals from the lower classes and the dismissal of weaklings from the ruling group. It is the process by which entirely new social interests and new social groups express themselves in the public life of the nation. The transition from colonial status to independence of African nations is one illustration of this process. Much more is involved in this process than the rise of a few talented natives to positions of authority; the entire composition and structure of the ruling group undergoes significant changes. The interests of the previously colonized peoples are now expressed by a new elite which comes directly from their midst. Another illustration of how new social interests come to power was detailed in the first chapter, where we made reference to Joseph Schumpeter's thesis that changing economic conditions call forth new types of skill groups. Thus feudal lords were replaced by entrepreneurs, and industrial barons are currently being replaced by managers.

Various conditions can stimulate the type of elite circulation Mosca emphasizes. Changes in technology and economic arrangements, population movement and migration, wars of attrition or conquest, and other causes bring new elites to the fore. If the social order is to remain stable in the midst of such flux, outlets are necessary for these new interests and the groups that press them. These outlets are provided by the circulation of elites.

Mosca, like Pareto, is concerned with the debilitating consequences of aristocracies. "If all aristocracies had remained steadfastly closed and stationary, the world would never have changed, and mankind would have stopped developing at the stage that it had attained at the time of the Homeric monarchies, or the old Near Eastern empires." But progress has not been arrested, and for Mosca the reason is to be found in elite circulation. "The struggle between those who are at the top and those who are born at the bottom but aspire to climb has been, is, and will ever be the ferment that forces individuals and classes to widen their horizons and seek the new roads that have brought the world to the degree of civilization that it attained in the nineteenth century."[4]

Not only does the aristocratic principle of closed recruitment impede social progress, it can lead to social cataclysm. Nations die, writes Mosca, "when their ruling classes are incapable of reorganizing in such a way as to meet the needs of changing times by drawing from the lower and deeper strata of society new elements that serve to give them new blood and new life."[5] The relatively open class structure of Western democracies is singled out as particularly conducive to social progress and social stability. The democratic principle of elite selection (not, it should be emphasized, the democratic principle of egalitarianism, which, to Mosca, was a dangerous excess) combined with upward mobility through the various social strata keeps the ranks of the ruling class open, and this "has made it possible for almost all political forces, almost all social values, to participate in the political management of society."[6]

This last point underscores the extent to which Mosca anticipates the latter-day stress on political pluralism. To the political pluralist, as to Mosca, social stability is protected in political arrangements which permit great variety of social interests to have some voice in governing the society.

Thus, to summarize, the circulation of elites is the process wherein the ability to govern and the powers of government are matched in the same persons (Pareto) as well as the process wherein social interests of a great variety are given room to express themselves in the elite circles of society (Mosca). Elite circulation should be unfettered by artificial restraints of the aristocratic variety. To impede circulation is to endanger society.

THE PROCESS OF ELITE CIRCULATION

Drawing on both Pareto and Mosca, we see that there are two major ways in which new elites can come to power: (1) gradually through processes of assimilation, co-optation, and modifications of the criteria of elite recruitment; and (2) suddenly through processes of rebellion, revolution, and other forms of violent take-over. The latter mode of entry is more likely if the former mode is denied. That is, if the established elite does not make room for those who are giving leadership to new social interests, then the counter-elite will turn to extralegal, usually violent, methods of claiming the power which is their due. In Mosca's language:

> When the aptitude to command and to exercise political control is no longer the sole possession of the legal rulers but has become common enough among other people; when outside the ruling class another class has formed which finds itself deprived of power though it does have the capacity to share in the responsibilities of government —then that law has become an obstacle in the path of an elemental force and must, by one way or another, go.[7]

If there are two distinct modes of entry for the new elites, there are also two different results for the distribution of power: (1) The old and the new elites can share power, or (2) the old can be wholly displaced by the new. As we shall see, the United States typifies the first pattern; witness the gradual marriage between big business and big labor. Revolutionary regimes, such as those that took over the Soviet Union in 1917 or China in 1949, typify the latter pattern; the old elite are banned, exiled, shot, or, if lucky, forgotten, and the new elite take full charge. It might be thought that violent entry and total displacement are inseparable, as are gradual entry and the sharing of power. But this is not always the case. But before giving examples, we shall present a simple figure to pose the question more sharply.

| | | Mode of Entry of New Elite | |
		Gradual (peaceful)	Sudden (violent)
Resulting Distribution of Power	Shared Power Between New and Old Elite	A	B
	New Elite Displaces Old Elite	C	D

A. From the short term view, American political history is full of examples of the circulation of elites. We noted the case of labor and business. A similar story can be told of Yankees and ethnics, of Easterners and the "frontier" people, and will someday be told, we suspect, of whites and blacks, men and women, producers and

consumers. This topic will interest us again as we turn more specifically to the relationship between elite and non-elite, especially
as that relationship is mediated by elections in the American context.

B. Some people may think that sudden and violent entry can hardly
be compatible with subsequent sharing of power between the new
and the old elite. But such people have not considered the rapid
transition from "decolonization" to "neo-colonialism" in many
parts of the third world. Consider, for example, Kenya. Violent
guerrilla warfare directed at the British colonists was followed by
total independence a few years later (and the release of detainees
who assumed full political control). This is the story that is usually
told. But the story stops too soon. The British did not leave, and
did not relinquish control of huge tracts of land or ownership of
the major industries. For that matter, troops remain stationed in
Kenya and many top officers in the police and military are British.
There are Africans in powerful positions, but they have only
nudged the colonialists aside, not sent them packing.

C. If one's time span is long enough, one would observe that most
changes put into cell A would eventually belong to C; the old
elites do not stay forever, but are finally relegated to oblivion by
the new social forces. Thus historians, such as Henri Pirenne, talk
of historical periods in language that suggests complete if gradual
replacement:

With every change in economic development, there is a break in
continuity. The capitalists who have been active up to that point
recognize, one may say, that they are incapable of adapting themselves to the circumstances produced by hitherto unknown needs,
which require new means for their satisfaction. They retire from
the struggle, and become an aristocracy whose members, if they
participate at all in the management of affairs, participate only
in a passive way by providing capital. In their place new men
arise, bold and enterprising individuals who sail audaciously before the winds of change . . . .[8]

Pirenne identifies four turning points: "The rise of the town merchants from the eleventh century, the development of international trade in the thirteenth century, the emergence of new industries and of manufacturing towns in the sixteenth century, and
finally the industrial revolution of the eighteenth century"[9]; his

message being that each transformation was accompanied by new leaders rising from the lower classes.

D. Here the illustrations are easy, and, at any rate, have been fully conceptualized in Marx's theory of class conflict and revolution. Sudden and violent entry of a new elite followed by the complete routing of the old elite is characteristic of the successful class revolution. It is not a case, as in "palace revolutions" or military coups, where new faces are exchanged for old faces but the same interests dominate. The change is more profound; it produces a true circulation of the elites in which wholly new interests are represented and completely different social groups have access to political elite positions.

In all four of these cases, elite circulaton involves more than the movement of individuals into and out of the ruling group. Economic, cultural, demographic, and technical changes, which seldom are under the complete control of the elite, result in the formation of new social groups, and these groups assert themselves politically. The proletariat are the classic example; brought into being by the industrial revolution, the proletariat has come to share power with that elite that initiated the chain of events that created the proletariat. The proletariat has used a variety of techniques to achieve this status; these techniques range from strikes and labor violence to the formation of labor parties and emphasis on electoral politics. In American political history, especially along the Northeastern seaboard, migrants were attracted to the new industries, and these ethnics eventually organized themselves politically and came to share power with the Yankee entrepreneurs who had lured them into industry in the first place.

WHAT ELITE CIRCULATION IS NOT

Personnel turnover should not be equated with elite circulation, although this mistake is often made. There is always personnel turnover; men achieve and depart from high positions for a variety of reasons. There are natural causes; sickness, old age, and death of leaders make room for new recruits. There are also legal considerations, such as mandatory retirement policies in bureaucracies and tenure limitations for elected positions. To learn that no American President (since the Twenty-

Second Amendment) serves more than eight years is hardly instructive about elite circulation, and it is not much more instructive to learn that members of his staff and Cabinet often serve even fewer years.

Personnel turnover also occurs because of intra-elite competition for the biggest prizes. The struggle to reach top positions can be very competitive and tenure for any given individual may be insecure. In political life, election defeats lead to personnel turnover, although election defeats occur less frequently in American politics than campaign fervor might indicate—about nine of every ten Congressmen who stand for re-election are successful, and the rate is equally high at other levels of government. Nevertheless, men do on occasion lose high office by election defeat, and carry with them the many appointees holding patronage posts. High positions in the corporate world can also be lost due to competition, although the mechanisms by which, for instance, a corporation president loses power are less public than the devices of electoral politics. But poor management, loss of confidence by stockholders or those who execute management decisions, and even the "voting power" of the purchasing consumer can help ease a boss out of power in favor of his senior vice-president, although, in many cases, the boss will be elevated to a higher if only honorific post.

Thus, natural causes, voluntary retirements, legal restrictions, and competition may explain personnel turnover; however, changes in personnel may or may not be linked to elite circulation. Elite circulation is not necessarily the replacement of high officeholders by different persons; it is, instead, the replacement of officeholders by different *types* of persons. While the movement of men into and out of the command posts of society is highly consequential for the participants and their allies, it has no connection with the rise of new talent or the emergence of new social groups to power. This is the transferal of power described by the term "palace revolution"; in such revolutions, leadership is changed to satisfy career ambitions or a shift in alliances, but the turnover need have no relationship with elite circulation. The exchange of one military junta for another, as is the pattern of coups in many South American countries, again is a matter of personnel turnover and is not connected with any movement from lower strata to elite positions.

Consider a simple situation in which there are two types of persons in society, the Xs and the Zs. If investigation shows that political elites are always Xs, even though different persons hold power at different times, then no circulation of elites has occurred:

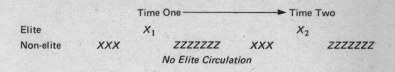

Time One ————————→ Time Two

Elite X_1 X_2

Non-elite   *XXX*   *ZZZZZZZ*   *XXX*   *ZZZZZZZ*

No Elite Circulation

But if we learn that Zs find their way into top positions, then can it be said that elite circulation has occurred. This is true whether Zs have entered by gradual assimilation or by the sudden use of force, and whether power is then shared between X and Z, or Xs are completely banished from elite positions.

Time One ————————→ Time Two

Elite X *(Z, X)* or *(Z)*

Non-elite   *XXX*   *ZZZZZZZ*   *XXX*   *ZZZZZZZ*

Elite Circulation

The difference in emphasis between Pareto and Mosca can now be more clearly seen. Neither would equate personnel turnover with elite circulation. But they differ in what is implied by the movement of Zs into the elite; Pareto stressed the rise of talented and ambitious individuals from the lower classes, and Mosca stressed the emergence of new social groups and interests demanding a voice in government.

ELITE CIRCULATION AND AMERICAN POLITICS

There has been and continues to be significant amounts of elite circulation in American politics. Talented and ambitious persons have risen from the lower strata to positions of considerable political and economic power; there undoubtedly are at the moment these words are being read some persons of modest social origins who are ascending the relevant hierarchies, perhaps even among those who are reading these words. Of course, social mobility, especially upward mobility, is not as prevalent as many commentators have assumed; and, of course, the more advantaged strata in society will continue to contribute more than their share to the ruling group. But even accepting these qualifications, we still conclude that talented individuals starting with modest economic resources but having strong egos, appropriate skills, and luck are in the process of displacing persons who no longer have the stamina or ability to maintain their control. Elite circulation of the type that concerned Pareto is an ongoing process in American political and economic life.

We come to the same conclusion if we follow Mosca's broader construction of elite circulation. New social groups have in the past and continue in the present to edge their way into elite circles. During the past two centuries, a diversity of social groups have dominated society or have shared this power with other groups. Certainly, the landowners and men of the professions who founded the nation did not expect that by its 100th birthday "their nation" would be run by aggressive, extremely wealthy industrialists and capitalists; and these same entrepreneurs, so much in control in the latter part of the nineteenth and first part of the twentieth century, hardly expected that they would someday have to recognize the leaders of giant labor unions who presume to speak on behalf of the working class.

Today, elite circulation is still occurring, for example, among black people. By 1971, there were sufficient black members of Congress to form a caucus and demand, and partially receive, preferential treatment in committee assignments, and to have an audience with the President in order to deliver their own programs for executive consideration. At local levels, the changes since the early 1950s have been equally dramatic, with several of the largest cities in the U.S. now having black mayors and with many more cities having a sizable number of black aldermen or councillors. The ascendancy of blacks in the corporate world is increasing as well, largely as a result of co-optation by white-owned companies. Of course, the number of blacks in positions of power is still not proportionate to their population size. The fact that more black faces appear in board rooms, in city, state, and national legislatures, in executive bureaus, and indeed across the positions of peripheral power should not be interpreted as meaning that the large black population is having its grievances and needs attended to. As noted before, simple changes in the composition of the ruling groups does not automatically imply changes in the policies that affect the non-elite. But this issue can be bypassed for the moment as the present task is simply to underline that elite circulation is an ongoing fact of American politics.

It is too early to know whether elite circulation along the dimension of sex is to affect public policy in any significant way; however, there undoubtedly will be a rapid and fairly extensive movement of women into increasingly powerful positions in society over the next few decades. It is unlikely that females will some day dominate polity and economy as the males do today, and it is even unlikely that parity will be reached with females occupying half the directing positions in society; however, that women as a group will gradually displace a certain percentage of males from controlling positions seems assured, even at this early stage in the process of elite circulation.

Documenting instances of elite circulation, however, is not the same as explaining the process itself. Political analysis seeks to understand what accounts for changes in the composition of elites, and what explains how different values and interests come to be represented among the rulers. We have available two very different, although not incompatible, interpretations which have been advanced by students of American society. One interpretation stresses political and especially electoral factors. The other stresses economic and social structural factors. For purposes of convenience, we shall term the first the "electoral thesis of elite circulation" and the second the "economic thesis of elite circulation," although these labels simplify what are extraordinarily complex phenomena.

THE ELECTORAL THESIS OF
ELITE CIRCULATION

This thesis emphasizes the part played by the American electorate in altering the composition of ruling groups. It is aptly illustrated in Robert Dahl's review of nearly two centuries of political history in New Haven, Connecticut, and we can use his account to describe how elections might affect elite circulation.[10]

From its incorporation as a city in 1784 until the early 1840s, New Haven was controlled by an elite of the established and prestigious families. This patrician elite was drawn almost exclusively from Congregational ministers, from lawyers and other professionals, and from men with respectable business enterprises. Yale University was the major recruiting ground for the elite, and the proving ground for their abilities. This was an elite of wealth, education, and family standing, and it completely dominated the political life of New Haven:

> They were of one common stock and one religion, cohesive in their uniformly conservative outlook on all matters, substantially unchallenged in their authority, successful in pushing through their own policies, and in full control of such critical social institutions as the established religion, the educational system (including not only the schools but Yale as well), and even business enterprises.[11]

But this oligarchy for all its prestige and resources was to give way in the 1840s to a new elite of different origin and outlook from the patricians they replaced. The new elite, which ruled until the turn of the century, were industrialists and capitalists; and although rich in their own right, they did not benefit from the family connections and specialized education of the genteel class they shoved aside. Dahl calls this elite the "entrepreneurs" and states:

> With the growth of manufacturing a new kind of man rose to the top in the local economic order. Typically he came from the same stock as the patricians; like almost any New Englander he could trace his forebears back to the early colonial period or even to the Mayflower. But he frequently came from humbler origins, quite probably from poverty, turned his hand to hard physical work at an early age, had little opportunity for formal education, got in on the ground floor of some new enterprise, and one day found himself a man of substance. He was, in short, the epitome of the self-made man.[12]

This passage illustrates the two dimensions of elite circulation. Talented and hard-working individuals, despite modest beginnings, edge aside the established but spent elite; and new social groups, in this case manufacturing and industrial interests, gain access to ruling circles. Like their counterparts across the young nation, the entrepreneurs of New Haven came to control the wealth and the political offices. But in assuming political control and in creating a new, industrial base for the accumulation of wealth, these entrepreneurs transformed society in a way that was to establish new social groups who, in turn, obtained political control.

The brickyards and mills, the casket and carriage manufacturing plants, the lumbering and ship building industries, all needed workers; because just as there can be no agricultural society without farmers, there can be no industrial society without workers. And, in the case of New Haven, and much of nineteenth-century America, the workers came from abroad. And, in the twentieth century, it was men of working-class origins, born of immigrant Irish and Italian families, who took over the leadership of the political parties and hence ascended to public office in New Haven.

Thus, three social types have governed New Haven—established, prestigious families during its early days, aggressive and successful entrepreneurs during the latter part of the nineteenth century, and party professionals adept at the game of ethnic politics beginning around 1900. This description of elite circulation, however, is not as important as the factors that Dahl introduces to explain it—specifically, the growth of electoral politics.

The old established families of the Congregational Church gave way to the self-made entrepreneurs because the former were clumsy and the latter adept in the electoral politics sweeping the nation during this period of Jacksonian democracy. As soon as dissident groups began to challenge the patricians, the control of the old elite was doomed, because "they were too few in number to maintain control over public office in a political order where office could be contested in elections. . . . Sooner or later, leaders who knew how to mobilize sheer numbers were bound to prevail over the old oligarchy."[13] Dahl suggests five factors that hastened the elite circulation: the secret ballot, the spread of the suffrage, the growth in population, mobilization of the voters by the political parties, and the ideological rigidity of the oligarchy that was so unsuited to democratic ideas and competitive politics.

If electoral politics explain the transfer of power from the patricians to the entrepreneurs, even more do they explain the transfer of power from the entrepreneurs to professional politicians, whose strength was rooted in a working-class, ethnic population. "Like the patricians before them, the entrepreneurs suffered from one acute political vulnerability— they necessarily lacked numbers. This weakness was now to be exploited by another band of new men, the [proletariat] who made up in popularity with their fellow citizens what they frequently lacked in wealth and social standing."[14] Dahl then again turns to the electorate to account for the removal of one elite and the entrenchment of another.

> Since political leaders hoped to expand their own influence with the votes of ethnic groups, they helped the immigrant overcome his initial political powerlessness by engaging him in politics. Whatever else the ethnics lacked, they had numbers. Hence politicians took the initiative; they made it easy for immigrants to become citizens, encouraged ethnics to register, put them on the party rolls, and aided them in meeting the innumerable specific problems resulting from their poverty, strangeness and lowly position. To obtain and hold the votes, the political leaders rewarded them with city jobs. They also appealed to their desire for ethnic prestige and self-respect by running members of the ethnic groups as candidates for elective office.[15]

This, in a nutshell, is what every American schoolchild is taught about "elite circulation." The men who govern the society are those who have the broadest popular support; remove that support and a new, more suitable group will rise to take their place.

But the thesis is not altogether satisfactory. In its simpler versions (although not the version offered by Dahl), it seems to hold that elite circulation is a matter of the electorate tiring of one elite and searching around for another. Certainly this version, although not unknown in civics textbooks, is but a parody of American politics. But even the more sophisticated accounts, which stress that electoral support is fashioned by a counter-elite and is not a spontaneous change of heart by the masses, overlooks too much. There is more to the circulation of elites than the waxing and waning of electoral strength. Let us then consider an alternative thesis, one which pays scant attention to elections and voters in accounting for elite circulation.

THE ECONOMIC OR STRUCTURAL THESIS
OF ELITE CIRCULATION

An economic thesis of elite circulation notes that it is not shifts in electorate preferences but changes in the economic organization of society which preface and account for transfer of control from one elite to another. To explain why one elite falls and another rises, it is necessary to investigate changes in the system of property relations and in the forms of economic production, not, as Pareto insisted, changes in the psychology of the dominant minority, and not, as many democratic theorists insist, changes in the preferences of the non-elite. Thus, for instance, if the patrician elite are replaced by the successful capitalist elite in New Haven, it is because the entrepreneurs control the means of production and own the means by which wealth is amassed. In short, they own the institutions on which the livelihood of the masses depends; and it is this fact, not electoral politics, which primarily accounts for the capitalist's ascendancy in New Haven politics.

The economic thesis, of course, owes much to marxian analysis. The introduction of new productive techniques is what leads to social change. The social class which owns the outmoded productive forces has its control of society loosened by the rise of a new class which is responsible for, and owns, the economic institutions that come to dominate production in the society. The old ruling class cannot prevent its own downfall, because structural changes in the society have an inevitability and logic of their own which is never completely under the control of any single minority.

We need not follow Marx totally to appreciate the corrective his analysis brings to an undue emphasis on electoral politics. But as we shall see shortly, it will not do to ignore wholly elections in the study of elite circulation in the United States.

In a peculiar way, the book by C. Wright Mills, which we have cited so often, *The Power Elite,* is marxian in its account of elite circulations. According to Mills, it is the "institutional landscape" of the society which determines who the elite are. Men have power by virtue of their positions at the apex of the controlling institutions. And although Mills has no self-conscious theory of elite circulation, mostly because he considers only a single period in American political history, his general hypothesis includes an implicit thesis. He writes that, "The power elite has been shaped by the coincidence of interest between those who control the major means of production and those who control the newly enlarged means of violence."[16] Military capitalism is the foundation of the elite which have dominated American society since World War II.

If Mills is correct, it follows that if the institutions singled out for attention lose in influence, the conditions are established for elite circulation. Thus, if the United States turns to neo-isolationism and develops a generalized antagonism toward the "military-industrial complex," then the institutional basis of the present elite evaporates. On the other hand, one can hear references to the "health-industrial complex" and the "educational-industrial complex" and even the "welfare-industrial complex," which suggests that the new elite may be formed as a result of the coincidence of interests between those who manage the social services of society (technical bureaucrats in the private and public sector) and again the corporation chiefs.

But Mills nowhere elaborates a thesis about elite circulation, and it is only by taking liberties with his analysis that it serves for illustrative purposes. A work that more deliberately explains elite circulation with reference to economic and social structural factors is *The Managerial Revolution.*[17] James Burnham wrote this book in the early 1940s in an attempt to synthesize marxian and elitist notions so as to provide a coherent statement about a new type of elite which was bound to control all the industrial societies of the world.

The book follows in the elitist tradition insofar as politics is viewed as a struggle between small groups for the dominant positions in society. Social change occurs as one elite replaces another. But the book is also marxist influenced. The basis of any elite's power is its control over the chief means of production. The circulation of elites, then, is understood in terms of shifts in economic structures, particularly shifts in property relations (what constitutes ownership of "private" property) and shifts in the means of production (the basis of wealth in society). According to Burnham, membership in the ruling class belongs to those who have control over access to the instruments of production and who determine the distribution of what is produced. Control is property rights, the right to acquire and dispose as one sees fit. There are two critical phases of control:

First, the ability either through personal strength, or, as in complex societies, with the backing—threatened or actual—of the state power acting through the police, courts, and armed forces to prevent access by others to the object controlled (owned); and, second, a preferential treatment in the distribution of the products of the objects controlled (owned).[18]

To use language introduced in the first chapter, the elite are those who own the instruments which produce social surplus and who receive a disproportionate share of that surplus.

Having thus defined elites in marxian influenced categories, Burnham turns to the issue of elite circulation. His thesis is simple: The "managerial revolution" is nothing more and nothing less than the replacement of the capitalist elite by a managerial elite. Many different names are given to the managers, Burnham notes, but

> We may often recognize them as "production managers," operating executives, superintendents, administrative engineers, supervisory technicians; or, in government (for they are to be found in governmental enterprise just as in private enterprise) as administrators, commissioners, bureau heads, and so on. I mean by managers, in short, those who already for the most part in contemporary society are actually managing, on its technical side, the actual process of production, no matter what the legal and financial form—individual, corporate, governmental— of the process.[19]

The ascendancy of this new elite can be traced to their functional importance to society. Modern technology places a high premium on men who manage giant corporations, such as General Motors, and giant governmental bureaucracies, such as the Pentagon. The route to power by the new managerial elite is not amassing personal wealth, as was the case for the early capitalist, but is gaining control of the State itself. This becomes possible as a fusion of State and economy occurs, as the State moves into the economy and the economy penetrates the State. There is direct takeover by the State of certain productive enterprises (Atomic Energy Commission), there are contracts and subsidies that support entire industries (defense related aerospace industry), there are administrative controls (Federal Trade Commission), and there are symbiotic relations between sectors of the economy and State bureaucracies (transportation and communication).

> The active heads of the bureaus are the managers-in-government, the same, or nearly the same, in training, functions, skills, habits of thought as the managers-in-industry. Indeed, there is less and less distinction between the two: in Russia, managers-in-industry and managers-in-government are one and the same, since there is no [important] industry apart from government.[20]

We need not here be concerned with the accuracy of Burnham's thesis, because our purpose is to show that elite circulation can be explained with reference primarily to the changing structure of society. Therefore, it should not surprise us to read through Burnham's study and find no serious attention to elections and political parties. Such attention would be superfluous; rulers are the direct product of structural developments in modern economic organization. For Burnham,

> With the consolidation of the managerial structure, which includes the state monopoly of all important enterprise, the position of the managers is assured. . . . Far from being incapable of constituting a ruling class, the managers, by the very conditions of modern technology and contemporary institutional evolution, would have a hard time avoiding rule.[21]

One looks in vain for the role of a mass electorate in such a sweeping proposition.

It would be foolish to overlook the important truth in structural interpretations of elite circulation, but it would be equally foolish to describe American politics without including electoral considerations. Certainly, reform groups, such as the black movement, believe that elite circulation is facilitated by building electoral coalitions and bringing about changes in existing voter habits.

COMBINING THE ELECTORAL AND ECONOMIC
THESIS OF ELITE CIRCULATION

The emphasis on elections and the emphasis on economic arrangements can be merged in terms of two broad generalizations about elections— generalizations which help us understand processes underpinning elite circulation in American politics.

1. Elections facilitate the rise of individuals from the lower stratum into elite positions. Each political generation has a few men who start with modest resources but increase their holdings with each election victory until they reach the elite circles. Lyndon Johnson and Richard Nixon are clear examples, as indeed are their Vice-Presidents, Hubert Humphrey and Spiro Agnew. This type of upward mobility is made possible by the resource of popularity, the ability to attract the affec-

tion and support of large numbers of voters. And because popularity is not a political resource that directly varies with wealth (although, to some degree, money can help manufacture popularity), electoral politics has long been viewed as an avenue of upward mobility. Perhaps surpassed only by professional athletics and higher education, the political sphere affords the opportunity for some individuals located in less advantaged social groups—immigrants, Jews, workers, blacks—to "rise above their station in life." In city politics, as noted in connection with New Haven, immigrants of working-class origin have been strikingly successful in mobilizing electoral support to improve their position. Contemporary black politics reflects also the coincidence of electoral politics and elite circulation, as political advancement, electoral success, and upward mobility join in the careers of successful black politicians. Indeed, as early as 1946, twice as many black parents as white parents were favorably disposed to politics as a career for their sons, a fact indicating some awareness of what ladders existed for the climb out of the ghetto.

The contribution of electoral politics to elite circulation has implications for more than the fortunate or talented few whose own status is enhanced. Because in this connection it can be said that elections contribute to gradual, peaceful changes in the composition of the ruling groups. The long-range effect is to stabilize the political order, much as Pareto and Mosca predicted. In American politics, the phrase "working within the system" has exactly this meaning. The system is protected as the talented few are able to work their way into the establishment by virtue of electoral successes. Not only does this co-opt the talented leaders of the lower stratum, it also creates linkage between the rulers and the ruled. Mosca clearly saw the importance of such linkages:

> A ruling class is more prone to fall into errors . . . the more closed it is, actually if not legally, to elements rising from the lower classes. In the lower classes the hard necessities of life, the unending and carking scramble for bread, the lack of literary culture, keep the primordial instincts of struggle and the unfailing ruggedness of human nature alive.

A ruling class morally and intellectually isolated from the mass will lose "its ability to provide against its own danger and against those of the society that has the misfortune to be guided by it."[22]

2. If we accept a broader construction of elite circulation, we can show also that elections can hasten the transfer of power from one elite to another, or hasten the sharing of power between an established elite and a previously excluded group. This is so because elections put into the hands of an emerging elite a resource which serves to publicize the stakes involved in changing the type of men ruling the society. That elections provide a public forum derives from the fact that nothing in political life attracts as much attention as does the fate of powerful men.

In the U.S., the transfer of power (although not necessarily the circulation of elites) is closely associated in the public mind with the drama of elections. This allows the possibility of publicly displaying what is at stake when critical turning points are reached, that is, when elite circulation is taking place. If it is true that today we are in the midst of a shift from the military-industrial complex to a social services-industrial complex, this shift will be partly due to the fact that the militarists responsible for cold war policies and a very unpopular war are under attack *in the campaign oratory* of new challengers who promise to direct national resources in a wholly different direction.

This does not mean that the electorate creates this new elite, just as it did not "create" the militarists in the first place. But elections do involve the masses in the process of elite circulation, and the moods and preferences of average citizens are not without some consequences. That the masses participate is at once the most and the least significant fact about elite circulation in American politics. It is the most significant because it suggests that the structure of power and the set of men who hold power rest upon a mass base, but it is the least significant because the "institutional landscape" is always the final arbiter of elite circulation. Electoral choices are surface, although not superficial, phenomena. The electorate does not establish the alternatives, but it can choose among them and in this way hasten the shift from one elite to another.

The principle involved can thus be summarized as follows: Economic and social conditions loosen the hold on society of established elites and strengthen the claims of counter-elites, and elections facilitate the access of counter-elites into the ruling groups. At least for political societies in which competitive elections prevail, it is necessary to extend Mosca's commentary when he writes that "Ruling classes decline inevitably when they cease to find scope for the capacities through which they rose to power, when they can no longer render the social services which they once rendered, or when their talents and the services they render lose in importance in the social environment in which they live."[23] We extend this functional account of the fall of ruling groups by appending the thought that elections can hasten their downfall, and can help establish a peaceful transfer of power from the old to the new elites. This extension does not deny Mosca's core insight. Elections themselves do not explain why it is that the talents and services of a given ruling group decline in social significance. Elections only record this fact.

We can return to New Haven's political history to further illustrate the benefits of merging the economic thesis and the electoral thesis of elite circulation. Dahl identifies two major periods of elite circulation: the 1840s, when the entrepreneurs pushed aside the traditional ruling families, and the early 1900s, when ethnic and worker-based party machines replaced the industrial leaders in political office. In both instances, shifts in electoral conditions and relative voter strengths are cited as reasons for the circulation. However, not just any group was in a position in the 1840s or again in the 1900s to take advantage of electoral conditions.

Dahl writes of the period when the established, prestigious families were elbowed aside by the new capitalist class, "Who else, then, should occupy public office if not the new industrialists? Not the urban workers, who though they more and more outnumbered all the rest were immigrants lacking in status, political know-how, and economic resources."[24] Because of the changing economic conditions in New Haven and, we repeat, throughout urban America, it was the entrepreneurs who had the political resources to gain control of the city. Urban workers, despite their greater numbers, were not favored by the economic conditions and were not to share in political control for more than half a century.

When the working class does assume some control over New Haven political life in the 1900s it is largely because of changing conditions which favor their ascent, including, it should be noted, changing political technologies such as were provided by the urban party machine.

Elite circulation is not a simple matter of the electorate tiring of one elite and looking around to see who is available to take over. It is a much more complex matter of shifts in property relations, in ownership of the means of production, in the demographic composition of the population, and of available political technologies.

It is for this reason that when we trace the patterns of elite circulation we might assign little significance to the role of elections. The weakening of an established elite and the momentum of a counter-elite is rooted in economic and technological conditions. Just as the various competing elites are limited in their resources by these conditions, the electorate is limited in its choices. Thus, it is an oversimplification to cite shifts in voter sentiment as the explanation for elite circulation.

Yet elections cannot be denied, which is the mistake theorists such as James Burnham have made. At least in American politics it is clear that elections mediate between social structural transformations and processes of elite circulation. The transformations in the society are not under the control of the electorate, or even under the control of elites. Transformations in the demography, the technology, the economy, or the institutional landscape of American society result from and promote conditions only partly planned, at best, and never fully foreseen in their initial stages. For example, current scientific research into the basic biological processes is setting in motion today social forces and new interest clusters which are bound to have profound effect on the type of leadership skills required in a half-century; however, none can foresee what social issues will dominate as the society moves into the twenty-first century.

If social structural transformations establish the ground rules for elite circulation, the pace of circulation and the extent to which new elites share power with, rather than wholly displace, previous elites are certainly affected by voter preferences and attitudes. The electorate shifts and picks and chooses in line with many considerations, and these considerations cannot be ignored in an account of who governs.

Notes

1 Vilfredo Pareto, *The Mind and Society,* Arthur Livingston, ed. (New York: Dover, 1963), paragraph 2027. This is a two-volume republication of the original four-volume publication by Harcourt, Brace and Co., 1935, under the sponsorship of The Pareto Fund. Pareto numbered his paragraphs consecutively; we follow common footnoting practice and cite, by number, the paragraph quoted.

2   *Ibid.,* 2031.
3   This four-part classification is suggested by Piet Thoenes, *The Elite in the Wel-fare State,* English edition edited by J. A. Banks (London: Faber and Faber, 1966), p. 48.
4   Mosca, *The Ruling Class,* pp. 415-416.
5   *Ibid.,* p. 460.
6   *Ibid.,* p. 474.
7   This is taken from Mosca's earlier work, *Teorica dei governi e governo parle-mentare,* and is cited in T. B. Bottomore, *Elites and Society* (Middlesex, England: Penguin, 1966), p. 55.
8   Henri Pirenne, "The Stages in the Social History of Capitalism," *American Historical Review* (1914); reprinted in R. Bendix and S. M. Lipset, eds., *Class, Status, and Power,* 2nd ed. (New York: Free Press, 1966), p. 97.
9   This summary statement is that of Bottomore, *Elites and Society,* p. 57.
10 Dahl, *Who Governs?* (New Haven: Yale University Press, 1961), especially Chapters 2 through 4.
11 *Ibid.,* p. 16.
12 *Ibid.,* p. 25.
13 *Ibid.,* pp. 18, 20.
14 *Ibid.,* p. 31.
15 *Ibid.,* p. 34.
16 Mills, *The Power Elite,* p. 276.
17 James Burnham, *The Managerial Revolution* (Bloomington: Indiana University Press, 1941).
18 *Ibid.,* p. 59.
19 *Ibid.,* p. 80.
20 *Ibid.,* p. 150.
21 *Ibid.,* pp. 280, 281.
22 Mosca, *The Ruling Class,* p. 119.
23 *Ibid.,* pp. 65, 66.
24 Dahl, *Who Governs?,* p. 30.

CHAPTER 8
THE ACCOUNTABILITY
OF ELITES

"Representation is the grand discovery of modern times," wrote James Mill. And his sentiment is shared by very many contemporary students of politics. Political representation is a system of government which accepts that the few always govern the many, but intends to make a virtue of this fact. If the tiny elite that direct the society do so on be-half of the mass citizenry (if they are "representative"), then the principles of democracy are salvaged despite the persuasive argument of elite theorists.

What made political representation such a grand discovery was the realization, even in liberal democratic circles, that direct, participatory democracy is an impossibility in large societies. Citizens cannot meet, deliberate, and resolve matters of state if there are very many citizens, and there are very many even in relatively small political communities, let alone in the enormous nation-states which are the effective jurisdictions for most in the world. The golden days of Athenian democracy are often cited with nostalgia by those who prefer direct to representattive democracy. But this nostalgia ignores certain obvious arithmetic. The city-states of classical Greece had approximately 20,000 citizens (nonslaves and males). But consider, as one political theorist has, what happens if even this many persons attend public meetings: "Allowing two minutes for each speaker in a meeting lasting six hours, less than one percent of the citizens would have an opportunity to speak." Indeed, if speakers were given a longer period to advance their position, and defend it from counterclaims, say ten minutes to present and five minutes to rebut, only 24 citizens could participate in the six-hour meeting. In a public meeting, then, "the larger the number of citizens, the less the chance that every citizen with a different viewpoint would be given the opportunity to present his views. Thus the greater the num-

bers, the more the town meeting runs the risk of becoming unrepresentative."[1] Any who have sat through the marathon meetings called on so
many campuses to discuss and debate whether to "close it down" can
appreciate the point. A system of political representation is, as *Federalist Paper No. 52* noted, "a substitute for a meeting of the citizens in
person." Simple arithmetic shows that it is a necessary substitute if the
number of citizens is at all large.

The fact is that some form of political representation is here to stay.
In the United States alone, there are more than 80,000 different governing units in which a small number are selected to "represent" the larger
number. There are school boards, special district commissions, town-
ship and city councils, state and national legislatures, and many other
types of governing bodies—all called "representative assemblies." The
same phenomenon—governing by a few in the name of the many—pervades nongovernmental sectors of society as well: Every organization
from the neighborhood clubs to giant corporations, from the local
P.T.A. to million-member labor unions, are run by a small number of
members designated to represent the interests of the larger membership.
The concepts and institutions of political representation pervade the
culture and organization of American society to a degree largely un-
recognized. We forget that as far back as grade school we elected "representatives" to represent the home-room on the student council. Perhaps
no political notion, with the exception of decisions by majority vote, is
so deeply a part of our thinking as is political representation.

Early democratic thinkers recognized that democratic government
was being profoundly affected by the specialization of labor, the growth
of bureaucracy, and the increased part played by the State in organizing
collective action and dispensing the social surplus created. Commentators such as Weber and Michels and Mosca noted that democracy as a
political system was not immune to the modes of organizing and exercising authority associated with the industrialized, rationalized society.
These modes penetrated political life as quickly and effectively as they
penetrated economic life, and techniques of organization and mass
manipulation gave all the advantages to the ruling few over the ruled
masses, despite the rhetoric of democracy. As we have seen, Mosca's
ruling class and Pareto's political elite, Weber's professional politician or
Michels's oligarchy are variants on a common theme: Power cannot be

equally dispersed, even in a democratic society, but will tend always to be concentrated in a few hands—those who are delegated, or usurp, leadership in managing collective affairs.

But, reasoned liberal democrats, just because there are always rulers distinct from the ruled need not mean a relationship of domination and submission. Political representation provides the tool for those who advance democracy as a counterpressure to elite rule. If elites can be made to be representative of the masses, then the democratic principles are not lost despite the unequal division of political power in the society. It has been held for the last two centuries that although rule might always be in the hands of a tiny fraction of the population, arrangements can be devised to insure that these few will represent the true interests and welfare of the people. Thus, if it is no longer possible to have government *by* the people, the goals of government of and for the people are still within reach.

We shall shortly turn to the actual arrangements, institutions, and values which in American politics are thought to bring about representative democracy, and we shall offer some critical comments about these practices. But first it is necessary to have a clearer idea of what political representation is and what it is not. For it is a term used very loosely, and often incorrectly.

WHAT IS POLITICAL REPRESENTATION?

A common although unsatisfactory usage of "representation" emphasizes the social and economic makeup of the elite. This is the populist tradition which asserts that a ruling group should have proportionate numbers of each and every variety of group in the society. Thus, a spokeswoman for the National Women's Political Caucus, Rep. Bella S. Abzug, defines "a truly representative Congress" as one which is half women, 11 percent black, younger, and containing more working people, teachers, artists, and other presently "unrepresented" types of people. Such an argument stresses the typification of Congress, and questions whether it mirrors in social and economic traits the population from which it is selected. Once this populist position is taken, it is a simple matter to demonstrate that the elite in the United States are unrepresentative, and are likely to remain so. We noted in our discussion of recruitment some of the reasons for the domination of middle and upper-middle groups in the formation of the ruling groups.

The social typicalness of a ruling group is, however, not a very satisfactory definition of political representation, even if replication on a miniature scale were possible. The weakness in the social composition argument has been noted already in our discussion of recruitment: Social origin does not guarantee political outlook. The self-made man who reaches the top may be much less concerned about the fate of those he left behind than the man born to wealth and position.

Of course, most who advance the populist claim and wish for a demographically representative ruling group have something in mind other than social composition. They contend that the interests of a social group will be truly represented only if it has its own members among the ruling circles. The trade union movement in Great Britain claimed that social policy would reflect the needs of the working class only if Parliament could be made more "representative" by the election of working-class members, and from this doctrine the Labour Party was born. Here is a classic instance of the assumption that social origin is highly correlated with political viewpoint and, incidentally, with the political ability necessary to press effectively the claims of the workers. This may be so (although the record of the British Labour Party is checkered, to say the least, and it is true also that the leadership of this party is firmly in the hands of nonworkers), but there is no guarantee that a man working in a factory has the interests of the workers at heart, just as there is no guarantee that all blacks are equally concerned about serving the black population or that all women are equally ready to defend women's liberation causes.

Because reformers recognize this simple truth, their real concern is not with social composition *per se* but with how the social origins and social status of rulers might affect activities and policies. This being the case, it is necessary to conceive of representation in a broader context than what is suggested by the focus on social composition.

Political representation is acting in the interests of the constituency, and in a manner responsive to it. An elite that serves the interests of the broader public is representative whereas an elite that considers parochial and self-serving interests is not. Moreover, an elite that governs in response to citizen preferences is being representative in contrast to the elite that ignores or manipulates citizen demands.[2]

This admittedly is a vague formulation, but it serves our present purposes. What we underscore is that the social composition of the elite may increase its willingness or ability to represent the public but that social composition is not itself a definition of political representation. When black power groups demand that more blacks serve on governing boards, they do not want the "Uncle Toms" who are acceptable to white leaders, but want members who will represent the cause of the black power movement. And the National Political Women's Caucus admits that it is not composition as such, but the policies which count; thus the Caucus aims "at the election of women but also of men who declare themselves ready to fight for the needs and rights of women and all underrepresented groups."

Turning attention to the responsiveness of the elite rather than their social origins has one distinct advantage. It bids us to consider the conditions that foster elite responsiveness on the assumption that in a democracy leaders are held to account for what they do and not who they are. Thus, the issue of political representation merges into the issue of political accountability, at least in democratic theory. The purpose of holding an elite accountable for their actions is to insure that their actions will represent the "general welfare."

Commentary on responsiveness and accountability in American politics is of three general types. There is, first, comment about whether the values that animate the power-holders might not be adequate or at least important in bringing about a responsive elite. There is, second, even more extended comment on whether institutional arrangements—especially competitive elections—establish the desired values of democracy even though a small group has great powers. There is, finally, the idea that the numerous access points between the non-elite and the elite, especially through the pressure-group system, guarantees responsiveness and accountability. Although these three topics overlap to a degree, it is profitable to discuss them as somewhat separate notions. This permits us to take a close look at each point of view, and to review the weaknesses of each.

INWARD CONVICTIONS AND REPRESENTATIVE DEMOCRACY

In Plato's ideal state, rule is to be in the hands of the Guardians. No elaborate institutional or constitutional machinery is necessary to insure faithfulness to the public trust because the Guardians will be imbued with an "inward conviction that they must always do what they believe to be best for the commonwealth."[3] This inward conviction is the special property of the ruling elite; it is nurtured as the Guardians are exposed to special training and rigorous challenges which fit them for the responsibilities to be assumed. The values and the norms of these philosopher-rulers are the best insurance a community can have against injustices and arbitrary rule. They insure that the elite are committed to the public good, not narrow class interests; insure that the elite are motivated by civic responsibility, not self-aggrandizement; and insure that rule is passed on to persons similarly committed and motivated, not to relatives, friends, or other ambitious associates.

Plato was particularly adamant about the succession question, as revealed in a passage which anticipates by some 2,000 years the concern of Mosca and Pareto with elite circulation:

So the first and chief injunction laid by heaven upon the Rulers is that, among all the things of which they must show themselves good guardians, there is none that needs to be so carefully watched as the mixture of metals in the souls of children. If a child of their own is born with an alloy of iron or brass [therefore being ill-fitted to rule], they must, without the smallest pity, assign him the station proper to his nature and thrust him out among the craftsmen or the farmers. If, on the contrary, these classes produce a child with gold or silver in his composition, they will promote him, according to his value, to be a Guardian or Auxiliary. They will appeal to a prophecy that ruin will come upon the state when it passes into the keeping of a man of iron or brass.[4]

The Republic, then, is protected from tendencies toward irresponsible rulers or decay in the ruling class *by the values of the ruling class itself.* It is to the inward convictions of the elite that we turn for an explanation of how to stabilize the just society. That is, the safeguard against unjust rule was to have just rulers. And the way in which to get these rulers is to educate and nurture them in the values of the Republic.

In somewhat disguised forms, the Platonic ideal lingers on in contemporary thought. Certainly there are strains of Platonism in various interpretations of the viability and stability of representative democracy in America. These interpretations proceed in four steps.

1. The mass public in the United States has an uncomfortably low regard for democratic rights and procedures. Although the public agrees to an abstract democratic creed, when the issue of specific application faces it, the public has low levels of tolerance for free speech, deviant political opinions, judicial processes, and the like. More than a quarter of the general electorate feel that the majority has a right to outlaw minorities if it wants to; and, again, a quarter of the populace reports that we cannot afford to depend on the slow and unreliable methods of courts in dealing with dangerous enemies like the communists. Approximately half the population would deny the vote to those who cannot do so intelligently; and again half the populace would prevent publication of a book that contains "wrong" political views, while nearly three-fifths reject the idea that freedom implies the right to teach "foreign ideas" in our schools.[5] These and similar survey findings have caused some question about the mass public as a repository of the values of democracy.

2. The same surveys, however, show the political leadership to have a consistently firmer grasp of and commitment to the democratic creed. Writing of political influentials, one commentator notes that this commitment to democracy is "evidenced in their stronger approval of democratic ideas, their greater tolerance and regard for proper procedures and citizen rights; their superior understanding and acceptance of the 'rules of the game,' and their more affirmative attitudes toward the political system in general." This author continues,

> Compared with the electorate, whose ordinary members are submerged in an ideological babble of poorly informed and discordant opinions, the members of the political minority inhabit a world in which political ideas are vastly more salient, intellectual consistency is more frequently demanded, attitudes are related to principles, actions are connected to beliefs, "correct" opinions are rewarded and "incorrect" opinions are punished. . . . The net effect of these influences is to heighten their sensitivity to political ideas and to unite them more firmly behind the values of the American tradition.[6]

3. The manner in which the elite come to hold to the democratic values bears more than a little resemblance to Plato's hopes in *The Republic.* The political influentials constitute, in effect, "a subculture with its own peculiar set of norms of behavior, motives, and approved standards. Processes of indoctrination internalize such norms among those

who are born to or climb to positions of power and leadership; they serve as standards of action, which are reinforced by a social discipline among the political activists."[7] Another student of American democracy reasons in a similar vein about the effects of political recruitment: The political professional

> is likely to support the existing norms because his own endorsement of existing norms was initially a criterion in his own recruitment and advancement; complex processes of political selection and rejection tend to exclude the deviant who challenges the prevailing norms of the existing political system. Most of the professionals might properly be called democratic "legitimists."[8]

An emphasis on recruitment, training, and education also accounts for the failure among the public to appreciate and defend the principles of democracy:

> Democratic beliefs and habits are obviously not "natural" but must be learned; and they are learned more slowly by men and women whose lives are circumscribed by apathy, ignorance, provincialism and social or physical distance from the centers of intellectual activity. In the absence of knowledge and experience—as we can readily observe from the fidgety course of growth in newly emerging nations —the presuppositions and complex obligations of democracy, the rights it grants and the self-restraints it imposes, cannot be quickly comprehended. Even in a highly developed nation like the United States, millions of people continue to possess only the most rudimentary understanding of democratic ideology.[9]

4. The inference drawn from these three observations is reminiscent of the Platonic concept. Democratic viability and social stability are saved by the elite, not by mass participation. Indeed, it is to the benefit of society that "those who are most confused about democratic ideas are also likely to be politically apathetic and without significant influence. Their role in the nation's decision process is so small that their 'misguided' opinions or non-opinions have little practical consequence for stability."[10] Their passive role is countered by the active defense of democracy by the elite.

> The longer one frets with the puzzle of how democratic regimes manage to function, the more plausible it appears that a substantial

part of the explanation is to be found in the motives that actuate the leadership echelon; the values that it holds, in the rules of the political game to which it adheres, in the expectations which it entertains about its own status in society, and perhaps in some of the objective circumstances, both material and institutional, in which it functions.[11]

The skill with which the elite maintain the democratic tradition rests somewhat on the extensive political resources they command; "consequently, a challenge to the existing norms is bound to be costly to the challenger, for legitimist professionals can quickly shift their skills and resources into the urgent task of doing in the dissenter."[12] Given the resources of the elites, it is fortunate that their values bid them to serve the public welfare rather than their own parochial interests. The modal norms of the ruling classes of a democratic order have been described in the following terms: "Fundamental is a regard for public opinion, a belief that in some way or another it should prevail. . . . The basic doctrine goes further to include a sense of trusteeship for the people generally and an adherence to the basic doctrine that collective efforts should be dedicated to the promotion of mass gains rather than of narrow class advantage."[13]

The thesis paraphrased and summarized in the previous four points reduces to the simple proposition that representative democracy depends on the values of the elite more than the actions of the non-elite. It recalls Plato's insistence that the cause of justice is served by the "inward conviction" of the guardian and not by the moods and manners of those on whose behalf justice pervails.

Before commenting on the difficulty inherent in this particular defense of democracy, note should be taken of one reason for its wide attraction. It can be applied as easily to nongovernmental as to governmental elites. That is, because it emphasizes the inward convictions of the elite rather than the institutions of elections, there is reason to consider the values of economic or military power-holders in the same light as the values of elected officials. And this has been done. Thus, in some circles, it is argued that the enormous powers of corporation executives are cause for no great concern, because these men are as committed and motivated to preserve the American democratic traditions as are the governmental elite. Economic leaders are the product of schooling that stresses corporate responsibility, just as they are a product of social experiences that stress the values of a free and open society. Their association with governmental elites is to some degree responsible for their acquiring these values. McCloskey, although not speaking directly of corporate executives, described the process by which influentials become familiar with the convictions appropriate to governing the society: Influentials

> are distinguished from the mass of the electorate by their above-average education and economic status, their greater political interest and awareness, and their more immediate access to the command posts of community decisions. Many of them participate not only in politics but in other public activities as well. This affords them, among other benefits, a more sophisticated understanding of how the society is run and a more intimate association with other men and women who are alert to political ideas and values.[14]

The concept of a properly indoctrinated, and therefore beneficent, elite has been extended to the military elite as well. The military leadership is, above all, professional. And, in the American context, to be a professional military man is to be bound by and committed to the democratic creed, including most especially the doctrine of civilian control over the military. American citizens need not fear that the military elite will misuse their enormous powers or be neglectful or devious in their adherence to the democratic rules, because the men who command the military are professionally trained and thus imbued with the virtues of the American way of life.

These then are aspects of the Platonic doctrine which have returned to haunt us 2,000 years later as we seek to evaluate the representativeness and responsiveness of the elite in America. Can we rely on the "inward convictions" of the elite to protect the democratic tradition? There are two reasons for expressing doubt.

First, and most important, the record of the elite is not promising. Compliance with democratic rules demands great self-restraint, especially for the elite. It requires that they forebear from using their immense resources of patronage and media control to stifle groups seen as repugnant. Further, it requires also that they consider public preferences even when they, the elite, "know best" what the society needs. It requires that they refrain, as individuals, from furthering private interests through their access to contracts, contacts, and the public treasury. And it requires that they resist the tendency to isolate themselves from the broader public and resist the temptation to select their own successors on narrow grounds. On all counts, and others which could be listed, the elite fail to achieve the standards Plato expected of the Guardians, and fail as well to measure up even to the requirements established by those contemporary theorists who would force American democracy into the mold of Platonic elitism. Consider a few dramatic, although not atypical, cases.

Senator Joseph McCarthy of Wisconsin in the name of uprooting un-American activities disregarded democratic traditions for nearly half a decade. He was contemptuous and destructive of exactly those "rules of the game" which the elite are supposed to preserve. And he had enormous influence on American politics, an influence weakened but not yet expurgated two decades later. Richard Rovere provides a useful summary to help us recall the early 1950s:

> He held two presidents captive—or as nearly captive as any Presidents of the United States have ever been held; in their conduct of the nation's affairs, Harry S. Truman and Dwight D. Eisenhower, from early 1950 through late 1954, could never act without weighing the effect of their plans upon McCarthy and the forces he led, and in consequence there were times when, because of this man, they could not act at all. He had enormous impact on American foreign policy at a time when that policy bore heavily on the course of world history, and American diplomacy might bear a different aspect today if McCarthy had never lived. In the Senate, his headquarters and his hiding place, he assumed the functions of the Committee of the Whole; he lived in thoroughgoing contempt of the Congress of which he was a member, of the rules it had made for itself, and—whenever they ran counter to his purposes—of the laws enacted for the general welfare.[15]

That one U.S. Senator should show flagrant disdain for reasoned discourse, for free speech, for due process, and for the principle of innocent until proven guilty does not, of course, prove anything about the broader elite. But if this broader elite either passively permitted or actively supported transparent violations of procedural democracy, then there is reason to doubt the commitment of the Guardians. And the evidence gives ample support to the notion that McCarthy was sustained by exactly those persons thought to be the repository of the democratic creed. Political elites

> helped dramatize his issues and fight his fights. Conservative Republican activists provided money and enthusiam for the Senator's cause. In Wisconsin, for example, McCarthy did not mobilize the mass of voters. But he did mobilize the local elites of the Republican Party. . . . He had succeeded in harnessing respectable elites and respectable institutions to which the populace paid deference.[16]

The elite in government were slow to judge their own, reasoning, as did Senator McClellan of Arkansas, "I do not want to do unto one of my colleagues what I would not want him to do unto me under the same circumstances."[17]

It is not necessary to go back 20 years to find evidence that the commitment of the political elite to democracy is more tarnished in practice than in theory. We need not impugn the motives of the small clique who took American society deeper and deeper into the Vietnam war; perhaps they were men of good intentions sincerely attempting to serve their country. But there can be little doubt that the public was deceived and Congress deliberately misled, and that this was accomplished on a massive scale, with little more than quiet grumbling from all but a handful of Senators and Congressmen. If the Kennedys and McNamaras and Rostows and Johnsons can conceive, plan, and initiate a "secret war," how are we to remain confident that the principles of representative democracy rest secure in the inward convictions of the elite? How the elite responded to political, often aggressive dissent on the War gives concern as well. We need not here take sides one way or the other with Attorney General Mitchell's political views to raise questions about his commitment to due process when some 800 antiwar demonstrators were arrested, with his approval, although no charge was pressed against them. The attempt to transform political dissent into treason, which is an old trick, of course, cannot but raise doubts about the wisdom of relying on the good faith of the elite to sustain the First Amendment freedoms.

But if there are doubts about the government elite, there are even more reasons for pessimism about the economic elite. There certainly are many corporate executives who have a sense of responsibility and who care about the society they so substantially influence, but it is doubtful whether these personal values adequately establish anything remotely approaching the responsiveness and accountability promised in the democratic creed. Instances of public fraud are uncovered every day, and it is safe to say that there are many that have not been uncovered. Even the hallowed commitment to "free enterprise" is undermined by price-fixing and related arrangements.[18]

Certainly it is comforting to be told that the military elite, being professionals, know their place in relation to civilian control. But the comfort evaporates when the role of the Joint Chiefs of Staff is carefully examined, because the Joint Chiefs of Staff have great latitude and near autonomy in matters of intelligence, of military strategy, and of expenditures and weapon development. Whatever their professional norms, the admirals and generals protect their spheres of influence with a tenacity that questions their concern with civilian control. Moreover, the realm of military justice gives evidence that the "democratic principles" are defined very differently within than without the military. Officers and soldiers alike who have attempted to exercise their rights as citizens have learned, to their dismay, that the Bill of Rights does not extend to even their off-duty activities.

If we are less than sanguine about "inward convictions" as the guarantor of democracy, it is largely because of the record itself. The survey data testifying to the special political culture of the elite are important, but they do not tell the entire story. The commitment of the elite seems to crumble when pressures mount, as they did in the McCarthy era and as they did again in the late 1960s. That is, it is exactly in those times of crisis when the democratic procedures are most vulnerable that the presumed defenders weaken.

We should briefly record a second flaw in the contemporary versions of Plato's dream state. The thesis has a curious if little noticed logical property. The standards by which the elite measure themselves are often self-generated. To have political power is to have at least some control over the institutions, such as media and schools that shape and give operational meaning to the values of society. And, in this regard, the elite hold themselves accountable to standards that they themselves fix. Note, for instance, that the four points listed above emphasize procedural issues to the almost total neglect of substantive issues. Thus, the elite is honored if it stoutly defends universal suffrage, First Amendment freedoms, and due process of law. And we do not wish to make

light of how important it is that the elite do, in fact, defend these principles. But it is possible for the elite to take their stand on procedural
issues while pursuing policies (or nonpolicies) that lead to decay of cities,
imperialistic adventurism, entrenchment of racist institutions, and a
growing disparity in income and living conditions between those below
and those above the poverty line. And if the elite themselves are assigning blame and credit, it is unlikely that they measure themselves in
terms of social deterioration.

AN INSTITUTIONAL THESIS

It has been correctly stated that it was a conservative group of 55 men
who gathered in Philadelphia two centuries ago, and who wished upon
the American citizenry a Constitution which continues to regulate and
shape our politics. But it is a mistake to see their conservatism only as
an expression of men of property and wealth trying to fight off the radical tendencies unleashed by an egalitarian war for independence. They
were in this limited sense "conservative," but they were conservatives in
a broader and more significant sense as well. They held a basically conservative view of human nature, and to this day the Constitution reflects
that view.

Very simply, the framers of the Constitution saw man as an untrust-
worthy creature. Given a chance, men would break contracts with one
another. Their passions and ambitions would dominate their reason and
self-restraint. Minorities, when they controlled the means of coercion,
would tyrannize majorities, plunder from them in order to expand on
their own privileges. Majorities, when unrestrained, would destroy the
rights of minorities and force them to conform to majoritarian wishes.
Man outside of society and unencumbered by institutional restraints
was vicious and exploitative. The veneer of civilization was thin indeed,
and it took perseverance to maintain it.

Listen to John Adams writing to his radical cousin, Samuel Adams,

> Human appetites, passions, prejudices and self-love will never be con-
> quered by benevolence and knowledge alone. . . . "The love of
> liberty," you say, "is interwoven in the soul of man." So it is [also]
> in that of a wolfe; and I doubt whether it be much more rational,
> generous, or social in one than in the other. . . . We must not, then,

depend upon the love of liberty in the soul of man for its preservation. Some political institutions must be prepared to assist this love
against its enemies.

This passage shows clearly the transition from a pessimistic view of
human nature to a conservative although benign view of social institutions. Conservatives hold that social institutions backed by the authority
of the State are necessary to restrain men. If the founders were pessimistic about man, they were optimistic about social and civil institutions. Despite the unfortunate proclivities of the masses toward agitation
and impetuousness, a good political constitution could bring about social order.

It is to the credit of the Constitutional framers that they were consistent in applying their principles. They feared the unchecked ambitions of the elite just as they feared the excesses of the masses. Thus, as
they instituted the authority necessary to govern the masses, they also
imposed constraints on those who would exercise the authority. No
single group, be it a minority within the government, an extragovern-
mental minority, or the majority outside the governing circles must be
allowed final (unchecked) control over the coercive instruments and
institutions of society. *Federalist Paper No. 51* succinctly states the
theory:

> Ambition must be made to counteract ambition. . . . It may be a
> reflection on human nature, that such devices should be necessary
> to control the abuses of government. But what is government itself,
> but the greatest of all reflections on human nature? If men were
> angels, no government would be necessary. If angels were to govern
> men, neither external nor internal controls on government would be
> necessary. In framing a government which is to be administered by
> men over men, the great difficulty lies in this: you must first enable
> the government to control the governed; and in the next place
> oblige it to control itself.

Two major institutional devices were envisioned by the framers:
First, an elaborate system of checks and balances and separation of
powers wherein men who administered one program would be given
Constitutional means to resist encroachment by others, thus keeping
any single interest from dominating the whole of government authority;
and second, the exterior control (control by the nonruling masses) of

elections, the essence of the representative system of democracy. In this chapter, we are concerned only with the second of these institutional devices, because 200 years ago, as now, political theorists saw in periodic elections the guarantor of political representation despite the unavoidable separation of society into elites and masses.

The Constitution held that public officials should serve limited terms; they do not "own" the offices but are only temporary occupants who at regularly scheduled times must face the electorate which initially granted them power. The purpose, as *Federalist Paper No. 57* stated, was to instill in leadership a "habitual recollection of their dependence on the people." In words that recall Lord Acton's axiom that "power corrupts," *Federalist 57* continues: "Before the sentiments impressed on their minds by the mode of their elevation can be effaced by the exercise of power, they will be compelled to anticipate the moment when they must descend to the level from which they were raised; there forever to remain unless a faithful discharge of their trust shall have established their title to a renewal of it."

This passage outlines the assumptions which yet today sustain a belief that representative government is made possible by elections. Being elected to office is to be "elevated" and being evicted from office is to be "punished." Officeholders, therefore, exercise power in a manner faithful to the trust placed in them by the electorate. The underlying thesis has elsewhere been called "the theory of electoral accountability."[19] Because of the substantial import of this theory for the political formula in the United States, it merits extended review.

What, in brief, the theory of electoral accountability does is link the elitists' observation that the few rule the many with the democrats' observation that the few represent the many. This marriage comes about as follows: To be sure, a very few men direct and control the society, but this tiny elite is not indifferent to public needs and preference. Because the public is an electorate, the few, being either elected officials or dependent for their powers and privileges on elected officials, stand in fear of the wrath of the electorate. The accountability of the few to the many is insured because men are ambitious to gain and control the apparatus of the State, and such ambitions can be realized only by paying due attention to the electorate. Because the electorate, through periodic elections, grants or withholds the privilege of government, men who enjoy governing pursue policies they believe will satisfy the voters.

In American political thought, this thesis stretches back to the Constitution itself, and beyond that, of course, to the political thinkers of the seventeenth and eighteenth centuries. The thesis also has its contemporary proponents, most of whom begin with a definition of democracy penned by Joseph Schumpeter in his classic, *Capitalism, Socialism and Democracy*. "The democratic method is that institutional arrangement for arriving at political decision in which individuals acquire the power to decide by means of a competitive struggle for the people's vote."[20] In this view of democracy, the "role of the people is to produce a government," a view Schumpeter expands as follows:

> It should be observed that in making it the primary function of the electorate to produce a government (directly or through an intermediate body) I intended to include in this phrase also the function of evicting it. The one means simply the acceptance of a leader or group of leaders, and the other means simply the withdrawal of this acceptance.[21]

Commentary on American politics has been greatly influenced by Schumpeter's definition. In a widely read essay on democracy, Seymour Lipset views democracy as "a social mechanism which permits the largest possible part of the population to influence the major decisions by choosing among contenders for political office."[22] Or, as more succinctly formulated by Anthony Downs, contestants for office "formulate policies in order to win elections, rather than win elections in order to formulate policies."[23] We earlier cited portions of Robert Dahl's study of New Haven politics, and noted then that Dahl emphasizes elections in accounting for elite circulation. In this same study, Dahl also writes that "elected leaders of New Haven keep the real or imagined preferences of constituents constantly in mind in deciding what policies to adopt or reject."[24]

This anticipation of voter responses is what links elite rule and political representation; the electorate, in these formulations, does indeed control their governors. Schumpeter writes that "electorates normally do not control their political leaders in any way except by refusing to re-elect them or the parliamentary majorities which support them,"[25] a point elaborated by Lipset when he writes that representative democracy is practically synonymous with the permanent insecurity of the governors: "Thus every incumbent of a position of high status within a truly democratic system must of necessity anticipate the loss of his position by the operation of the normal political process."[26] And it is the probationary tenure in office which leads Dahl to observe that the effective political elites operate within limits "set by their expectations as to the reactions of the group of political active citizens who go to the polls."[27]

It is easy to see why this line of argument is popular in defenses of America as a democratic State. The ancient task of preventing tyranny by an elite is solved by the simple institutional device of periodic elections. Not too much is expected, therefore, of the public, which is a good thing, because, in general, the average citizen is ignorant about political matters and largely indifferent to them. Most citizens will rouse themselves to vote every two or four years, but more than this should not be expected. Thus the thesis of "electoral accountability" is realistic; it makes no assumptions about the masses that are not confirmed by social surveys. It is realistic in a second sense as well. The fact that everywhere societies are "divided into two classes—a class that rules and a class that is ruled" need not be denied, but instead can be incorporated into a political theory that makes a virtue of this fact. Electoral accountability insures that political representation constrains elite rule, and thus saves democracy from the enemy within: The tendency of power to accumulate in the hands of a small group.

In short, the theory of electoral accountability replaces a commitment to participatory democracy (considered unworkable and unrealistic) with a faith in elite competition. The first requirement of representative democracy is an intra-elite struggle to control political office, and this struggle is periodically decided by the mass electorate. In choosing who shall govern them, the public is also choosing how it shall be governed.

There is an important point to be made about this conception of American politics. The "theory of electoral accountability" is much more than an academic notion. Rather, this idea and the package of assumptions it incorporates is integral to the operating political beliefs of many American citizens. "Electoral accountability" is a core term in what Mosca has called the "political formula," and what others have called the "symbolic universe of politics." For Mosca, the power of any political class rests on the political formula (set of moral principles) used to justify their rule. The formula in the United States is that "The powers of all lawmakers, magistrates and governmental officials in the United States emanate directly or indirectly from the vote of the voters, which is held to be the expression of the sovereign will of the whole American people."[28] This belief is held by the overwhelming majority of Americans. Studies of very young children show that voting is often chosen as a symbol of the government, and, indeed, that democracy is conceptualized in terms of voting privileges. One set of data about political beliefs of grade school children is summarized as follows:

> To young children, voting and elections are important democratic activities. The conflict which is present in every campaign is minimized. Throughout the age span there typically is a positive attitude toward candidates: they are viewed as concerned more with the public welfare than with selfish gains. Elections are perceived as crucial to the goals of the democratic process even though they may result in removal of incumbents for whom the child feels personal attachment. . . . The high value placed upon the election process may also encourage the acceptance of a newly elected President. Though the campaign winner may not be his personal favorite, a child's trust in the election process assures him that any person chosen by election will be capable and trustworthy.

This report continues by emphasizing how children believe that the defeated candidate "should help the winner to do a good job" and that citizens themselves should "go along with the man who was elected even if you didn't vote for him."[29]

That such beliefs are well-established even among ten-year-olds is perhaps not surprising. Elections are part of every American child's school experience. Even in the earliest grades there are elections to choose "representatives" to serve on the student council; there are elections to choose the captain of the safety patrol; there are elections to choose the head cheerleader; there are votes about what to do on a school outing. The child considers these elections to be important and attaches great value to the significance of his vote. As an adult, he may realize that such powers were fictitious and that the teachers and other authorities controlled all the important decisions. Thus, with maturity, his confidence in elections is weakened, but he still retains his basic belief that

representative democracy is insured by the competition of leaders for
the electoral support of the public.

The thesis of electoral accountability has several weaknesses. First,
the reader should recall one of our central conceptions—that critical
political decisions in America are made by important members of the
economic elite, especially the managers and directors of our largest corporations. When this is granted, it is readily seen that some of the important sectors of the governing elite are relatively untouched by the
central institution purportedly designed to promote responsiveness.

There are, to be sure, "elections" in other than political sectors:
Stockholders vote for corporation directors, trade union members vote
for union officials, and even consumers can be said to vote by investing
their capital. But these forms of elections do not begin to establish the
type of accountability and responsiveness necessary for representative
democracy to be workable. The reasons for this are well-known: Most
stockholder or union elections involve nothing other than the choice to
support incumbent leaders and their policies or to vote "no" by absten-
tion; two slates of candidates or two programs of actions are seldom if
ever presented. Attempts to wage "proxy fights" have usually proven
very unsuccessful because of the great advantages accruing to extant
directors due to their control of the organization. Moreover, not all citizens get to vote for the Board of Directors of General Motors; this privilege is given only to the stockholders (in proportion to the stock they
control). However, it is not just the stockholders who are affected by
the actions of General Motors. The same is true of union elections; the protectionist and racist policies of the building and construction unions are
possible because the blacks who cannot gain admittance to these unions
are also unable to participate in their elections. Thus, elections within a
particular sector, even if presenting alternatives and offering competing
slates, are necessarily limited elections.

But there is another substantial flaw to the theory of electoral accountability. Implicit in the model is the notion that the relationship
between elites and voters is akin to that of the traditional New England
town meeting: Elites articulate the reasons for their held positions in a
rational manner before the informed electorate, which then exercises its
collective judgment in choosing between the candidates on the basis of
reason.

Even a cursory comparison between this picture and the way in which American election campaigns are conducted will reveal a yawning chasm indeed. Those seeking office are more-often-than-not content to campaign on the basis of slogans, such as "law and order" or "support your local police," designed to elicit emotional responses from the electorate, rather than to form the basis for a rational debate. Moreover, candidates will often conceal their true positions on issues from the electorate; consider only President Johnson's 1964 Presidential campaign statements that he would not expand America's role in the Vietnam war when he had every intention of doing so at the time. Again, campaigns are also replete with false issues, as, in 1960, when candidate John Kennedy raised the spectre of a "missile gap" between the American and Russian arsenals, a gap which was in fact nonexistent. Finally, we only briefly note the recently developed manipulatory public relations techniques designed to present candidates with different personality characteristics than they actually possess.

On the other side of the ledger, as we shall discuss shortly, the voter is ill-informed. Thus, the election system is far removed from the rational model of an informed electorate choosing among candidates who present rationally held positions. It is often not a system whereby candidates are held accountable for their actions, but rather one in which there is frequently no accountability for *political* actions. Rather, accountability is a perverted conception involving elites' abilities to manipulate electorates through fear, deception, and distorted personality characteristics.

The democratic-accountability thesis has several other flaws as well. These flaws call into question whether even the elected leaders can be held accountable in the manner set forth by the theorists. Two weaknesses in the electoral institutions interest us here: One involves the ambitions and status of the elite and the other involves the choices presented to the electorate by the American political system.

If there is to be electoral accountability, the men who hold high office, and the men dependent on those who hold high office, must be intent on retaining those positions or on moving to even higher ones. Because if officeholders are indifferent to their political futures, why should their choices in policy matters be guided by the likely response of voters at the next election? Representative government, writes one political theorist, depends above all on a supply of men driven to hold office: "The desire for election and, more important, for re-election becomes the electorate's restraint upon its public officials. No more irresponsible government is imaginable than one of high-minded men unconcerned for their political futures."[30]

It is axiomatic for most political commentators that this condition holds, but a study of local-level politicians casts some doubts. A group of city councilmen was asked if it were easy or difficult to ignore majority preferences when determining community policy.[31] Listen to a few answers:

> Easy, I am an independent type of individual. I don't feel the weight of voter responsibility. I am not all fired up for a political career.

> You don't always follow the majority; you shouldn't give a damn whether you get elected or not. Don't be afraid to be defeated.

> I am free to do as I feel. In general it is easy to vote against the majority because I don't have any political ambitions.

Other officeholders reflect similar sentiments in explaining indecision about future political plans:

> I won't know [if I'll stand for re-election] until my time is up. I don't think a councilman can do a good job if he is concerned about counting votes. If something is best for the city, you have to go against some groups. And you don't want to have to worry that these groups may not vote for you in the next election if you vote wrong.

> I promised myself I wouldn't decide ahead of time whether to run or not. I don't want to do things to collect votes.

It should be emphasized that these remarks were made by city councilmen in one area of the country (the San Francisco Bay area) whereas our interest in electoral accountability refers to the national political elite. Still the quotations are interesting. They underscore the ambivalence with which American citizens approach the issue of electoral accountability. Thus, on nationwide television, President Richard Nixon explains his decision to invade Cambodia with the comment that he would rather be "a one-term President" than not do what he saw to be in the national interest. Nixon is here courting voters, not deliberately ignoring them, because he senses that the American electorate wants public leaders who "stand on principles" rather than just appease the voters in order to further their own ambitions. Consider the possible results in Nixon's popularity had he gone before the public and announced the following: "I have examined carefully and at length intelligence reports on the Vietcong sanctuaries in Cambodia, and I believe beyond a doubt that American lives will be lost and the cause of the South Vietnamese weakened unless military action is taken against those sanctuaries. Nevertheless, looking forward to the prospects of re-election in 1972, I will refrain from initiating the necessary action." Such a speech would be consistent with the premises of electoral accountability but, in practice, it would be absurd. And the absurdity reveals the ambivalence of the American, voter and official alike, in weighing principle against ambition.

The quotations from city councilmen are interesting in a second respect. They led to a search for possible reasons for nonambitiousness, and this search revealed one consideration that is as important for national as for local political elites. The thesis that officeholders can be held accountable by an electorate depends, as we have seen, on those officeholders being ambitious, and ambitiousness, in turn, is related to status considerations. Compelling reasons for holding onto office are the social status it confers or the wealth it produces. Indeed, it has been argued that if status inequality between officeholders and others is too great, those in office will resist challenges and will forestall any opposition movements. Peaceful transfer of power is jeopardized. The difficulties of establishing constitutional democracy in African nations, where officeholding confers immense status and opportunities for wealth, lends support to this reasoning.

But the proposition can be turned on its head. If political office confers no status, then the motive for seeking it may only be civic duty or some other altruistic concern. This is exactly what seems to occur in the cities where officeholders showed such little ambition. Holding a council position does not confer much status; rather it is a by-product of status acquired elsewhere, usually in the business or professional community. Civic duty motivates these upper-middle-class councilmen, and volunteerism explains how they come to hold office. There is a danger here. As noted, "No more irresponsible government is imaginable than one of high-minded men unconcerned for their political futures."

This finding at the local level is not entirely unapplicable to the national political elite, although few positions in society can offer the status conferred by a governorship, a Senate position, or certainly by the Presidency. But the same is not always true for top appointive offices. Robert McNamara took a tremendous cut in salary, from $400,000 to $25,000, to move from head of Ford Motors to the head of the Defense Department. Packard, Undersecretary of Defense in the Nixon administration, was forced to put his substantial wealth in trust to avoid conflict of interest charges. His three years in government are estimated to have cost him $17 million. And these are not isolated cases. Frequently, prospective appointees to the federal executive have to be lured from powerful and prestigious positions by appeals to their sense of civic duty and public responsibility. If they are not satisfied or not appreciated in public office, these men can simply return to the leading law firms or corporations they recently departed. They are not on a career ladder that the electorate can control, and electoral sanctions are far from their minds as they shift and choose among alternative public policies.

We do not wish to push the argument too far, but neither will it do to ignore the volunteerism in American politics, even at the highest level. The conditions that minimize career considerations for members of the political elite are conditions that also weaken the institutions of electoral accountability. It is inadequate political theory to presume that just because there is the threat of electoral eviction, the members of the political elite sense and concern themselves with this threat. The entire issue of voter punishment is surrounded by an ambivalence which stresses the "independent judgment and principles" of political leadership as much as it stresses responsiveness, accountability, and sanctions. Moreover, even if there were no such ambivalence, there is a healthy component of volunteerism and civic duty in American politics, and such sentiments relax the standards of electoral accountability.

Another flaw in the theory of electoral accountability involves the structuring of choices by the two-party political system. When writers stress the importance of intra-elite competition in maintaining representative democracy, they frequently review several well-known facts about the American public as a political animal. These facts can be summarized in terms of four general findings derived from survey research:

1. By any standard, the level of political information of the average citizen is very low. Voters are ill-informed about public issues, about the voting records of their representatives, and about the policy stands of persons who challenge incumbents. Thus, only about half the population has even an elementary knowledge of the number of Senators from a state, the length of term of a member of the House of Representatives, the size of the Supreme Court, etc. Fewer yet are informed about substantive issues. Even political personalities are less well-known than might be thought. More Americans can correctly identify entertainment figures and sports heroes than can tell you the name of their own Senators. When it comes to matching personalities with policies, the American public has a dismal record. In one study, it is noted that only about two-fifths of the voters had read *anything* about either of the candidates for Congress in their district; and when asked to tell what they did know, references to current legislative issues were barely noticeable, comprising "not more than a thirtieth part of what the constituents had to say about their Congressmen."[32]

2. Coupled with low levels of information are low levels of political participation, at least of participation in electoral activities. Slightly more than three of five citizens, on the average, vote in Presidential campaigns. Well under half regularly vote in off-year congressional elections, and city elections attract yet fewer voters to the polls. More demanding political activities, such as working in an election or contacting a public official, occur even less frequently than voting, of course. As summarized by one commentator:

> Really active political participation—for example, contributing financially, or with one's own efforts, to the election of a candidate—was confined to fewer than 1 individual out of 9. After his election, the candidate could expect to receive letters or other communications from a similarly small proportion of his constituents. Even the simple indoor sport of talking politics proved to be unpopular; only a fifth of the sample described themselves as people who both frequently discussed public issues and who held their own in such conversations."[33]

3. Very few American citizens have elaborated "political ideologies" or conceptions of the political order. Even such vague and inconclusive labels as "liberal" and "conservative" fail to effectively categorize the

diverse positions taken by citizens on public issues. The average citizen cannot collect his political views in any coherent fashion, and changes his mind on the same issue from one year to the next. The extent to which Americans are consistent in political behavior can largely be attributed to their psychological affiliation with one or the other of the major parties. Much as with religion, the average citizen inherits his identification with the Democratic or Republican Party from his parents. This identification serves him well as an adult voter, because it provides him with a criterion for choosing between candidates and thereby relieves him of the burden of informing himself or thinking through his own policy preferences. More than two-thirds of the American voters consistently vote for the same party, and do so with seemingly little regard to the fluctuations in party positions in important issues.[34]

4. There are, of course, some voters who claim to be "independent" and who insist that they choose between the candidates rather than simply vote for the party of their childhood. But the so-called "independent voter," although often assumed to be more rational and informed than habitual party voters, proves on examination to be the least interested, least informed of voters. Although often switching his vote from one party to the other, and thus affecting electoral outcomes, the independent voter is ill-equipped to play this decisive role.

These four generalizations have been confirmed in numerous investigations, although they have also been qualified by data that report that participation, information, and voter rationality vary with context and that under certain conditions the American electorate shows more good judgment than the pollsters frequently attribute to it. But the qualifications are largely a matter of counterinterpretations of similar data. No student of voting behavior or of public opinion holds that the electorate even remotely approaches the active, knowledgeable, and rational body anticipated by the earliest proponents of democracy.

Thus, mass participation cannot be an essential ingredient of democracy to these theorists. What maintains the democratic tradition is not extensive participation in political policy-making by the public, but, instead, competition among elites whose behavior is regulated by periodic review procedures. Competition among elites and review procedures are provided by elections, and thus it is elections rather than mass political participation which "define" democracy. Moreover, mass ignorance and apathy are made into a virtue since elites can continue to support demo-cratic values without the pressure of mass authoritarianism.

The general proposition just reviewed holds that the masses are "irra-tional" but the system "rational." Two-party competition for the highest political offices provides for the accountability of elites, as they com-pete for electoral support, and ultimately for the responsiveness of the government to the public, as the policies pursued are calculated to win the affection of the masses. It is possible here to note only two consider-ations frequently ignored by those who see in intra-elite competition the salvation of democracy.

First, this thesis stresses the traits of individual voters (ignorance, apathy, irrationality) and of the elite group (commitment to demo-cratic procedures, internal competition), but pays little heed to the broader electoral arrangements and options. But consider the usual two-party presidential campaign. Voters have little control over the selection of candidates, that being largely in the hands of party professionals or, if we add in the few states with effective primaries, the somewhat larger group which is involved in primary campaigning and voting. Voters have only slightly more influence over the ranges of issues presented in the course of the campaign. For instance, a vast amount of survey data clearly indicates that the single most salient issue to the American elec-torate is the race question, and feelings remain sharply polarized despite official rhetoric about racial harmony. But the racial question is seldom presented to the American electorate as a matter of choice; both parties affirm the same liberal, integrationist values. It takes a third-party move-ment, such as that of George Wallace's American Independent Party, to force the race issue into the open, and even then the media shunts his platform aside as "inappropriate" for the American voter. Even if all the salient issues were discussed, the party leadership tends to converge to-ward a middle position, especially at election time. This reduces the op-portunity for the voter to form a coherent ideology which could become a criterion for electoral choices, and indeed reduces his motivation to determine just where the two parties stand. In that rare instance when a single issue does dominate an electoral period, and when the voters are sharply split, the positions of the major candidates may be such as to offer little choice. For example, opinion polls during the fall of 1968 show that Vietnam was the political issue of most concern to the majority of citizens. Yet on this issue the voters perceived few if any differences between the major candidates. In addition to this, many campaigns are centered around false issues, such as the "missile gap" of 1960; or slogans intended to elicit fear, such as "law and order" in 1968; or just simply the celebrity characteristics of the office-seekers. The voter has no way of knowing actual stands on real issues.

This suggests that it may be a failing of the election arrangements and campaign habits rather than the mass electorate (or in addition to the mass electorate) to which we might turn for explanation of the "withdrawal" of voters. There is no way of knowing, on the basis of available data, whether different electoral arrangements would have a marked effect on the involvement of the citizen in politics. But it is unquestionable that the present arrangement works to the advantage of elites.

A second, related observation about two-party politics and intra-elite competition is suggested by economic theory. Albert Hirschman has written that members of an organization (or a society) can complain, even rebel, against social deterioration in one of two ways: through voice or through exit. Voice is defined as

> any attempt at all to change, rather than to escape from, an objectionable state of affairs, whether through individual or collective petition to the management directly in charge, through appeal to a higher authority with the intention of forcing a change in management, or through various types of actions and protests, including those that are meant to mobilize public opinion.[35]

Exit is to quit the organization, or society, as a way of registering protest and escaping from the deteriorating conditions. The voice option is the traditional one in the political realm; it is costly and often impracticable to emigrate and therefore the *citizen* expresses his opposition to social deterioration or unfavorable conditions by exercising his voice in the political arena. By the same token, the exit option has traditionally been assigned to the economic realm; it is difficult to protest poor workmanship and inferior quality and therefore the *consumer* expresses dissatisfaction by making his next purchase elsewhere. It should be noted that the assignment of voice to political behavior and exit to market behavior is appropriate in theory only; political and market behavior each mix voice and exit to some degree.

We are here interested in applying these notions to a thesis about intra-elite competition in the political realm. Underlying the confidence in the two-party system are assumptions about the exit option. If the voters are unhappy with one set of political leaders, they shift their electoral support to the other party. This then keeps the leadership of each party alert to citizen dissatisfaction; in the language of representative democracy, it keeps the elite responsive. To the voter, it is said, "If you don't like the way things are going, vote the rascals out," but, above all else, "work within the system."

However, as Hirschman recognizes, radical critics of societies with stable two-party systems know that such "competition" can undermine the potent force of political voice: "The radical critique is correct in pointing out that competitive political systems have a considerable capacity to divert what might otherwise be a revolutionary ground swell into tame discontent with the governing party."[36] That is, much as commercial organizations can rid themselves of troublemaking customers by saying "go buy elsewhere," the political system rids itself of potential pressures by saying "vote the rascals out."

But voice, when we examine it more closely, proves to be somewhat more limited than it appears at first blush. Competition between two units must always be measured against the range of possible alternatives. Thus, if two industrial firms do not compete on the basis of price, service, or product quality, but only in the realm of advertising puffery, we would say that their competition is limited, indeed. Similarly, if the voters' only voice alternatives are between two political parties whose differences are small, we would again decry the quality of competition involved in the process. And, American politics has often been characterized by such limited competition. In 1968, the principal Presidential candidates—Nixon, Humphrey, and Wallace—virtually excluded the Vietnam war as an issue, while in years prior to that the major party candidates shared a wide consensus of views including belief in the capitalist system, the justice of America's cause in the cold war, and a very limited role for public enterprise. And yet these could have been major issues had they been introduced into the political arena.

Nor is this objection met by asserting that voters could have selected candidates from among third parties. First, it is extremely difficult for fledgling parties to get on the ballot in many states, and even when they can, they often dissipate their energies in getting on the ballot. And, it should be remembered, that it is Democratic and Republican officials who judge whether the new parties have met the technical requirements needed to obtain a ballot position. But, the far more formidable obstacle which exists for such parties is their severe money shortage. Such parties are not capable of raising sufficient money to mount a viable campaign in which their candidates will be exposed sufficiently to become known to the public. The sums required to mount Democratic and Republican campaigns ordinarily come in substantial part from large, very wealthy contributors. And these are precisely the kinds of individuals who, on ideological grounds, will have nothing to do with radical political groupings.

Finally, if all else fails, the political elite can repress such parties or simply describe them as "unpatriotic" or "treasonable" or beyond the pale of decent politics.

What this brief review of two modes of expressing political discontent indicates is that intra-elite competition, even when linked to a mass electorate through periodic elections, need not have only beneficial implications for the responsiveness of elites. The same competitive arrangements which intend to bring about responsiveness can also bring about protection of the elite from mass discontent and pressure. And, in this sense, the institutional guarantee of representative democracy can again work more to the benefit of elites than non-elites, thereby weakening the principles of "consent of the governed."

PRESSURE ORGANIZATIONS AND THE PETITIONING PROCESS

Americans, it has been said, are a nation of "joiners." They flock to the innumerable voluntary associations and organizations which dot the social landscape. And the extensive and complex group life which results is not without consequences, mostly benign, for representative democracy. At least, this is what one line of reasoning proposes. How do voluntary associations and pressure organizations contribute to checking the elite and forcing them to be responsive? An answer to this question comes out of a rich literature on American politics; we can provide only a brief overview as preface to expressing our own doubts about how well the "group process" establishes representative democracy.

The beginning point is to recognize the importance of group activity to political life, an importance which cannot be denied. As summarized by one observer, "Group interests are the animating forces in the political process. The exercise of the power of governance consists in the promotion of group objectives regarded as legitimate, in the reconciliation and mediation of conflicting group ambitions, and in the restraint of group tendencies judged to be socially destructive."[37]

This active role by groups benefits representative democracy in several respects. Organizations are linkages between the elite and the nonelite. Whereas the individual voter or petitioner may be scarcely noticed by elites, the citizen whose strength is augmented by collective pressure of a large and well-financed organization has less difficulty being heard. "Voluntary associations are the prime means by which the functions of mediating between the individual and the state is performed. Through them the individual is able to relate himself effectively and meaningfully to the political system," is the conclusion of two political scientists.[38]

This linkage role is particularly important to augment the electoral process. Elections occur infrequently, and when the excitement and flurry of the contest is past, the elite once again retreat into the company of peers and close advisors. But the lobbying activity of pressure groups reminds them of the wishes and demands of the public. And this reminder comes at an opportune time, for it is in the period between elections when laws are passed (or not), when public monies are spent, and when commitments on behalf of the entire society are made. The group process establishes a dual system of representation. Not only does the citizen have elected leaders to represent him, but he has group leaders and spokesmen to carry his wishes into the elite circles. In being "represented twice," the citizen has a double check on the elite. Group spokesmen press demands on the elite and report back the results to the group members.

But an active group life does more than take up the slack in the representational process. It facilitates social consensus and political moderation. This viewpoint is well summarized in the following passage:

The United States is a large and diverse nation with many different kinds of people holding many different values. The pursuit of these diverse values often occurs through the medium of interest groups which contend against one another for the influence and power to gain their values. The competition among so many groups moderates the claims and counterclaims by forcing compromise and bargaining. It disciplines the groups thereby and they adjust and adapt to one another. If any sector of society is aggrieved, it may organize and seek redress through the bargaining among groups. Freedom for each group is thus maximized, goals are moderated, and social consensus is promoted.[39]

Thus, an active group life moderates the conflicts and tensions that might otherwise be unmanageable in a society committed to the democratic principle that every viewpoint should receive a hearing.

Finally, it has been argued, organizations check tendencies that can be destructive to the political order within which representative democracy thrives. Associational activity mediates between the elite and the non-elite in a way that protects each from the excesses of the other. The excesses of the elite would be aloofness, isolation, arbitrariness, and, ultimately, tyranny. The excesses of the non-elite would be ill-informed and ill-formulated political viewpoints, shifting moods and unreasonable demands, sporadic and poorly considered political activities, and, ultimately, social anomie and alienation. Tyrannical elites and anomic masses are unlikely if the "space" between them is filled by an active group life. Organizations monitor and check the tendencies of elites, and they organize and stabilize the viewpoints and activities of the public.

We thus see that the antidemocratic possibilities when society is directed by an elite are modified, even prevented, in three different ways by an active group life. First, pressure organizations are a channel by which citizens express themselves to the elite and thus these organizations provide a necessary compliment to elections. Second, because of the variety of organizations, very diverse political viewpoints have the type of outlet that moderates social conflict and tension. Third, two of the severest dangers to a democracy—elite tyranny and mass anomie—are effectively checked by a layer of associational activity mediating between elites and non-elites, and reducing the antidemocratic excesses of both.

These, then, are some of the major propositions that have connected group politics with an understanding of representative democracy. While there is an element of truth in them, there are also some grave difficulties. Indeed, there are aspects of group politics that *reduce* the responsiveness of elites, and these aspects must be considered if our understanding of elites and political representation is to be complete. Let us then consider the evidence on organizations and their political role.

Not all Americans are joiners. Indeed the unorganized are nearly as numerous as the organized. One survey finds that as many as 43 percent of adult citizens belong to no organizations, and this despite including as organizations all of the following types of activities: trade or labor unions, business organizations, social groups, professional or farm organizations, cooperatives, fraternal or veterans' groups, athletic clubs, political, charitable, civic, or religious organizations, and any other organized group.[40] Given this shopping list of alternatives, it is striking that barely more than half the populace could come up with even *one* organization to which they belonged. If "group interests are the animating forces in the political process," as V. O. Key said, then a sizeable proportion of American citizens are disfranchised from this particular system. And insofar as social benefits are distributed in response to group pressures, such a large unorganized bloc calls into question the equity of the distribution.

Perhaps what we have in the United States is the politics of intense minorities. Individual groups press for selective benefits, leaving the unorganized to pick up the remains. The history of the labor movement is illustrative. Trade unions crystallized as a political force during a period when near total segregation of blacks was the prevailing pattern. Unions did come to wield significant power in American politics, but they were the mouthpiece of union leaders and not the working class. The benefits they gained for their members only partially and inadequately spilled over to the black workers or migrant agricultural workers. Indeed, parts of the organized labor movement have been deliberately (and successfully) fighting the worker interests of the unorganized, and, in particular, have been denying membership to blacks.

It is relevant to note that many of the benefits won by blacks over the past three decades have been won in the name of *citizenship rights* rather than in the name of organized interests. Supreme Court decisions on school integration, or legislation on voting rights, or executive programs to promote equal employment opportunities have been justified as extensions of basic citizenship rights to the black population. The unorganized always benefit more from the extension of citizenship than they do from a politics responsive to the pressure activities of groups.

Actually the unorganized are doubly disfranchised in American politics. First, in the sense just noted, they have no group spokesmen or organizational resources representing them. But second, nonmembers tend also to be nonparticipants in other respects. There is a consistently strong tendency for the politically active—those who regularly vote, who campaign for candidates, who directly contact officeholders—to be drawn from the ranks of organizational members. And this pattern is true in societies other than the United States. The reason is simple. Organizations not only represent group members, they urge them to become politically involved as individuals, and perhaps provide resources to this end. Thus the union member is barraged with information about elections, candidates and their records, and legislation before Congress; he is invited to political rallies and meetings organized by the union; and he can even be given time off to take part in politics. The nonunion worker is not, of course, similarly mobilized, especially given the way in which our political parties operate. Both of the major parties have direct and continuous links with organizations, but tenuous and even nonexistent links with the average citizen. It is a looseness of language which allows the American citizen to say that "he belongs to" the Democratic or Republican Party. Except for the party professionals, the political parties come to life only around election time; they are not mobilization parties which attempt to link the citizen with the elite on a continuous basis. Thus, the unorganized not only lack a group which could serve them as a channel to the elite, but also are denied a context which could involve them in politics on a regular basis.

It is more to the point that lower-status citizens are much less likely to belong to organizations than are upper-status citizens. Not only do the wealthier and well-educated belong to more organizations, they also participate in them more actively than do the poorer and less well-educated. And within most organizations, it is the well-to-do who occupy the leadership positions, and thus it is persons of the upper classes who largely decide the goals toward which group resources will be directed and who are in contact with the political elite.

Thus, insofar as an active group life connects citizen and elite, it does so more effectively for the middle and upper-middle classes than it does for the lower strata. The strong association between social status and organizational membership in the United States is particularly revealing when measured against data from other nations. The class bias in organizational membership is much higher in the U.S. than, for example, in Britain, Germany, or Italy. In each of these latter nations, lower-class citizens have greater opportunites to express themselves politically through the group process than they do in the United States. This discrepancy partly reflects the fact that in Britain, Germany, and Italy there have been deliberate efforts to mobilize and politically involve the lower classes by radical or working-class political parties.

America has simply never developed a lower-class organizational infrastructure. And thus an undue emphasis on group politics has a clear socioeconomic bias. It provides an additional resource and channel of access to those who already benefit from the social system, and it denies a linkage to those already penalized by lack of resources.

The correspondence in the United States between organizational membership and higher social status plus the tendency for those in organizations to participate more actively in politics than do non-members suggests that the group process very imperfectly connects the mass of citizens with the elite. The following table demonstrates the low levels of participation by those who are doubly penalized: first, by being without social and economic resources and second, by being without an organizational home.[41]

| | Organizational Involvement | | | | | |
| | High | | Medium | | Low | |
	High Social Status	Low Social Status	High Status	Low Status	High Status	Low Status
Proportion Who Are Politically Active	75%	67%	41%	27%	32%	10%

Only one out of every ten citizens penalized by low status and isolated from the interest-group system is likely to be politically active. In contrast, three of every four citizens who hold high status positions and who are involved in organizations are also politically active. It is evident, therefore, that, as we have already observed, the group process very imperfectly connects the mass of citizens with the elite. Intense minorities, especially those based in the middle and upper-middle classes, are advantaged by group politics. The majority is not so effectively served. As one critic summarized the evidence, "The vice in the groupist theory is that it conceals the most significant aspect of the system. The flaw in the pluralist heaven is that the heavenly chorus sings with a strong upper-class accent. Probably about 90 percent of the people cannot get into the pressure system."[42]

The class bias in membership and activity gives a conservative hue to the pressure system, but it is not the only factor contributing to this conservatism. Equally, if not more, important is the simple fact that well-established, entrenched organizations are more powerful than organizations in the process of being born. The established, organized interests have budgets, professional lobbying staffs, contacts in Washington and state capitals, and a long, often distinguished, record of public involvement. The upstart organization lacks all of these assets. But it is often the upstart organizations which represent dissatisfaction with the *status quo* and which enter politics to reform institutions and to change policies. They are met and more often than not beaten back by the conservative interests which have shaped the *status quo* and understandably intend to protect it. Thus, the N.A.A.C.P. has been more conservative and accommodating than the more recently formed Southern Christian Leadership Conference, which, in turn, has taken a more cautious stance than the newest entries into the black politics arena. Moreover, the newer organizations are disregarded by the parties bent on preserving the extant group system with which they have a long-standing accommodation.

The pressure-group system has a class and a conservative bias, both of which weaken its effectiveness in bringing about political representation and elite accountability. It would be in error to conclude that representation and accountability are not in some respects furthered by group politics, but it would be even more erroneous to conclude that just because a society has an active group life it has perfected and protected a representative democracy.

The thesis that an organizational layer between elite and non-elite insures representative politics is flawed in another manner as well. The thesis depends on active competition between different groups, but a plurality of groups does not necessarily imply group competition. As we noted in a previous chapter, powerful interest groups are capable of capturing entire sectors of public policy. The policy-making elites might be representative of a particular constituency, but it is often a constituency that is narrow and parochial in its demands. Agricultural policy provides a clear example. The powerful interest organizations that represent the farmer, especially the large, commercial farmer, have literally captured the public agencies that are supposed to regulate the agricultural sector.

In one extended criticism of pluralism and group politics, the author contends that the all-important distinction between private power and public authority has nearly been eliminated in American society: "This has been accomplished not by public expropriation of private domain—as would be true of the nationalization that Americans fear—but by private expropriation of public authority."[43] Powerful private interests rule their own fiefdoms with the blessing of public authority and with the largess of the public treasury.

To the extent that capture rather than competition describes group politics, political representation again suffers. Broad interests are sacrificed to narrow ones, and elites are cushioned from public reprisal by the protective envelope of friendly and powerful, if parochial, groups.

SUMMARY

Three separate arguments about political representation and elite accountability have been reviewed: (1) Elites are held in check by internalized values, which include a healthy respect for democratic norms and a commitment to serve the public interest. (2) Elites are held in check by a competitive election system, which penalizes and rewards according to how faithfully the public interest has been represented. And (3) elites are held in check by a vigorous interest-group system which provides a vast network through which the non-elite shape and constrain public policy in accord with majority preferences. Our review has revealed that each argument is flawed in major and minor ways, although each argument has some merit.

We conclude on a pessimistic note. Not only are elites well entrenched in American society, which is what we expect of any large-scale industrial nation, but they are more immune from popular control than the rhetoric of democracy implies. The nation talks a more democratic game than it plays. The elite, of course, are not all-powerful; they clearly operate within limits established by what the broader public is willing to tolerate. An elite will not long persist in the face of active Constitutional opposition, but the infrequency and ineffectiveness of such opposition must be noted.

In the final chapter, we turn again to the issue of elites and democracy, and there attempt to answer the question of which is greater the degree to which social policy in the U.S. derives from the elite or the degree to which it derives from the elite as it stands in some sort of representative relationship with the non-elite?

Notes

1. Robert A. Dahl, *After the Revolution* (New Haven: Yale University Press, 1970), p. 71.
2. This formulation owes much to the explication of political representation found in Hanna Fenichel Pitkin, *The Concept of Representation* (Berkeley: University of California Press, 1967). See, for instance, p. 209. A further elaboration of political representation along the lines suggested here can be found in Kenneth Prewitt and Heinz Eulau, "Political Matrix and Political Representation," *American Political Science Review,* vol. 63 (June 1969), pp. 427-441.
3. Plato, *The Republic,* Cornford translation, p. 105.
4. *Ibid.,* p. 107.
5. These findings are reported in Herbert McClosky, "Consensus and Ideology in American Politics," *American Political Science Review,* vol. 58 (June 1964), pp. 361-382.
6. *Ibid.,* p. 375.
7. V. O. Key, *Public Opinion and American Democracy* (New York: Knopf, 1961), p. 537.
8. Dahl, *Who Governs?* p. 320.
9. McClosky, "Consensus and Ideology in American Politics," p. 375.
10. *Ibid.,* p. 376.
11. Key, *Public Opinion and American Democracy,* p. 537.
12. Dahl, *Who Governs?,* p. 320.
13. Key, *Public Opinion and American Democracy,* p. 538.
14. McClosky, "Consensus and Ideology in American Politics," p. 374.
15. Quoted in Michael P. Rogin, *The Intellectuals and McCarthy: The Radical Specter* (Cambridge: The M.I.T. Press, 1967), p. 1.

16 *Ibid.,* pp. 250, 253.

17 *Ibid.,* pp. 254-255.

18 One of the more famous cases is that of the price-fixing widely practiced by the electrical industry, led by General Electric, Westinghouse, and Allis-Chalmers in the 1950s and early 1960s. Prices were fixed at a level approximately 40 percent higher than what a competitive market would have produced, and the government itself was the purchaser most victimized. The price-fixing itself was perhaps even less scandalous than the defense prepared by the electric companies. Thus a president of one of the defendent companies expressed himself as follows: ."No one attending the gatherings [to fix prices] was so stupid that he didn't know the meetings were in violation of the law. But it is the only way a business can be run. It is free enterprise." Quoted in John G. Fuller, *The Gentlemen Conspirators* (New York: Grove, 1962), p. 91.

19 The next few pages paraphrase an argument initially developed in Kenneth Prewitt, "Political Ambitions, Volunteerism, and Electoral Accountability," *American Political Science Review,* vol. 64 (March 1970), pp. 5-17.

20 Joseph Schumpeter, *Capitalism, Socialism and Democracy* (New York: Harper & Row, 1947), p. 269.

21 *Ibid.,* p. 272.

22 Seymour M. Lipset, *Political Man* (New York: Doubleday, 1960; Anchor Books Edition, 1963), p. 27.

23 Anthony Downs, *An Economic Theory of Democracy* (New York: Harper & Row, 1957), p. 28.

24 Dahl, *Who Governs?* p. 164.

25 Schumpeter, *Capitalism, Socialism and Democracy,* p. 272.

26 Seymour M. Lipset, Martin Trow, and James Coleman, *Union Democracy* (Garden City, N.Y.: Doubleday, 1962), p. 241.

27 Robert A. Dahl, *A Preface to Democratic Theory* (Chicago: University of Chicago Press, 1956), p. 72.

28 Mosca, *The Ruling Class,* p. 70.

29 Robert D. Hess and Judith V. Torney, *The Development of Political Attitudes in Children* (Garden City, N.Y.: Doubleday, 1968), pp. 88-89.

30 Joseph A. Schlesinger, *Ambition and Politics* (Chicago: Rand McNally, 1966), p. 2.

31 Taken from Prewitt, "Political Ambitions, Volunteerism, and Electoral Accountability."

32 Donald E. Stokes and Warren E. Miller, "Party Government and the Saliency of Congress," *Public Opinion Quarterly,* vol. 26, (Winter 1962), p. 543.

33 Fred I. Greenstein, *The American Party System and the American People* (Englewood Cliffs, N.J.: Prentice-Hall, 1963), p. 11.

34 Supporting evidence can be found primarily in Angus Campbell, et al., *The American Voter* (New York: Wiley, 1960).

35 Albert O. Hirschman, *Exit, Voice, and Loyalty* (Cambridge: Harvard University, 1970), p. 30.

36 Ibid., p. 28.

37 V. O. Key, *Politics, Parties and Pressure Groups,* 3d ed. (New York: Crowell, 1956), p. 23.

38 Gabriel A. Almond and Sidney Verba, *The Civic Culture* (Princeton, N.J.: Princeton University Press, 1963), p. 245.

39 Robert H. Salisbury, ed., *Interest Group Politics in America* (New York: Harper & Row, 1970), p. 2. Salisbury is summarizing a point of view, not aligning himself with it.

40 Almond and Verba, *The Civic Culture,* p. 301.

41 Taken from Norman H. Nie, G. Bingham Powell, Jr., and Kenneth Prewitt, "Social Structure and Political Participation: Developmental Relationships, Part II," *American Political Science Review,* vol. 63 (September 1969).

42 E. E. Schattschneider, *The Semi-Soverign People,* p. 35.

43 Theodore J. Lowi, *The End of Liberalism* (New York: Norton, 1969), p. 102.

PART FIVE

CONCLUSIONS

CHAPTER 9
ELITE THEORY
REVISITED

If your image of the relationship between elites and non-elites has been formed by reading the newspapers, it is likely an inaccurate image. Whereas news headlines proclaim a victory of the women's liberation movement, the actual facts are that a tiny group of self-selected females concerned with feminist issues have established themselves as a counter-elite in a male-dominated society. The mass media refers to the youth movement, but there is no politically viable organization of youths. There is instead a small minority who act and speak forcefully on a variety of youth-related questions. Even the so-called labor movement is more the actions of a few labor leaders than it is the actions of a mass rank-and-file worker's movement. By describing the actions of these small groups as mass movements, the media distort the truths of American politics.

This distortion is aided and abetted by the elites themselves. Elites are fond of metaphors that describe them as willing representatives of mass movements, electoral majorities, or active constituencies. But this is seldom the case. The leaders of miniscule black groups who speak on behalf of all blacks are a counter-elite battling established leaders more than the spearhead of a black political movement. It is not even self-evident that the views of this largely self-selected counter-elite correlate very closely with the wishes and preferences of the bulk of the black population. The elected leader is prone to similar exaggeration when he justifies his actions by stating that "his constituency" prefers such a policy or that he is simply reflecting the desires of the "silent majority."

Even in a democracy, politics is only indirectly the politics of mass movements or of active constituencies or of electoral mandates. Political masses largely sit on the sidelines, infrequently being mobilized by one elite or another. When we read and hear of mass political action our suspicions should be aroused. We very likely are reading and hearing of elites and counter-elites.

To insist on the analytic usefulness of the elite perspective is not to make a moral judgment. Although fascist theorists, such as Mussolini's intellectual mentor, Giovanni Gentile, will always apply the elitist perspective, it is poor intellectual history to think that the elite theory belongs only to the ideological right. The elite perspective has been adopted by theorists of radical, liberal, and conservative persuasion: C. Wright Mills urged radical changes in American society; Gaetano Mosca was a liberal in his preoccupation with democratic selection and social stability; Alexander Hamilton questioned the wisdom of popular democracy and supported constitutional provisions which allowed for strong, centralized leadership.

If elite theorists are spread along the ideological continuum, the ideologies of actual political elites are even more diversified. The Russian Revolution of 1917, the first major social revolution of the twentieth century, was led by a man dedicated to the thesis that only a vanguard can make a revolution. Lenin distrusted spontaneous unguided mass action but he can hardly thereby be placed in the camp of the enemies of the Russian revolution. Mao Tse-tung and his associates have more confidence in mass action, yet they nevertheless organized a political system in which immense powers are concentrated in very few hands. The history of race relations in the United States provides a different type of illustration. For two centuries, political power has remained concentrated in a relatively small political-economic class and yet the substance of race policy has changed enormously—from chattel slavery to Jim Crow arrangements, to integrated public facilities, to civil rights legislation, and now to black power politics. Elite rule has been compatible with nearly every conceivable type of relationship between blacks and whites, and if ever that relationship should become one of true black autonomy and racial justice, it will not be because political elites have evaporated. The clue to historical change will still be found in elite circulation.

Elite theory is not a normative theory. It does not describe the kind of society we should prefer. But this does not mean that elite theory is without consequences for normative theory. Elite theory raises the type of questions that have to be answered when we debate about the kind of society we want. Who are the elites on a critical policy issue? Are they opposed by an effective counter-elite? What resources do elites and counter-elites command? What is the vision of the future held by different elites? These questions are consistent with questions about public opinion or electoral choices or mass movements, but they are broader in scope than the latter topics. Large numbers of people become politically important when they are mobilized by elites, but mobilization of mass action is only one of many resources available to elites or counter-elites. To write history as if mass political action is never a resource utilized by elites is to miss much that is important, but to write history as if mass political action equals politics is to miss even more. Social science has yet to locate social laws in the same sense that physical scientists have located physical laws, but just as the engineer can build only in accordance with the laws of physics so can the political actor view history and the future only in terms of the "laws" of social behavior. Elite theory claims to have discovered a regularity in politics, and this regularity reduces the number of normative alternatives we need to consider realistically.

If normative political thinking is influenced by the elite perspective, so also is historical thinking. Indeed, it is in connection with the philosophy of history that elite theory makes a valuable contribution. Often we are so impressed by the dramatic events of history that we accept as theories of history perspectives that assume that change is always taking place. Marxism, with its emphasis on continuous class conflict, is an example of such a theory; so also is Hegelian idealism, which finds the unfolding of the spirit according to dialectical principles to be the central agency of historical change.

But not all history is social change, at least not social change in the sense intended by Marx or Hegel. History is also stability, stagnation, and decay, and each of these processes as well as historical change can be illuminated with the perspectives of elite theory.

Let us begin with historical change, which would include not only cataclysmic events, such as revolutionary upheavals, but also substantial modifications of the social or economic system which occur without significant disruption. The Russian Revolution of 1917 is an example of the former type of historical change, while the fundamental rearrangement of the relationship between the State and the economy in the

United States since the 1930s is an example of the latter type. Elites are the significant actors in bringing about both types of change. The Russian Revolution took place when counter-elites mobilized the resources necessary to overthrow the ruling elites; the integration of polity and economy and the introduction of welfare state measures took place in the U.S. as the ruling elite redirected the resources at the command of government.

In these as well as other cases of major historical change, the masses have awakened from their normal state of political lethargy. But the mass marching and shouting was organized by elites and counter-elites. When the marching and shouting ends and, as in Russia, a new elite is installed, it is the first action of the new elite to demobilize the masses and insist that they return to their quiescent state. It is then the new elite which sets about organizing the revolutionary regime and henceforth governs the society. Recent history provides a clear illustration of this principle in the first action of Sheikh Mujibur Rahman, popular leader and first President of Bangla Desh, who when he formed a new government requested the guerrilla bands who helped bring his regime to power to turn in their arms to the authorities and to disband.

Spontaneous mass actions do take place, of course. But they are not common and seem to cluster in any given society within a relatively short time period. When spontaneous agitation is not quickly organized by a counter-elite, it is invariably crushed. Thus, the several peasant uprisings in seventeenth-century France were suppressed, but when the bourgeoise elite subsequently led the French Revolution, the monarchy was overthrown.[1] The bourgeoise elite not only organized the Revolution, it organized the successor regime. In looking even at revolutionary change we should devote as much or more attention to the struggle between elites and counter-elites as to the mobilized masses.

Most of history, however, does not involve social upheavals or even substantial, if peaceful, modification of society, economy, or polity. The persistent trait of political regimes is stability: an elite performing its day-to-day chores. This performance only tangentially involves mass participation, perhaps only when the electorate chooses between competing members of the elite every few years. Stability it should be noted is not the opposite of change. Often the ruling elite directs the pace of social change in a way that maintains the integrity of the society's basic institutions. For nearly 200 years the American institutions of government have remained intact, and although the Constitution has been amended and stretched, it is still in important respects the same document that was framed in 1787. The elites entrusted with the care and control of the government have effectively maintained the institutions from generation to generation, making the adjustments necessary to insure political stability.

There are times when the paired conditions of moderated change and social stability do not coalesce. One possible outcome when a regime is unable or unwilling to effect the necessary adjustments is revolutionary overthrow. Another possible outcome is stagnation in which practically no change occurs in a society. The technology, the social structure, the means of livelihood, the power arrangements, and the cultural beliefs are duplicated from one generation to another. Notwithstanding his belief in a dynamic theory of history, Karl Marx decried the stagnation of Chinese and Indian societies in which nothing of significance changed for many centuries. New beliefs and new social arrangements came about only after incursions from the West. There are nomadic societies in the deserts of Northern Africa which live today much as their ancestors did 2000 years ago. And there are small tribes of hunters and gatherers scattered around the globe whose technology and religion and polity differ very little from those of similar peoples who lived 8000 years ago.

Social stagnation occurs when elites lack either the will or the resources to transform traditional ways of doing things. Or, of course, it can occur when the established elite successfully resists the efforts of counter-elites to introduce new outlooks or new technologies. Usually, the established elite can combine repression and co-optation to maintain their control. Such was the case when the Chinese Imperial regime simultaneously repressed peasant rebellions and circulated talented elements into the elite through the civil service examination system.

A regime may not only stagnate, it may actually decay as the Roman Empire or Spain of the seventeenth century amply document. A number of reasons connected with elite conduct can explain such decay. Laziness, corruption, or inefficiency can render an elite incapable of coping with society's problems. A defective vision of social trends can blind the elite to the consequences of current policies. A quest for creature comforts can siphon off needed investment capital and eventually the entire society will have to pay the cost. These types of weaknesses within the ruling elite often result from failures to recruit capable people with new ideas from outside the ruling class. Seventeenth-century Spain is perhaps a classic example of a nation declining because degenerate elements dominated in the ruling elite. As a result of the decay of the elite, the government was unable to foster policies that might have promoted national growth.[2] Because royal squander was preferred to social investment, the potential Spanish Empire never really materialized. To put it bluntly, a ruling elite in the aggregate can be every bit as stupid as many people are individually.

Although the elite perspective provides insight into historical change, social stability, stagnation, and even decay, it by no means is a complete theory of history. History may have a single ultimate efficient cause, such as class conflict, or, more likely, it may be shaped by a variety of factors, such as belief systems, biological determinism, technological conditions, heroes in history, and fortuitous circumstances. Elite theory cannot tell us what finally accounts for the movement of history, and probably no general theory ever will. But elite theory is consistent with various perspectives on historical causation and can itself add considerably to our understanding.

Elite theory compels us to focus on specific groups who organize and direct events, and who block or retard other events. If we are to reduce history to technological changes, then it is elites who discover and apply new technologies. If we are to reduce history to man's inherent aggressiveness or some other form of biological determinism, then it is elites who shape the organized manifestations of this aggressiveness and direct it toward this or that social goal. If we are to reduce history to class conflict, then it is elites and counter-elites who arouse class consciousness and excite mass action. If we are to reduce history to the gradual transformation of social policy, then it is elite circulation which explains the demise of one outlook and the emergence of another.

ELITES AND POWER

We run the risk of being misunderstood in thus insisting on the usefulness of the elite perspective. It is an incorrect reading of our discussion to conclude that elites are all-powerful. To see elites as the central actors in history is not to see them as unconstrained and operating without limits. Elites are seldom all-powerful and completely autonomous of restrictive social processes. Elites are limited, in the first place, by the policy priorities and political procedures already established in the society, especially where these priorities and procedures are widely accepted. As social scientist Piet Thoenes observes:

> . . . political priorities . . . are already fixed; and insofar as there are still any political decisions to be taken, they are only decisions of a secondary nature. The main purpose of political leadership is to act as guardian for aims which have been once and for all agreed upon; a guardianship, this, which does not involve particularly onerous duties, in view of the fact that the aims are scarcely exposed to any criticisms on the home front. Thus, as regards the internal social order, political leadership is hardly any longer of importance. Hence quite a fierce struggle can arise regarding the possession of key positions. For the most part this is a struggle of factions, a dynastic argument extraordinarily stirring for those taking part in it, but of less consequence when viewed from the angle of the historical development of society.[3]

The point is undoubtedly overdrawn, because any social-economic order can be dismantled just as it once had to be constructed. But the central argument is nevertheless important. There are political priorities and social arrangements that constrain and hamper the elite of any society. Political elites in the United States are not "powerful" enough to call off elections; political elites in the U.S.S.R. are not "powerful" enough to reject the metaphors of communism; political elites in the Union of South Africa are not "powerful" enough to suddenly introduce programs of racial justice. Although the electoral policy of the U.S., the economic policy of the U.S.S.R., and the racial policy of South Africa can alter over time, no single elite standing at a particular point in time has the power to reverse policies and procedures that are widely accepted in the society.

Constraints on elite rule are particularly evident in democracies, as we can readily see by considering just a few examples from U.S. politics. We can for the present characterize the U.S. as a procedural democracy, taking this phrase to mean a society that permits competitive elections, relatively unhampered rights of political association and organization, and basic freedoms of speech and press. Elites who govern societies that are organized under the rules of procedural democracy do behave differently than do elites of other societies. This does not mean that the public somehow sets the agenda of social priorities or that mass preferences are the deciding factor in selecting public policies. We have dismissed the idea that the public has political power in this sense, or at least dismissed the idea that it has power in cases other than when it is mobilized by elites. But we do not conclude that democratic procedures are just a façade behind which social resources are manipulated for the sole benefit of powerful elites. Democratic procedures act to restrain or at least deter the authoritarian tendencies of some members of the elite.

Further, procedural democracy facilitates the emergence of counter-elites. It is an undeniable fact of politics that freedom of speech and press and the right of political association greatly aid the growth of opposition political movements. The antiwar activities in the 1960s provide a clear demonstration of this point. These activities were organized by a counter-elite strongly opposed to the Vietnam adventure, an elite initially restricted to college campuses but eventually able to encompass religious and business leaders and finally to attract sections of the top political leadership. The antiwar activities that resulted in the displacement of the Johnson regime would hardly have been possible had not freedom of association protected the teach-ins, the marches and demonstrations, and the public rallies, and had not freedom of the press led to the fantastic outpouring of antigovernment literature and to the increasingly critical stance of the national news media, and had not freedom of speech defended the voice of outspoken antiwar leaders in the classroom, the pulpit, and finally on the campaign trail. Of course, this must be balanced with the political trials of the 1960s and the many examples where dissent was stifled and force was used to repress antigovernment activities. But it is poor political analysis to hold to the position that procedural democracy has no bearing on the successful emergence of a counter-elite.

American history is replete with examples of repressive tactics employed by powerful elites and of political demagoguery that bordered on the tyrannical. It was only two decades ago that the U.S. lived through a period of extensive repression and demagoguery. Initiated by

President Truman and brought to fruition by Senator Joseph McCarthy, the doctrine of anticommunism was invoked and abused until the nation was on the verge of political hysteria. Not only were political liberals victimized, but persons whose deviancy expressed itself in nothing more sinister than odd reading habits or unusual leisure time activities found themselves harangued in front of a Congressional committee. Political careers were broken and intellectuals penalized simply because of refusal to testify before Congressional committees or administrative boards. And the 1960s were not entirely free of repressiveness; opposition to American involvement in Vietnam has been transformed into "anti-Americanism" by political elites; and leaders of black militant organizations have been harassed, intimidated, and in a few instances summarily executed by zealous law enforcement officers.

Procedural democracy cannot entirely eliminate these antidemocratic tendencies by threatened and frightened elites, but procedural democracy does constrain the elites at many points and prevents them from consolidating their hold over American society. Constitutional checks and balances, First Amendment freedoms, due process, periodic elections, and legitimated political opposition do prevent authoritarian tendencies from degenerating into Stalinism. A Joseph McCarthy can be a powerful man in American society, and the Senator was. But if he intimidated many, he never quieted all political opposition; if he influenced election outcomes, he never had an election called off; if he terrorized anxious State Department officers, he never commanded a private army which randomly terrorized an entire population; and in the final analysis he had no recourse when he was censored by his own colleagues in the Senate. Political repression, demagoguery, intimidation, and even victimization are likely to always be with us, but no American elite has managed to consolidate its power to the point that a Stalinist system of terror has governed the nation.

There is a final point to stress about the consequences of political democracy for elite rule. The incumbency of particular political elites is to a degree probationary. Competitive, periodic elections do provide an avenue by which mass action can eliminate conspicuously ineffective or pernicious elites. If democratic elections are not as democratic as some hope, they are not inconsequential. The small circles that formulate and execute public policies are not totally isolated from public pressures.

When the mistakes of an elite group are especially devastating, mass public action, organized by a counter-elite it should be emphasized, can hasten elite circulation. Such was the case when Republican fiscal policy could not salvage the economy after the stock market crash of 1929 or when President Johnson and his advisors were unable to terminate the Vietnam war in the mid-1960s.

This aspect of democracy may be of small comfort to persons whose utopian image of democracy is characterized by phrases such as "popular sovereignty" or "participatory democracy," but it is not a minor accomplishment in the history of political societies. Should they have the misfortune to be governed by bad elites, most societies are more or less stuck with them. At best, they must await for an opposition movement to become sufficiently well-organized and well-equipped so that it can effect a succesful coup. Democratic societies also suffer the mistakes of their elites, but they need not suffer as patiently or as long as do non-democracies. Moreover, democratic societies have devised a method of eliminating one elite and installing another with a minimum of bloodshed. This also is not an insignificant accomplishment, as any reader of history, past or present, must appreciate. Violent overthrow of established elites is painful and costly, and it often is the masses who pay the most. The birth of Bangla Desh was hailed as a victory for the forces of liberation against the evils of a military tyranny, and maybe it was. But the observer of these events could not but feel sorrow and anger at the price paid by the respective societies. Had the election returns been heeded by the military elite of West Pakistan, the discredited elite and their policies could have been eliminated with much less personal tragedy and social destruction. As it was, guerrilla warfare, civilian bombings, military intervention, and partial genocide were needed to accomplish what might otherwise have transpired by means of peaceful elections. Procedural democracy, then, can facilitate the emergence of counter-elites, can check the excesses of established elites, and can introduce an element of public voice in the circulation of elites. Elites are powerful, but only within limits. To conclude otherwise is to err in the direction of assigning too much power to elites.

Elite theory pinpoints the central political actors. It does not tell us how much power they have with respect to any given social policy, and it does not tell us what social goals they will pursue. Elite theory cannot in itself explain why one part of the American political-military elite led the nation into the costly Vietnam adventure while another part vigorously opposed this foreign involvement; it cannot tell us why some elites resist racist institutions and policies while other elites remain relatively indifferent to racial injustice. It does make us focus on elites and, after identifying them, ask why their interests are what they are. Like any social theory there are limits to what the elite perspective can accomplish, and these limits may well preclude its usefulness in analyzing many social processes. Indeed, one should be wary of any theory which seeks to explain too much. What elite theory does explain entitles it to the highest standing in social science.

Notes

1 See Barrington Moore, Jr., *Social Origins of Dictatorship and Democracy* (Boston: Beacon Press, 1966), p. 70.

2 See James V. Vives, "The Decline of Spain in the Seventeenth Century," in Carlos M. Cipolla, ed., *The Economic Decline of Empires* (London: Methuen, 1970), pp. 165-167. And Earl J. Hamilton, "The Decline of Spain," *Economic History Review,* 1st Series, vol. VIII (1938), pp. 168-179.

3 Piet Thoenes, *The Elite in the Welfare State* (New York: Free Press, 1966), p. 172.

SELECTED BIBLIOGRAPHY

The following works are among the numerous books and articles which have been written on elite theory and the distribution of power in America. They were selected for inclusion either because of their significant contribution to elite theory or because of the importance of their statement about power in American society.

Bachrach, Peter, *The Theory of Democratic Elitism,* Boston: Little, Brown, 1967.

Baran, Paul, and Sweezy, Paul, *Monopoly Capital,* New York: Monthly Review, 1966.

Baratz, Morton S., "Corporate Giants and the Power Structure," *Western Political Quarterly* (June, 1956).

Berle, Adolph A., *Power Without Property,* New York: Harcourt Brace Jovanovich, 1959.

Bottomore, Tom, *Elites and Society,* Baltimore: Penguin, 1966.

Brady, Robert, *Business as a System of Power,* New York: Columbia University Press, 1943.

Burnham, James, *The Machiavellians,* New York: Gateway, 1943.

Burnham, James, *The Mangerial Revolution,* Bloomington: Indiana University Press, 1941.

Connolly, William E. (ed.), *The Bias of Pluralism,* Chicago: Atherton, 1969.

Dahl, Robert A., *A Preface to Democratic Theory,* Chicago: University of Chicago Press, 1956.

Dahl, Robert A., *Who Governs?,* New Haven: Yale University Press, 1961.

Domhoff, G. William, *The Higher Circles,* New York: Random House, 1970.

Domhoff, G. William, *Who Rules America?,* Englewood Cliffs, N.J.: Prentice-Hall, 1967.

Domhoff, G. William, and Ballard, Hoyt B., *C. Wright Mills and the Power Elite,* Boston: Beacon Press, 1968.

Engler, Robert, *The Politics of Oil,* New York: Macmillan, 1961.

Galbraith, John K., *American Capitalism,* Boston: Houghton Mifflin, 1967.

Galbraith, John K., *The New Industrial State,* Boston: Houghton Mifflin, 1967.

Horowitz, David (ed.), *The Corporations and the Cold War,* New York: Monthly Review, 1969.

Hunter, Floyd, *Top Leadership U.S.A.,* Chapel Hill: University of North Carolina Press, 1959.

Kariel, Henry S., *The Decline of Pluralism,* Stanford: Stanford University Press, 1961.

Keller, Suzanne, *Beyond the Ruling Class.* New York: Random House, 1968.

Kolko, Gabriel, *The Roots of American Foreign Policy,* Boston: Beacon, 1969.

Kolko, Gabriel, *The Triumph of Conservatism,* New York: Free Press, 1963.

Kolko, Gabriel, *Wealth and Power in America,* New York: Praeger, 1962.

Latham, Earl, *The Group Basis of Politics*, New York: Octagon, 1965.

Lenski, Gerhard, *Power and Privilege,* New York: McGraw-Hill, 1966.

Lowi, Theodore J., "American Business Public Policy Case Studies and Political Theory," *World Politics* (July 1964).

Lowi, Theodore J., *The End of Liberalism,* New York: Norton, 1969.

Lundberg, Ferdinand, *America's 60 Families,* New York: Vanguard, 1937.

Lundberg, Ferdinand, *The Rich and Super Rich,* New York: Lyle Stuart, 1968.

McConnell, Grant, *Private Power and American Democracy,* New York: Knopf, 1967.

McCoy, Charles A., and Playford, John (eds.), *Apolitical Politics,* New York: Crowell, 1967.

McFarland, Andrew, *Power and Leadership in Pluralist Systems,* Stanford: Stanford University Press, 1969.

Meisel, James H., *The Myth of the Ruling Class,* Ann Arbor: University of Michigan Press, 1968.

Michels, Robert, *Political Parties,* New York: Collier, 1962.

Miliband, Ralph, *The State in Capitalist Society,* New York: Basic Books, 1969.

Mills, C. Wright, *The Power Elite,* New York: Oxford University Press, 1956.

Mosca, Gaetano, *The Ruling Class,* New York: McGraw-Hill, 1939.

Pareto, Vilfredo, *The Mind and Society,* New York: Dover, 1963.

Pareto, Vilfredo, *The Rise and Fall of the Elites,* Totowa, N.J.: Bedminster, 1968.

Pareto, Vilfredo, *Sociological Writings,* New York: Praeger, 1966.

Parry, Geraint, *Political Elites,* New York: Praeger, 1969.

Perlo, Victor, *The Empire of High Finance,* New York: International, 1957.

Prewitt, Kenneth, *The Recruitment of Political Leaders,* Indianapolis: Bobbs-Merrill, 1970.

Reisman, David A., *The Lonely Crowd,* New Haven: Yale University Press, 1961.

Rochester, Anna, *Rulers of America,* New York: International Publishers, 1936.

Rose, Arnold, *The Power Structure,* New York: Oxford University Press, 1967.

Schattschneider, E. E., *The Semi-Sovereign People,* New York: Holt, Rinehart and Winston, 1960.

Schumpeter, Joseph, *Imperialism, Social Classes,* Cleveland: World Publishing, 1951.

Sereno, Renzo, *The Rulers,* New York: Harper & Row, 1968.

Smoot, Dan, *The Invisible Government,* Belmont, Mass.: Western, 1962.

Stanley, David T., Mann, Dean E., and Doig, Jameson W., *Men Who Govern,* Washington: Brookings Institution, 1967.

Swomley, John M., *The Military Establishment,* Boston: Beacon, 1964.
Theones, Piet, *The Elite in the Welfare State,* New York: Free Press, 1966.
Truman, David, *The Governmental Process,* New York: Knopf, 1951.
Wolff, Robert Paul, *The Poverty of Liberalism,* Boston: Beacon, 1968.

NAME INDEX

SUBJECT INDEX